Mrs. Macleod Wylie

**The Gospel in Burmah**

The story of its introduction and marvelous progress among the Burmese and

Karens

Mrs. Macleod Wylie
**The Gospel in Burmah**
*The story of its introduction and marvelous progress among the Burmese and Karens*

ISBN/EAN: 9783337240899

Printed in Europe, USA, Canada, Australia, Japan

Cover: Foto ©Lupo / pixelio.de

More available books at **www.hansebooks.com**

# THE
# GOSPEL IN BURMAH;

THE

STORY OF ITS INTRODUCTION

AND

MARVELLOUS PROGRESS

AMONG

## THE BURMESE AND KARENS.

BY

MRS. MACLEOD WYLIE.

NEW YORK:

SHELDON & COMPANY, 115 Nassau Street.

BOSTON: GOULD & LINCOLN.

1860.

# CONTENTS.

### INTRODUCTORY.

Sources of Information; Burman Geography; Government, Races, and Religions of Burmah; the Karens and their Traditions: the Talaings; the Shans; Success of the Mission; Openings for the Gospel; Prayer needed.

Pages 7–18

### CHAPTER I.

Establishment of the American Board of Missions; the Missionaries reach India; Mission commenced in Rangoon; the first Convert, Moung Nau; unsuccessful Visit to Ava; first Burmese War; heroism and death of Mrs. Judson.

Pages 19–35

### CHAPTER II.

The first Karen Convert, Ko-tha-byu; Visit to the Karens of Dongyan; their Desire for God's Book; the Karen Alphabet formed; Karen Mission in Tavoy; singular Worship of an unknown Book; Labors, success, and illness of Mr. Boardman; Enquirers and Converts; Mr. Boardman's Death.

Pages 36–52

### CHAPTER III.

Arrival of Mr. and Mrs. Mason at Tavoy; Mrs. Boardman's excellent schools; the Sgau Karens and their chief; Mrs. Mason's classes and schools; Mrs. Helen Mason's illness and death; her habits of devotion. Pages 53–66

### CHAPTER IV.

Ko-thah-a, a distinguished Burman Convert, baptized and ordained; the Rangoon Mission re-established; translation of the Burman Scriptures; crowds of Visitors from the Interior; Mr. Wade at Mergui; Labors of Mr. Kincaid;

his journey to Ava; Persecution of the Burman Converts in Pegu; Baptisms at Maubee; the Christian Governor of Bassein; enlargement of the Mission; Mr. Kincaid's Journey beyond Ava; his perils and deliverance.

Pages 67–82

## CHAPTER V.

The Mission in Arracan; its commencement and early growth; death and character of Ko-thah-byu; Mr. Abbott at Sandoway; immigration of Christian Karens, driven by persecution from Burmah; death of Mrs. Abbott; Akyab; the Mountain Chief; trials of the Mission; Death of Missionaries; "Six Men for Arracan;" Review of the various Missions in Burmah.

Pages 83–94

## CHAPTER VI.

Illness of the Judsons; the Burmese Dictionary; Mrs. Judson's Works; her Missionary Labors; Mrs. Judson's illness, voyage, and death; Dr. Judson's return; progress among the Kemmees; vain attempt to re-establish the Rangoon Mission; last illness, death, and character of Dr. Judson.

Pages 95–108

## CHAPTER VII.

Nomination of Native Pastors; Wah Dee; the village of Thay Rau; Native Labors; Pastors in Tavoy; Tavoy Association; its rules of conduct and of worship; Persecution in Pegu; Martyrdom of Thagua; Progress in Bassein; wonderful history of Myat Kyau; his labors, character, and death.

Pages 109–127

## CHAPTER VIII.

Return to Rangoon; Visit from a Priest; Trials of the Karen Converts; Visit to a Monastery; War with the English; conduct of the Governor; his consternation; message from the Commodore; the Governor consults Mr. Kincaid; tyranny of the Governor; disorders in the city; arrival of the new Governor; the English deputation insulted; the King's ship captured; the English retire; Battle of the Stockades; interview of the Missionaries with Lord Dalhousie; Pegu annexed; Prospects of the future.

Pages 128–151

## CHAPTER IX.

The Tenasserim Provinces; Matah; a Sabbath at Matah; the teachers Klana and Kolapau; Mrs. Mason's journey to Longpung; thence to Chongquait and its heathen people; Visit to Palatot; discussions with the heathen; results of the journey.

Pages 152–170

CONTENTS. v

## CHAPTER X.

Mr. Ingall's labors at Rangoon; progress there; a strange Blacksmith; numerous Converts; the History of Moung Shway Pau; his conversion and baptism; Ko-thah-a and Mau Sa; Peace under the English rule; Mr. Ingalls' last journey, illness and death; Losses in the Mission. Pages 171-194

## CHAPTER XI.

Dr. Mason's first journey to Toungoo; the town of Shwaygyeen; death of the first Mrs. Harris; the city of Toungoo; its important position; the Mission commenced; Visit from the Taubeah Chief; Thako Mosha; the Chief's Verses; Visit from a Toungoo Lady; Conversation with her; Visits from other Ladies; their religious difficulties; their anxiety to learn; zeal of Shapau. Pages 195-211

## CHAPTER XII.

The history of Sau Quala; his parents; his boyhood; his conversion; his Mother's conversion and death; residence with his brother; their earnest studies; his public profession; his first efforts for others; he is present at Mr. Boardman's death; studies under Dr. Mason and Dr. Judson; collects the Karen Traditions; and assists in the translation of the Bible; writes Karen books; his marriage; his preaching and discussions; his frequent journeys; he becomes a pastor; progress among the Karens in the Tenasserim Province; Dr. Mason's opinion of Sau Quala; Revivals at Pyeekhya and Newville; Quala is ordained; Story of Dumoo; Dumoo and Quala set off for Toungoo; Quala's marvellous successs; his devoted labors; offer of Government employ; the offer declined. Pages 212-245

## CHAPTER XIII.

Sau Quala and his assistants; earnest spirit of these native Missionaries; Mr. Whitaker at Toungoo; Mr. and Mrs. Harris at Shwaygyeen; Death of Mrs. Harris; remarkable progress at Toungoo; earnestness of the people; Pwaipau's success; Dr. Mason's return; jungle travelling; his visit to the mountain Churches; support of the native teachers; the Bghai Association of Churches; number of the Converts and their families; ability of the Preachers; extraordinary liberality of the Churches; marvellous progress; the Bghai tribes; their ancient feuds; the independent Bghais; Border tribes; Much land to be possessed; Shapau's success; Mrs. Mason at Toungoo; the Female Normal School founded; its plan; the first scholars; letters from the people promising to support it; lawlessness of the tribes; Quala's letter; letter to the American Churches; progress of the Normal School; the teacher Sauka; his visit to the Sgaus; lawlessness of the tribes; many become Christians; murders among them; blood-revenge; Pwaipau ordained in Toungoo; his history; enquiries of the young teachers; Shapau ordained; wide doors of usefulness; Mrs. Mason visits the jungles; goes into the mountains; Mopgha house; timber collected; Christian village at Toungoo; Bghai public spirit; their improved manners; report of the Toungoo Mission for 1857; statistics; contributions. Pages 240-294

## CHAPTER XIV.

Position of the Missionaries: TAVOY native Pastors; the origin of evil illustrated; a Karen convert; disappearance of the Priests; a Burman village: MAULMAIN; the Theological Seminary; the Karen Churches: SHWAYGYEEN: BASSEIN; Report of the Karen Churches; their liberality; desire for the Bible; grounds of discouragement; the Burmans of Bassein; the northern Karens; native Missionaries sent to them: HENTHADA; progress made; native assistants; the Henthada Normal School; increase of Converts: PROME; conversion of a young Burman priest; general progress in the district: RANGOON; the Burman preacher, Moung-thet-nau; his conversion and baptism; death of Mr. Vinton; his numerous Churches; growth of the Mission; openings for usefulness, and his earnest appeals; his character, influence, and zealous labors; his last journey, illness, and sudden death; mourning of the Karens; conclusion; Apostolic preaching, plans, and precedents, followed by Apostolic success. Pages 295–332

# THE GOSPEL IN BURMAH.

## INTRODUCTORY.

"For from the rising of the sun even to the going down of the same, my name shall be great among the Gentiles; and in every place incense shall be offered unto my name, and a pure offering: for my name shall be great among the heathen, saith the Lord of hosts."—MAL. i. 11.

THE idea suggested by the New Testament, of a Mission to the heathen, has been in a remarkable degree realized by the AMERICAN MISSION TO BURMAH. Commenced in faith; unaided by wealth or worldly power; achieving its choicest victories, as well among the speculative Burmans as the unsophisticated Karens, by the simple preaching of the Gospel, and that mainly by native evangelists; blessed in its progress by a succession of faithful believers, who patiently fulfilled their course, not counting their lives dear unto them; exerting a wide influence through the whole Christian Church by the example and the memory of its labors and its success; this Mission has special claims to the sympathies and the love of the whole household of faith.

Other Missions have been blessed too. Not in primitive times alone, nor in the succeeding darker ages when Christianity in the forests of Germany, and amidst the din of war throughout Europe, won some of her noblest and least remembered triumphs, but in modern times also, from the

Missions of Eliot and Brainerd, of Ziegenbalg and Swartz, to those of Vanderkemp, Carey, and Martyn. In all these the Spirit of God worked variously according to the purpose of His will. By Him the laborers were prepared; by Him the doors of entrance and utterance were opened; by Him the word was made effectual to the saving of all who believed; and at the present time He has still His witnesses and His agents, in a vast diversity of circumstances, with widely differing gifts, occupying each one his allotted sphere of labor, " making increase of the body unto the edifying of itself in love " But it has pleased Him that in the work in Burmah His grace should be especially manifested, and His power felt; that there, the Church might behold a prelude of that promised shower of blessing which shall redound through the thanksgiving of many to the glory of God.

The history of this Mission lies scattered in the valuable memoirs of Dr. Judson, embodying the record of his first heroic wife; in the delightful memoirs of Sarah Judson's peaceful, holy course; in American periodicals; in the Tract Society's " Karen Apostle;" in Malcom's " South Eastern Asia;" in Gammell's History of the American Baptist Mission; in the memoirs of Helen M. Mason and Boardman; in the Rev. J. Baillie's recent work, " Rivers in the Desert," and other publications. But no where is there a connected narrative of the whole Mission. In the following pages an attempt has therefore been made to present a continuous, though not complete series of sketches, drawn not from those materials alone, but also from private information and records, obtained from intimate personal communication with several of the missionaries themselves.

The Kingdom, or as it used to be called the Empire of Burmah, occupies a great portion of the immense peninsula of Farther India on the eastern side of the Bay of Bengal.

Before the English conquests in 1826, it consisted of Burmah Proper, Cathay, Arracan, Pegu, Tenasserim, and the extensive country of the Shan Tribes. By those conquests, and the subsequent war of 1853, Arracan, Pegu, and Tenasserim, with the entire sea coast of the country, have been incorporated into the British territory, and the kingdom has been humbled and shattered. The population, though numerous, probably amounting to five or six millions in the entire country, is disproportioned to its immense extent, fertility, and resources. Two great rivers, the Irrawaddy and the Salween, with the Sitang and many other lesser streams, and the Yoma and other ranges of mountains, intersect the country. A large portion is covered with pathless jungle, and a great portion of the extensive plains is liable to inundation. The principal British settlements are at Akyab in Arracan; Rangoon, Bassein, and Dalhousie, as ports of the Irrawaddy; Shwaygyéen, Toungoo, Henthada, Prome, Thyat Myu, and Meaday in the interior of Pegu; and Maulmain, Amherst, Tavoy, and Mergui in Tenasserim. The rapid progress of Tenasserim under the British rule, inspires the hope that all the British Provinces will form points of attraction to the population still under the King of Burmah, who feel that neither life nor property is secure; and recent intercourse with the Red Karens, and increasing intercourse with the Shans, will probably lead to an extension both of British territory and of Christian missions.

The GOVERNMENT of Burmah is a despotism, administered chiefly by inferior officers in different districts, with unscrupulous and exacting cruelty; but the present King's personal influence appears to be beneficial, and his intelligence and mildness of character, render the continuance of peace, during his reign, probable. But other counsels may at any time prevail, and former scenes of revolution and civil war may be renewed. All such commotions will drive more emigrants into the British provinces, and the restless spirit of commercial enterprise while peace lasts, will carry further and further into Burmah up the Irrawaddy, probably to the borders of China, fresh disturbing elements. A recent splendid publication, (Capt. H. Yule's narrative of a Mission to Ava in 1855,) opens to view the prospect of a rich country, destined, it may be, to amazing developments of future wealth and prosperity. But such lands abound in the glorious East, rich with boundless and undeveloped resources, stored to profusion with the choicest gifts of nature, and capable of sustaining innumerable myriads of the human family.

The PEOPLE of Burmah consist of various distinct races.—The Burmans, Karens, Peguans or Talaings, and Shans, are the principal. Of these the Shans and the Red Karens live in a state of semi-barbarism. The principal exports of the country are rice, timber, silk, and lacquered ware. The principal cattle are buffaloes and ponies. Elephants are also very numerous and valuable. Of late years the demand for rice, especially from Arracan and Bassein (in Pegu,) has been so great, that a powerful impulse has been given to the mercantile spirit of the people : and silver, to the amount probably of not less than five millions sterling, has been imported within the last five years.

The prevalent RELIGION of Burmah, and the established religion of the court of Ava, is BUDDHISM, the faith alike of China, Siam, Ceylon, Thibet, and Tartary. Buddh is a general term for divinity, and not the name for any particular god. In this world, it is said, there have been four Buddhs or incarnations, the last of whom was Gaudama. One is yet to come, Arumaday. Gaudama was born about B. C. 626, having previously lived in four hundred millions of worlds, and passed through innumerable conditions in each. The narratives of his adventures in former states are preserved, and form a considerable part of the sacred books. He became a Buddh in the thirty-fifth year of his age, and remained so forty-five years, at the end of which time, having performed all kinds of meritorious deeds, and promulgated excellent laws, he obtained "nigban," that is, entered into annihilation.

No laws or sayings of the first three Buddhs are extant, but those of Gaudama were orally transmitted until about A. D. 94, when they were reduced to writing in Ceylon.— These are the only sacred books of the Burmans, and are all in the Pali language. The whole are called the Betagat.

The sins which are to be avoided are described in a moral code consisting of five principal and positive laws :—1. Thou shalt not kill. 2. Thou shalt not steal. 3. Thou shalt not commit adultery. 4. Thou shalt not lie. 5. Thou shalt not drink intoxicating drink.

Of any Supreme God, or any eternal self-existent being, Buddhism affords no intimation ; nor of any creation or providence. Merit consists in avoiding sins, and cultivating virtues, and the reward of it is the sole hope of the Buddhist. He knows nothing of eternal life, anticipates ultimate annihilation, is ignorant of the doctrine of forgiveness of sins through an atonement, and of the gift of righteousness through faith. Antecedently to annihilation he anticipates a prolonged existence in various conditions and degrees of happiness, but his creed has practically little influence upon his moral conduct. The Burmans generally are cruel and deceitful, and have made very slight advances in civilization, though generally endowed with singular acuteness and ingenuity.

The origin of the Karens is still doubtful, and various

theories have been propounded, based upon their remarkable traditions. They chiefly inhabit villages in the jungles and mountains, and notwithstanding all the power and oppressions of the Burmans, they have for the most part maintained their independence, and lived apart as a separate people. Their traditions embody remembrances of the creation, the deluge, and the promise of a deliverer. They speak of God in his sovereignty, unity and eternity, his perfection and holiness. They include a large portion of the moral law, and they minutely specify white messengers from the sea, and God's own book, as the means of their recovery, enlightenment and salvation. Of these traditions some are given by Dr. Mason in the "Karen Apostle." They appear to be unexampled in the records of heathen nations, in these modern times. The following are striking specimens:

### THE CREATION AND FALL, IN VERSE.

"In ancient times God created the world;
All things were minutely ordered by him.
In ancient times God created the world;
He has power to enlarge, and power to diminish.
God created the world formerly;
He can enlarge and diminish it at pleasure.
God formed the world formerly;
He appointed food and drink.
He appointed the fruit of trial;—
He gave minute orders.
Satan deceived two persons;
He caused them to eat the fruit of the tree of trial.
They obeyed not, they believed not God;
They ate the fruit of the tree of trial;—
When they ate the fruit of trial,
They became subject to sickness, old age and death.

Had they obeyed, and believed God,
We should not have been subjected to sickness;
Had they obeyed, and believed God,
We should have prospered in our doings.
Had they obeyed and believed Him,
We should not have been poor."

### DISPERSION OF MEN.

"Oh children and grandchildren! men had at first one father and mother; but because they did not love each other, they separated. After their separation they did not know each other, and their language became different; and they became enemies to each other and they fought."
"The Karens were the elder brother,
They obtained all the words of God,
They did not believe all the words of God,
And became enemies to each other:
Because they disbelieved God,
Their language divided.
God gave them commands,
But they did not believe him and divisions ensued."

### RESURRECTION.

"O children and grandchildren! you think the earth large The earth is not so large as the entada bean. When the time arrives, people will be more numerous than the leaves of the trees, and those who are now unseen will then be brought to view. O my children, there will not be a hiding place for a single thing on earth."

### IDOLATRY.

"O children and grandchildren! do not worship idols or priests. If you worship them you obtain no advantage thereby, while you increase your sins exceedingly."

### LOVE TO ENEMIES.

"O children and grandchildren! if a person injure you, let him do what he wishes, and bear all the sufferings he brings upon you with humility. If an enemy persecute you, love him with the heart. On account of our having sinned against God from the beginning, we ought to suffer."

### NATIONAL TRADITIONS.

#### *A people beloved of God.*

"O children and grandchildren! formerly God loved the Karen nation above all others, but they transgressed his commands, and in consequence of their transgressions we suffer as at present. Because God cursed us, we are in our afflicted state, and have no books. But God will have mercy on us, and again he will love us above others. God will yet save us again; it is on account of our listening to the language of Satan, that we thus suffer."

### RETURN OF GOD.

"At the appointed season God will come;
The dead trees will blossom and flower:
When the appointed season comes, God will arrive:
The mouldering trees will blossom and bloom again:
God will come and bring the great Thau-thee;\*
We must worship both great and small.
The great Thau-thee, God created;
Let us ascend and worship.
There is a great mountain in the ford,
Can you ascend and worship God?
There is a great mountain in the way,
Are you able to ascend and worship God?
How many evenings have you ascended to worship God?

---

\* A mountain so called, which is to be the seat of future happiness, according to some statements.

You call yourselves the children of God,
How often have you ascended to worship God?"

Such a people were prepared to receive the Gospel with all readiness of mind. Their character was frank and manly, though intemperance and predatory habits had tended greatly to debase them.

Their numbers are uncertain, but it is believed that they extend far beyond Ava, and Mr. Kincaid traces an affinity between them and bordering tribes of China. Under the British Government, they have generally submitted to the establishment of law and order, and the warm sympathy of Major Phayre, the able Commissioner of Pegu, with this interesting people, affords the best guarantee that British authority, even when confided to the hands of Burman subordinates, will not be perverted to their oppression in that province. They are divided into several tribes: the Red Karens, and the Sgaus, being the principal. The most important other tribes, appear to be the Pwos, and the Bghais. All have distinct dialects, which seem at present to require somewhat various alphabets.

The Peguans, or TALAINGS, long oppressed after their conquest by the Burmans, became special objects of hatred after the British forces unhappily withdrew from Pegu in 1826, and left these people, who had manifested their friendly sympathy with them, to Burman vengeance. The subsequent years, till the British annexation, in 1853, witnessed increasing severities, and the race is now greatly diminished.

Among the SHANS, no European settlement has been formed, and very little is known with certainty, of their numbers, or their habits. They frequently kidnap and carry children into slavery, and hitherto appear to have resisted even the approach of civilization.

The habits and manners of the population of Burmah, generally, present a marked contrast to the customs of India, and singular facilities for the work of Missions. There is no hereditary priesthood like Brahmanism; no anti-social system like caste, presenting a barrier to the introduction of every change; and no seclusion of the female sex. Among the Burmans there is a considerable amount of intelligence and education, and the whole population is accessible to the Missionary. Intercourse is comparatively open and unreserved, and the people usually are peaceful and courteous; but the Buddhist religion, with its monasteries, and gorgeous temples, its gay processions, and festivals, strongly fascinates the popular Burman mind, and too commonly enthrals it with a fatal spell.

Such is the sphere of labor, such are the hearers of the Gospel, we shall contemplate in the following pages. Of many of the hearers it certainly seems that the Lord has said, " This people have I formed for myself, they shall show forth my praise ;" and in many of the remote wilderness scenes of rugged beauty, where the Gospel has reached the untutored and unsubdued Karen, His message seems to have been as of old : " Let the inhabitants of the rock sing ; let them shout from the top of the mountains, let them give glory unto the Lord, and declare His praise," (Isaiah xlii. 11, 12.) His word has been clothed with power, and lawless men have sat at the feet of Jesus, like children, to be nourished with the milk of truth, and have fed on it in the simplicity of their hearts. They have been touched, not by the superior learning or intelligence of their teachers, for very often the messengers of the Gospel have been men entirely like themselves, but by the story of the cross, and that alone, —by the first principles of the Gospel of Christ. This has fired their hearts, convinced their judgments, and directed their wills. Once, " thieves, covetous, drunkards, revilers, extortioners, they are washed, they are sanctified, they are justified, in the name of the Lord Jesus, and by the Spirit of our God." (1 Cor. vi. 10, 11.)

And what shall we say of those who have gone from America to give their lives to this labor of love? They have been "as a dew from the Lord in the midst of many people," (Micah v. 7.) And their fruit remains. But one after another has been taken away. Many hindrances have arisen. It has been God's will oftentimes to bring their usefulness to a close, and to work in other, and unexpected ways, that He alone might be exalted: "sealing up the hand of every man, that all men may see *His* work," (Job. xxxvii. 7.)

This Mission then needs our prayers. It has been highly favored, but if the praises were to be given to man, and not to God, if pride were to take the place of humility, if God's Spirit were to be forgotten as the author of every good and perfect gift, soon, very soon, would Ichabod, "the glory is departed," be written as the inscription on its tomb. Rather let all the Church of Christ not only rejoice in the manifestation of God's gracious kindness to this Mission, but unite in *prayer*, that His Spirit may not be grieved, and that the beloved brethren in Burmah, may be blessed with that single eye which is full of light, and the gift of a holy and faithful dependence upon the grace of Christ alone.

Many and urgent are the calls for this prayer on behalf of Missions. The Missions in Burmah, in Tinnevelly, in Chota-Nagpore, in Turkey, and in Western Africa, seem to be full of promise that God is preparing to honor the preaching of His word in a new and remarkable manner. And by the discoveries in Southern Africa; by the approach of His heralds to Central Asia, at Peshawur; and by the weakening of Mohammedan kingdoms, is not the Lord pointing to new fields of labor, and saying to His people, "Go forward?" Is He not causing them to lay to heart the long desolations, and to yearn with lively sympathy over the lands of cruelty and darkness? They see by far the greater part of this earth closed to the Gospel, and filled with violence, millions in slavery, the female sex degraded, and Satan worshipped under countless forms, by whole successive generations, and they cry: O Lord, how long? how long shall the wicked triumph? Remember thy promises, the hopes and prayers of thy people, and do thou work for the glory of thy name, in thy faithfulness and truth! Surely, if we thus continued pleading with Him, we should see the blessing which is now descending upon a few favored spots, widely extending through the earth, opening paths in the wilderness, and rivers in the desert, and bowing down the greatest obstacle of all, the heart of the proud and lofty. How swiftly and how soon He would fulfil the desires of our hearts we cannot tell, but as His ways are higher than our ways, and His thoughts than our thoughts, there would be wonders wrought, such as we cannot imagine in these days of the "hiding of His power." For all the discoveries of modern times transcend all the conceptions of our forefathers, much more will the forth-putting of divine strength in the energy of love accomplish changes that will shame the feebleness of man. The great day of the descent of the Holy Spirit indicated in the conversion of three thousand, the mighty influence of divine grace: but greater blessings are promised, and on a wider scale the preaching of the glorious Gospel will be clothed with power. We see now only the first indications of those brighter days, but our children's children may witness results, that will teach them at once to rejoice in our earlier labors, and to wonder at the weakness of our faith. Confident in these hopes let us not faint, but toil and pray on, joyfully serving our generation according to the will of God, and resting on the promise, that "They who sow, and they who reap, shall rejoice together."

## CHAPTER I.

### EARLY DAYS.

"I know thy works: behold, I have set before thee an open door, and no man can shut it: for thou hast a little strength, and hast kept my word, and hast not denied my name."—Rev. iii. 8.

NEARLY fifty years have passed away since a few young students, gathered from different parts of the country, met in the Seminary at Andover, Massachusetts, with hearts inflamed with the love of Christ, and with a burning zeal to make known His Gospel to the perishing heathen. With some this sentiment had been the growth of years; with others it had started into existence on reading Claudius Buchanan's sermon entitled "The Star in the East;" but with all, the settled purpose of their lives was to obey that command of Christ, "Go ye into the world, and preach the Gospel to every creature." It was during a solitary ramble in the woods at the back of the college, with no eye but that of God resting upon him, that one of that little company came to the determination to obey that command. That one was ADONIRAM JUDSON, afterwards so distinguished as the Missionary to Burmah, and it was from that little company, that an Institution sprang, whose name has been associated with some of the noblest triumphs of the cross, the "American Board of Commissioners for Foreign Missions."

Antecedently to this movement in America, the Church Missionary, London Missionary and the Wesleyan Missionary Societies, had been formed in England; and the Baptist body had already sent out those pioneers of Missions in Bengal, Carey, Marshman, and Ward. The American Board was no sooner constituted, than it was considered expedient to send Mr. Judson to England, to endeavor to obtain the co-operation and assistance of the London Missionary Society. He was received with every mark of kindness by the Directors, but although they professed their entire willingness to assist with funds, until the American Board could raise sufficient for the support of their own missionaries, they wisely considered that separated as they were by the Atlantic, it would be impossible to carry on the two Societies satisfactorily in conjunction. It was therefore decided on Mr. Judson's return to America that he and Mrs. Judson should proceed at once in company with Messrs. Newell, Hall, Nott and their wives, and Mr. Rice, to Bengal, and from thence if practicable to proceed to Burmah, or any other field in India, which in God's providence was opened to them. It was on the 19th February, 1812, that the brig weighed anchor, which was to convey these devoted missionaries to the land of their adoption. How evident it was that the Spirit of God had been working after the counsel of His own will, upon different individuals, and in different countries, preparing the way for those great missionary movements, which have since been the glory of both British and American Churches, and which will continue to grow and increase, until the kingdoms of this world become the kingdoms of our Lord, and of His Christ!

Arrived in India, the little band of missionaries were received at Serampore, with true Christian hospitality.

The British government was at this time strongly opposed to the introduction of Christianity, and watched with jealous eye any movement on the part of the Mission at Serampore. Upon the American missionaries presenting themselves to the authorities, they were informed that they must without delay return to the United States. After many difficulties and disappointments, they secured a passage to the Isle of France. On the way thither Harriet Newell breathed her last, and Mr. Rice became so seriously ill, that it was deemed advisable that he should return to America; Messrs. Hall and Nott proceeded to Bombay; and at last of all that devoted band, who sailed with the message of divine mercy to Burmah, Mr. and Mrs. Judson alone remained to land at Rangoon on the 13th July, 1813. Very touching is the expression of their feelings at this time. "Instead of rejoicing as we ought to have done, in having found a heathen land from which we were not immediately driven away, such were our weaknesses that we felt we had no portion left here below, and found consolation only in looking beyond our pilgrimage, which we tried to flatter ourselves would be short, to that peaceful region where the wicked cease from troubling, and the weary are at rest. But if ever we commended ourselves sincerely, and without reserve, to the disposal of our heavenly Father, it was on this evening."

The Serampore missionaries had from the year 1807, sought to establish a Mission in Burmah, and like the advanced guard, had prepared the way for those who followed. When the Judsons arrived at Rangoon, they were received by Mrs. Felix Carey at the Mission House, which was situated in a retired spot without the walls of the city. Mr. Carey was at the time absent at the court of Ava. It was here that Judson commenced the study of the language, and the translation of the Scriptures, and the preparation of tracts. Mr. and Mrs. Hough joined them in 1816, with a printing press and fonts; and in the following year Mr. Judson embarked for Chittagong, in the hope of securing the services of one of the native Christians as an assistant in preaching the Gospel to the people. During his absence, and when their minds were distressed by the intelligence that the vessel in which he had sailed had not been heard of at Chittagong, Mr. Hough was suddenly summoned to appear at the court house. There he was detained day after day, without knowing the charges preferred against him. It appeared afterwards, that he had been arrested upon suspicion of his being connected with some Portuguese priests, whom the king had banished. To increase their anxieties, rumors reached them of an impending war between the English and Burmese Governments, and the cholera which for the first time had broken out in Rangoon, was accomplishing its fearful work around them.

In these circumstances Mr. and Mrs. Hough resolved to go up to Calcutta, but Mrs. Judson clinging to the hope that her husband might yet return, remained at her post; and before the ship had sailed with the Houghs to Calcutta, to the great joy of all, Mr. Judson returned, having encountered great perils, from contrary winds and storms.

This sketch brings us to one of the most interesting points in the history of the Burmah Mission. More than five years of preparatory work had passed away, and Mr. Judson in that time had not only made himself familiar with the language to a remarkable degree, but had prepared and published some portion of the Scriptures, and a tract briefly and clearly explaining the doctrines and duties of Christianity, in the vernacular. Familiar teaching had been carried on to some extent in private, but no attempts had yet been made to carry out the message of God to the highways and crowded thoroughfares; and it was to this, that Mr. Judson now determined to give his attention.

In April, 1819, a zayat, a small low thatched building, was

completed, and opened for this sacred and important purpose. It was built by the way side, on the road leading to the Great Pagoda, which is continually thronged by busy crowds. With what feeling must the missionary of the cross have first lifted his heart and hands in devotion beneath that roof, dedicating it to the service of the Living God! From this time we began to notice a spirit of inquiry, and on the 1st May, we have mention of MOUNG NAU, the first Burman convert. He was a man silent and reserved by nature, and seems to have excited little hope or attention, but the grace of God had reached his heart, and had made him feel his exceeding sinfulness, and the preciousness of Christ's salvation. He was a poor man, obliged to labor for his daily bread, but he so hungered and thirsted after righteousness, that he counted all but loss, if he might win Christ. Not long after he became an inquirer, he had an advantageous offer to go to Ava, in the employ of a boat-owner, but like Simon and Andrew, who left their fishing and their nets to follow Jesus, he determined not to leave those who would lead him in the way, where he might find Him. On the 27th June, 1819, on the Sabbath evening, after a simple service in the zayat, they proceeded to a tank in the neighborhood. An enormous image of Gaudama is upon the bank, and there Moung Nau was baptized in the name of the triune Jehovah. It was but a small beginning, but precious in the sight of Him "who taketh pleasure in His people, and will beautify the meek with salvation."

Moung Nau became a valuable assistant to Mr. Judson, and through all the trials to which the Mission was afterwards exposed, he remained firm and steadfast, a faithful soldier and a servant of Jesus Christ to the end. On the 7th November of the same year, two more converts were baptized. Mr. Judson in writing of this event says, "No wondering crowd crowned the over-shadowing hill. No hymn of praise expressed the exultant feelings of joyous hearts. Stillness and solemnity pervaded the scene. We felt on the banks of the water, as a little, feeble, solitary band. But, perhaps, some hovering angels took note of the event; perhaps Jesus looked down on us, pitied and forgave our weakness, and marked us for His own; perhaps, if we deny Him not, He will acknowledge us another day more publicly than we venture, at present, to acknowledge Him."

From this time the tide of inquiry continued. Very interesting was the case of Moung Shwa Goung, a teacher of considerable distinction. He appeared to be half deist and half skeptic, a man of considerable powers, and very argumentative. Even his proud heart and lofty intellect bowed to the supremacy of divine grace. His frequent visits to the zayat attracted the attention of the priests, and of the officers of the viceroy who reported him to their master. They were told "to inquire further about him." This had such an effect upon Moung Shwa Goung, that he ceased to visit the zayat, and many others also who had manifested considerable interest were afraid to do so any longer.

This incident forced upon the missionaries the painful conviction, that the disapprobation of the Government might, at any moment, blight the buds of fairest promise, and lay their hopes in the dust. They accordingly decided to go at once to the capital, and plead their cause with the Emperor, in the hope that they might at least secure toleration for themselves, and the converts to Christianity.

At the close of 1819, Mr. Judson and Mr. Colman, who had joined the Mission in Rangoon, proceeded to Amarapura, at that time the capital of the empire, taking with them the faithful Moung Nau as their attendant. After some perplexing doubts as to the most suitable present for the Emperor, without which no unauthorized person could appear before him, they decided upon a Bible in six volumes, covered with gold leaf, each volume enclosed in a richly wrought wrapper, wisely considering that their "holy book" was the most suitable offering for men in their circumstances. Mr. Judson writes: "The expedition on which we have entered, however it may terminate, is unavoidably fraught with consequences momentous and solemn beyond all conception.— We are penetrating into the heart of one of the great kingdoms of the world, to make a formal offer of the gospel to a despotic monarch, and through him to the millions of his subjects. May the Lord accompany us, and crown our attempt with the desired success." The passage up the river, a distance of three hundred and fifty miles, was completed in rather more than a month, and the day after their arrival at the Burman capital, they presented themselves to the former viceroy of Rangoon, Mya-day-men, in the hope that they might interest him in their behalf. His wife had shown much kindness to Mrs. Judson, and they now promised to use all their influence to obtain for them an audience of the king. The desired day at last arrived, and we cannot refrain from giving the account of the interview in Dr. Judson's own words—" January 27th, 1820. We left the boat, and put ourselves under the conduct of Moung Yo. He carried us first to Mya-day-men, as a matter of form; and there we learned that the Emperor had been privately apprised of our arrival, and said, 'Let them be introduced.' We therefore proceeded to the palace; at the outer gate we were detained a long time, until various officers were satisfied that we had a right to enter, after which we deposited a present for the private minister of state, Moung Zah, and were ushered into his apartments in the palace yard. He received us very pleasantly, and ordered us to sit before the several governors and petty kings, who were waiting at his Levee. We here for the first time disclosed our character and object; told him that we were missionaries, or 'propagators of religion;' that we wished to appear before the Emperor, and present our sacred books, accompanied with a petition. He took the petition in his hand, looked over about half of it, and then familiarly asked several questions about our God and our religion, to which we replied. Just at this crisis some one announced that the golden foot was about to advance; on which the minister hastily rose up, put on his robes of state, saying that he must seize the moment to present us to the Emperor. We now found that we had unwittingly fallen on an unpropitious time, it being the day of the celebration of the late victory over the Kathays, and the very hour when his majesty was coming forth to witness the display made on the occasion. When the minister was dressed, he just said, 'How can you propagate religion in this empire? But come along.' Our hearts sank at these inauspicious words. He conducted us through various splendor and parade, until we ascended a flight of stairs, and entered a most magnificent hall. He directed us where to sit, and took his place on one side; the present was placed on the other; and Moung Yo and another officer of Mya-day-men sat a little behind.

"The scene to which we were now introduced really surpassed our expectation. The spacious extent of the hall, the number and magnitude of the pillars, the height of the dome, the whole completely covered with gold, presented a most grand and imposing spectacle. Very few were present, and those evidently great officers of state. Our situation prevented us from seeing the further avenue of the hall; but the end where we sat opened into the parade, which the Emperor was about to inspect. We remained about five minutes, when every one put himself into the most respectful attitude, and Moung Yo whispered that his majesty had entered. We looked through the hall as far as the pillars would allow, and presently caught sight of the modern Ahasuerus. He came forward, unattended—in solitary grandeur—exhibited the proud gait and majesty of an eastern monarch. His dress was rich, but not distinctive; and he carried in his hand the gold sheathed sword, which seems to have taken the place of the sceptre of ancient times. But it was his high aspect, and commanding eye, that chiefly riveted our attention. He strided on. Every head excepting ours was now in the dust. We remained kneeling, our hands folded, our eyes fixed on the monarch. When he drew near we caught his attention. He stopped, partly turned towards us—'Who are these?' 'The teachers, great king,' I replied. 'What, you speak Burman—the priests that I heard of last night?' 'When did you arrive?' 'Are you teachers of religion?' "Are you like the Portuguese Priests?' 'Are you married?' These and similar questions we answered, when he appeared to be pleased with us, and sat down on an elevated seat, his hand resting on the hilt of his sword, and his eyes fixed intently on us. Moung Zah read the petition; and it ran thus:—'The American teachers present themselves to receive the favor of the excellent king, the sovereign of land and sea. Hearing that, on account of the greatness of the royal power, the royal country was in a quiet and prosperous state, we arrived at the town of Rangoon, within the royal dominions, and having obtained leave of the Governor of that town to come up and behold the golden face, we have ascended and reached the bottom of the golden feet. In the great country of America, we sustain the character of teachers, and explainers of the sacred scriptures of our religion. And since it is contained in those scriptures, that if we pass to other countries, and preach and propagate religion, great good will result, and both those who teach and those who receive the religion will be freed from future punishment, and enjoy, without decay or death, the eternal felicity of heaven,—that royal permission be given, that we, taking refuge in the royal power, may preach our religion in these dominions, and that those who are pleased with our preaching, and wish to listen to and be guided by it, whether foreigners or Burmans, may be exempt from Government molestation, they present themselves to receive the favor of the excellent King, the Sovereign of land and sea."

"The Emperor heard this petition and stretched out his hand. Moung Zah was called forward and presented it. His Majesty began at the top, and deliberately read through. In the meantime I gave Moung Zah an abridged copy of the tract, in which every offensive sentence was corrected, and the whole put into the handsomest style and dress possible. After the Emperor had perused the petition, he handed it back without saying a word, and took the tract. Our hearts now rose to God for a display of his grace, 'Oh, have mercy on Burmah! Have mercy on her King!' But alas! the time was not yet come. He held the tract long enough to read the first two sentences, which assert that there is one eternal God, who is independent of the incidents of mortality, and that beside him there is no God; and then with an air of indifference, perhaps disdain, he dashed it down to the ground; Moung Zah stooped forward, picked it up, and handed it to us: Moung Yo made a slight attempt to save us by unfolding one of the volumes, which composed our present, and displaying its beauty; but his majesty took no notice. Our fate was decided. After a few moments, Moung Zah interpreted his royal master's will, in the following terms: 'Why do you ask for such permission? Have not the Portuguese, the English, the Mussulmans, and people of all religions, full liberty to practice and worship according to their customs? In regard to the objects of your petition his majesty gives no orders. In regard to your sacred books, take them away: his majesty has no use for them.'

"Something was now said about brother Colman's skill in medicine, upon which the Emperor once more opened his mouth, and said, 'Let them proceed to the residence of my physician, the Portuguese priest; let him examine whether they can be useful to me in that line, and report accordingly.' He then rose from his seat, strided to the end of the hall, and there after having dashed to the ground the first intelligence that he had ever received of the eternal God, his Maker, his Preserver, his Judge, he threw himself down on a cushion, and lay listening to the music, and gazing on the parade spread out before him."

With hopes thus crushed and disappointed, they were hurried from the palace, and after some vain efforts to accomplish their object, they determined to return to Rangoon, feeling that for the future, they could expect no help or countenance from man. In the weakness of their faith, they were almost tempted to abandon Burmah, and to seek some country where the government would be more favorable; but God had other purposes, purposes of mercy to many in Burmah; and the failing hearts of his servants were strengthened by the young converts and inquirers, who, on hearing that they thought of leaving them, besought them with many prayers and tears to remain, and share their trials. It was finally arranged that Mr. and Mrs. Colman should go to Chittagong, so that if the storm of persecution rose, the missionaries and converts might find a refuge there. The

Judsons remained at Rangoon, the solitary occupants of the mission premises, but surrounded day by day with some few earnest inquirers. Amongst them was the teacher Moung Shwagoung, who, with six others, was in a few months admitted into the church by baptism, giving most satisfactory evidence of love to Christ and devotedness to Him. Thus things glided on more smoothly with the mission family, and all around began to wear a brighter aspect, when Mrs. Judson's failing health warned them that it would be necessary to seek its renewal in her native land, and that the bitterness of separation was before them. In vain the shorter voyage to Bengal was tried, and in August, 1821, she left the spot in which all her interests were centered, and in which her richest earthly hopes were treasured up.

In December, 1821, Mr. Judson was joined by Dr. and Mrs. Price; Mr. and Mrs. Hough also returned to Rangoon, and enabled him to carry on his work with renewed vigor. It was not long, before the knowledge of Dr. Price's arrival, and his skill as a physician, reached the Court of Ava, and he was summoned to the presence of the king. Mr. Judson was obliged to accompany him, and in one of their interviews was ordered to preach before his majesty, and had frequent conversations with the princes of the court, in which he had opportunities of commending Christianity to their notice. After spending several months at Ava, Mr. Judson returned to Rangoon to meet Mrs. Judson, who arrived there in December, 1823, accompanied by Mr. and Mrs. Wade. After some consideration, it was determined that the Wades should remain at Rangoon, and that Mr. (now Dr.) and Mrs. Judson should proceed immediately to Ava, and availing themselves of the favor shown to Dr. Price's medical skill, endeavor to establish a mission in the Capital itself. How little did they then foresee the bonds and imprisonment which there awaited them, and which drew forth into action those qualities in the character of Mrs. Judson, which rendered her one of the most remarkable women of her time! The war with England broke out in the beginning of 1824: on the morning of the 10th of May the British fleet had penetrated up the Irrawaddy to within a few miles of Rangoon, and war was openly declared with Burmah. The first violence of the coming storm broke upon the helpless mission families at Rangoon. In vain they remonstrated, and urged that they had no connection with the British Government; orders were issued for their arrest, and Mr. Hough and Mr. Wade were, with all the other European residents, hurried off to the common prison. There, chained together, and under the charge of armed men, they waited with intense anxiety the result of the engagement. As soon as the firing commenced, the guards, panic-stricken, fled, and just as hope again revived, and they looked for deliverance, fifty Burmans entered the prison house, stripped them of their clothes, and drove them to the place of execution. The dreaded moment had arrived. The executioner, with uplifted hand, stood ready for the signal, when Mr. Hough's voice broke the awful silence. It was in their own tongue that he entreated for a respite, and that he might be sent as the ambassador of peace on board the English frigate; an assent was given, and the rest of the unhappy prisoners were laden with irons and placed in confinement. The next day the English landed, and they were set free. The lives of Mrs. Hough and Mrs. Wade were, during all this time, wonderfully preserved. Insulted by the Burmans, compelled to conceal themselves in a little shed, exposed to a heavy fire of artillery, they were yet untouched, and rescued eventually by British officers, and placed in a position of safety. A malignant fever, which broke out after the occupation of Rangoon by the

British, and carried off its thousands, attacked the mission family, and determined them as soon as they were sufficiently recovered, upon going to Calcutta, where they remained until the conclusion of the war.

In the meantime intelligence of the fall of Rangoon had reached the court of Ava; and the British Army under Sir A. Campbell, was steadily and victoriously advancing towards the Imperial capital itself. Dr. Judson and Dr. Price were amongst the first victims of Burman cruelty. They were thrown into a dungeon known by the name of the "death prison," and so secured that they were incapable of moving.

It was now that the noble and heroic spirit of Mrs. Judson rose to the emergency. Feeble in health, but strong in purpose, she suffered no obstacle to daunt her energies, or to stand in the way of pleading for freedom and relief. For a time she was not allowed to leave her house; she was strictly watched and guarded, and exposed to cruel insults and extortions; but at length she succeeded in presenting a petition to the governor, and by her earnest appeals to his sympathy, obtained the privilege of visiting the prisoners, and at last of erecting a little bamboo hut within the precincts of the prison yard, in which for many months she lived, preparing their food, and ministering to their wants.

Nine weary months rolled on, but there was no weariness in the service of love; willingly, cheerfully was it rendered, but alas! one morning the prisoners were gone. Was it to torture and to death?

The governor, who had some pity for the sufferings of Mrs. Judson, had summoned her to his presence, that she might be absent from the prison, while the prisoners were driven out, and thus be spared the agony of a separation he had no power to prevent. But was she to be prevented discovering their retreat? In deepest admiration we follow her tracking their course, undaunted by the savage repulse, the fearful whisper, wending her solitary way by boat, or on the Burman cart, until at last she sank in the wretched village of Oung-pen-la, overcome with fatigue, anguish, and disease. Who can tell how great were the supports which her fainting spirit then received from Him who hath said, "I will not leave you comfortless?"

The prisoners had been thus hurried to Oung-pen-la, that they might be sacrificed in honor of Pakahwoon assuming the command of an army of fifty thousand men about to march against the English. By a remarkable interposition of God's providence, this awful catastrophe was prevented. The chief had been raised from a low condition to the rank of Woongye, but in the height of his power, and just as he was about to march at the head of his army, he was charged with treason, fell under the displeasure of the king, and was executed at an hour's notice. The fate of the missionaries was thus averted, and they were left uncared for at Oung-pen-la, when the near approach of the British army to the capital, induced the king to command the services of Dr Judson, as part of an embassy to the English camp with overtures of peace. The negociations were carried on entirely by the aid of Dr. Judson and Dr. Price. The release of the Christian prisoners was of course one of the conditions of the treaty, and on its conclusion the missionaries were once more free. So important were the services which they had rendered to the Burman Government, that they were solicited to remain, with the promise of advancement.

Dr. Price was subsequently induced to accept the proposals of the king; but Dr. and Mrs. Judson thankfully embraced the kind offer of hospitality from Sir Archibald Campbell and returned without delay to the British camp. We cannot forbear giving in Mrs. Judson's own words, the description of their departure from Ava.

"It was on a cool moonlight evening in March (1826), that with hearts filled with gratitude to God, and overflowing with joy at our prospects, we passed down the Irrawaddy, surrounded by six or eight golden boats, and accompanied by all we had on earth. We now for the first time, for more than a year and a half, felt that we were free, and no longer subject to the oppressive yoke of the Burmese; and with what sensations of delight on the next morning did I behold the masts of the steam-boat—the sure presage of being within the bounds of civilized life! We feel that our obligations to General Campbell can never be cancelled. Our final release from Ava, and our recovering all the property that had been taken, were owing entirely to his efforts. His subsequent hospitality, and kind attention to the accommodations for our passage to Rangoon, have left an indelible impression on our minds, and can never be forgotten."

Dr. Judson, on their arrival at Rangoon, accompanied Mr. Crawfurd, the English Commissioner, on a tour of inspection through the district ceded to the British Government by the recent treaty. A site was fixed upon as the future capital of the English possessions in Burmah, and received the name of AMHERST, in honor of Lord Amherst, who was then Governor-General of India. To this station Dr. Judson determined to remove his family, and there to unfurl the standard of the cross under the strong arm of British protection.

Soon afterwards, during Dr. Judson's absence at the court of Ava, whither he had gone as interpreter to Mr. Crawfurd's embassy, it pleased God to visit him with that affliction which so long clouded his heart and home. Mrs. Judson, whose constitution never recovered the shock it had sustained during her two years of suffering, sank under the effects of a remittent fever, and entered into rest on the 24th October, 1826; as deeply mourned by the English residents at Amherst, as by that little band of faithful Christians who had gathered round her. She was buried at Amherst.

A single hopia tree marks the resting place of Ann Judson. Many a Christian traveller has visited that hallowed spot, and given thanks to God for the grace granted to his servant. On Dr. Judson's return to Amherst, he found his infant daughter fast fading away. She had been born during their captivity, and was now his only remaining treasure, but she had to be yielded up. "Even so, heavenly Father: for so it seemed good in thy sight." .

> "Oh! who could bear life's stormy doom,
> Did not Thy wing of love
> Come, brightly wafting through the gloom,
> Our peace-branch from above?"

## CHAPTER II.

### EARLY DAYS WITH THE KARENS.

"Sought out......not forsaken."—Isaiah lxii. 12.

It was at the beginning of 1827, that the Mission was strengthened by the arrival of Mr. and Mrs. Boardman from America, who joined the brethren at Amherst. This place, which had been originally selected as the seat of the British Government, was found to be inconveniently situated, and Sir Archibald Campbell determined to remove the headquarters to Maulmain. We find therefore, in 1828, the missionaries, Dr. Judson, Mr. and Mrs. Wade, and Mr. and Mrs. Boardman, settled there; and the history of this period we shall give in a sketch sent us by Mrs. Wade, now one of the oldest surviving members of the Burman Mission.

"In Maulmain we had a boarding-school for Burman girls, and Dr. Judson had a bamboo zayat at the north end of the town, while Mr. Wade had a similar one at the south end, where they spent the greatest part of every day in the week, excepting Sunday, when we had regular worship in the Burman language, in the bamboo chapel near our own dwelling. Every evening in the week was devoted to the exposition of the Scriptures, and familiar conversation, for the benefit of the church-members, school girls, and any others who chose to attend. At that time the Karens were known only as tribes, more or less savage, inhabiting the mountains and valleys of the interior of Burmah. The few

Burman converts had, however, heard their missionary teachers express a wish to become acquainted with them, and finding one who was a debtor slave to a Burman, Ko-shwa-ba paid the small debt, and took him into his family. He proved, by being excessively rude and passionate, a very unpleasant accession to that Christian family, and though he gave some attention to the 'new religion,' Ko-shwa-ba felt constrained to put him away. This was the embryo "Karen Apostle." Dr. Judson, who was then a member of our family, proposed to pay Ko-shwa-ba the debt of poor Ko-THAH-BYU, if we would find employment for him, so that he might receive farther instruction; and it was not long after he came to live in our compound, that we began to perceive the influence of religion on his outward character, and that, by slow degrees, light dawned upon his dark mind, and the work of the Holy Spirit became perceptible on his hard heart. He seemed deeply penitent and confessed his sins, and sought earnestly by prayer, the pardon of sin, and reconciliation to God through our Saviour. It was to us a cause of deep interest, but when he expressed a wish to receive the ordinance of baptism, the members of the little Burman church who had not had the same opportunity of seeing the great change, both outward and internal, in this poor Karen, were slow to perceive that he was fit to be admitted into their church. And when at last he was cordially received by a vote of every member, and was to have been baptized the next Sunday, it happened to be the week that Mr. Boardman and family were leaving us for Tavoy; and they, wishing to take with them two little Karen orphan boys, who had been admitted into their school, could not induce them to go without their sister, who had lately been married to Ko-thah-byu. He therefore consented to go with his family to Tavoy, where he was soon baptized by Mr.

Boardman. Ko-thah-byu could speak Burman, and while with us learned to read that language, so that an excellent Catechism, written by the first Mrs. Judson, was his constant companion, and though his knowledge did not extend much beyond the contents of his little book, yet with the Holy Spirit's aid, he went forth and performed a great work. This was the 'first-fruits unto God' of the Karen Mission, whose churches now number some 14,000 regular communicants, while the nominal worshippers, and the readers of the blessed Bible, may be numbered by *tens of thousands*. While, however, this first Karen convert was yet on his way to Tavoy, Dr. Judson baptized a very respectable and intelligent Burman, by the name of Ko-myat-kyau, brother to the chief native Magistrate of Maulmain, who had formerly been Governor of Shwaygyeen, under the Burmese Government. When this brother was Collector of Customs among the numerous Karens of that province, he became familiar with their language, customs, &c. After his conversion, Ko-myat-kyau's mind reverted with deep interest to the Karens, and he often assured us that they would receive the gospel much more readily than the Burmans."

Mr. Wade says, "My impressions on this point were so strong that, with the advice of Dr. Judson, I set out with him, and two or three other Burman converts, to visit a Karen village at Dongyan, about twenty miles north of Maulmain. On our arrival every man, woman, and child had deserted their dwellings, and hid themselves in the jungle. We sat down in the shade of their houses, and after some time one or two of the men summoned courage to show themselves, and ask our object in coming to their village. Ko-myat-kyau told them our only object was to tell them about the true God, and the way of salvation. 'Oh, is *that* your object?' they replied, 'we thought you were

Government Officials, and we were afraid ; but if you are religious teachers, come to tell us of God, we are happy ; we will listen ;—Have you brought God's book ? Our fathers say : the Karens once had God's Book written on leather (parchment,) and they carelessly allowed it to be destroyed. Since then, as a punishment, we have been without books and without a written language. But our prophets say, the white foreigners have the book, and will in future time restore it to us. Behold, the white foreigners have come, as our prophets foretold ! Have you brought God's Book ?' (few of these simple villagers had seen a " white foreigner.") I replied, Yes, we have brought the Book of God, (shewing them a Bible) but it is in the language of the foreigners, though parts of it have been translated into the language of the Burmans. Can you read Burman ? ' No, we cannot ; you must translate it for us, as you have for the Burmans.' By this time the villagers generally had learned our object in coming, and ventured out of their hiding places, so that we had a large company of men and women and children around us ; some eagerly examining my strange dress ; others astonished at the whiteness of my face ; but more still, intent on hearing what I had to say about the Book of God, which they had so long expected the white foreigners to bring them. To their last request, I replied, ' I came from the land of the foreigners, to teach the Burmans the true religion. I have learned their language, but I do not understand Karen. I am obliged to speak to you through an interpreter ; but I will write to those who sent me out, to send a teacher for the Karens, who will study your language, reduce it to writing, and translate God's Word for you, if on your part you will agree to learn to read, and let your children learn ;. else the labor and expense will be lost. Will the Karens do it ?' ' Yes, we *will*, and we will worship

God, when we are taught his requirements. Our fathers have told that when the white foreigners bring us the lost Book, and teach us the true religion, we must listen and obey, then prosperity will return to us: but if we do not listen and obey, we shall perish without remedy. Long have we suffered, and prayed for deliverance, and now that the white foreigner has come with the lost word of God, according to the saying of the fathers, if we do not listen, we know that the threatening also will be fulfilled. Yes, we will listen and obey; but how long will it take for a teacher to come, learn our language, reduce it to writing, and translate for us the Book of God?' I said I thought it could be accomplished in ten years. 'Alas! it will not then be done in *my* day,' exclaimed a man who had nearly completed his three-score years and ten. 'But you must not wait for a new teacher, *you* must begin *at once.*' Many others joined in this request; but I could not then say, I will; for the idea of becoming a Karen Missionary had not yet occurred to my mind; my hands were full of work in the Burman department, and thirty converts were baptized and added to the Burman church in Maulmain, during that year.

"The Karen Chief, who had taken the lead in this conversation, invited us to his house, where we remained two weeks, teaching those who came to us, from all the region around. We were treated with great cordiality, as well as respect, but the Chief was cautious about committing himself to the cause of Christianity, until he knew more about it. His wife, however, imbibed at once a full conviction of the truth of what she heard, and she obtained the 'Pearl of great price.' From the labor of others in after years, this village became one of the most interesting stations of the Maulmain Karen Mission. Before leaving the Karens, I made some attempts to represent the Karen sounds by Burman characters, which I found entirely impracticable. On returning home, though I had no idea of attempting the work of reducing the Karen language to writing, my mind had received an impulse which led me on from step to step, though often interrupted for months, until with the aid of two Karens who understood Burman, I had analysed and classified the Karen sounds, and adopted a system of representing them, which embraced all the syllables occurring in their language. This work, strange as it may seem to others, as it does indeed to myself, was accomplished before I could speak a sentence in Karen; God gave the ability, and to Him be the praise. I adopted the Burman Alphabet, giving the characters a new sound so far as necessary; for the simple reason, that we had Burman type and no other in the printing office at the time, and its adoption would save expense and delay in printing. The inadequacy of the Burman alphabet to represent all the sounds in Karen, will be perceived by the single remark, that the Burman contains but ten vowel sounds while the Karen has fifty-four. A few new types, however, met the difficulty, and considering the ease with which the Karens learn to write, without instruction, I think no one regrets the adoption of the Burman character for the Karen language. In the prosecution of this interesting work, my mind became involuntarily absorbed, both while sleeping and waking, and having long suffered from liver complaint, my health failed, so that I was obliged to return to my native land for a season: not, however, until I had made many excursions among the Karen villages, received many visits in return, and had seen the happy result in fourteen baptized Karens, two or three of whom gave promise of becoming preachers of the gospel to their dark countrymen. The Spelling-book and Mrs. Judson's Catechism, had been printed in Karen, and a Karen school opened in Maulmain, which was left in the care of Dr. Judson. He likewise visited the Karen villages, and looked after the 'little flock,' as far as his numerous duties in the Burman department would permit, so that the good work went forward. The news of Books in the Karen language spread rapidly through the Karen villages, and brought many visitors to the school, where they first heard of a Saviour. From Tavoy, where Ko-thah-byu had been laboring with Mr. Boardman and Mr. Mason (now Dr. Mason), and where quite a large number had been baptized from the Karen villages of that region, two of their most intelligent young converts were sent to school in Maulmain to learn to read their own language; both could read Burman. One of these has long been a faithful ordained pastor of one of the largest churches in the region of Tavoy; while the other was Sau-Quala, the distinguished Karen missionary to Toungoo. Dr. Judson's Memoir truly says:—' The Karens had never before supposed their language capable of being represented by signs, like other languages; and they felt themselves, from being tribes of crushed, down-trodden slaves, suddenly elevated into a nation, with every facility for possessing a national literature.'"

Mrs. Wade proceeds:—" On Mr. Wade's return from the United States he was accompanied by the Rev. Messrs. Vinton and Howard, missionaries to the Karens. Both having studied the Karen language at home, and on the voyage to this country, they were prepared in a good degree to commence their labors on their first arrival. The Rev. Mr. Howard proceeded almost immediately to Rangoon, where a good work among the Karens of that region had been commenced by the Rev. Mr. Bennett, aided by Ko-thah-byu (who had now learned to read his own language) and two or three preachers from the Karen converts of Maulmain. Mr

Boardman had long been resting from his labors, and Mr Wade was directed to join Mr. Mason in his arduous and lonely labors in the jungles of the Province of Tavoy, with special reference also to a Karen literature.

"Dr. Judson had continued his labors for the Karens of Maulmain, as far as his duties in the Burman department would permit: so that one hundred and eleven had been baptized, churches had been formed, a good number had learned to read their own language, and several of the most intelligent and best instructed were already travelling from village to village, preaching the 'Gospel of the Kingdom,' or watching over the little flocks in the wilderness."

From this interesting letter we have a sketch of the first introduction to the Karens in the neighborhood of Maulmain, and we must now follow the footsteps of Mr. Boardman, and consider the commencement of the mission to this people in the province of TAVOY.

The city of Tavoy is one of the strongholds of Buddhism, and with its temples and shrines, its glittering pagodas and sacred groves, seems given to idolatry. Very picturesque is the scene upon their holy days, when the women gathering beneath the shade of the banyans, deck their spreading branches with flowers of richest colors, offerings to the unknown God; while, blending with the scene, is heard the music of innumerable bells suspended from the fairy spires of the pagodas, swelling or falling on the breeze, and echoing from hill to hill. How deeply must such scenes have kindled the desire in the missionary's mind to make known to them that God whom they ignorantly worshipped! Tavoy at this time was the residence of two hundred priests, and had upwards of a thousand pagodas: but Mr. Boardman rested upon the promise, and, strong in faith, looked forward to that day when even Burman idolaters should turn to the living God. Ko-THAH-BYU, the Karen convert mentioned by Mrs. Wade, who had accompanied Mr. Boardman to Tavoy, began his earnest labors among his countrymen in Tavoy. This remarkable man had been a robber and a murderer, and possessed such an ungovernable temper, that even after his conversion he had often to spend many hours in prayer for strength to overcome it, but he had been "forgiven much, and he loved much." One who knew him well wrote: "The preaching of Christ crucified was to his mind a work of paramount importance to all others. He was not only not ashamed of the gospel of Christ, but he gloried in being its humble messenger to guilty men. It has been said that if ever a man hated idolatry it was Ko-thah-byu. And I would add if ever a man loved the gospel, Ko-thah-byu was that man. It was his love for the gospel that kindled that unconquerable desire to proclaim its precious truths to his fellow-men. The word of the Lord was emphatically a fire shut up in his bones, so that whenever the inquiry was made, 'Whom shall I send and who will go for us?' he was always ready to respond, 'Here am I, send me!'" Another wrote: "In his beloved work he was unceasingly active, and seemed incapable of fatigue. In every other work he was indolent and inefficient; while in preaching Christ crucified, his soul would be wrought up with more than mortal energy. He was always planning some new excursion, and never was so happy as when he found individuals to whom he might preach from morning until evening. In seasons of special interest, he has not only continued his speech, like Paul, till midnight, but, not unfrequently, till break of day."

As the result of Ko-thah-byu's indefatigable labors, many of the Karens from the villages scattered over the mountains of Tavoy, flocked in from the distant jungles, with curious interest to see the white teacher, and to listen to the wonderful truths he taught. Mr. Boardman found that notwithstanding their rude exterior, they possessed minds susceptible of the most lively impressions, and remarkable teachableness of spirit. As an illustration of their susceptibility of impressions, we have an anecdote of a book which Mr. Boardman found had been left in one of the villages some years before by a Mussulman, who told them it was a sacred book, and commanded them to worship it. The person who had charge of it, though ignorant of its contents, had preserved it with the greatest care; and wrapped in muslin, and enclosed in a basket, the book became the object of veneration and worship. The most remarkable fact was, that they fully believed in the advent of a teacher, who would be able to teach and explain the mysteries of the sacred volume. On Mr. Boardman's arrival at the village, the chief of the tribe and the keeper of the book, came to ascertain his opinion of its character. An interview was appointed, when he was to have an opportunity of seeing it and judging of its contents; all seemed anxiously to await Mr. Boardman's decision. The day arrived, and with a long train of followers, the chief appeared bringing with him the venerated relic. The basket was opened, the muslin unrolled, and taking from its folds an old tattered worn-out volume, he reverently presented it to Mr. Boardman.

It proved to be the Book of Common Prayer and the Psalms, of an edition printed at Oxford. "It is a good book," said Mr. Boardman; "it teaches that there is a God in heaven, whom alone we should worship. You have been ignorantly worshipping this book: that is not good: I will teach you to worship the God whom the book reveals." Every Karen countenance was alternately lighted up with smiles of joy and cast down with inward convictions of having erred in worshipping a book instead of the God whom it reveals. I took the book of Psalms in Burman, and read such passages as seemed appropriate, and having given a brief and easy explanation, engaged in prayer. They stayed two days and discovered considerable interest in the instructions given them.

The aged sorcerer who had been the keeper of the book for twelve years, on hearing Mr. Boardman's decision, perceived that his office was at an end; he relinquished the fantastical dress he had worn, and the cudgel which for so long had been the badge of his spiritual authority, and subsequently became a humble believer in the Lord Jesus Christ.

When Mr. Boardman was able to visit the Karens in their own villages, they received him with joy and respect, and hailed him as one who, they believed, would show to them a more excellent way. From this time we find constantly in his journals entries like the following. "A good number of Karens are now with us, and Ko-thah-byu spends night and day in reading and explaining to them the words of eternal life. It seems as though the time for favoring this people had come."

Amongst the Burmans also there seemed to be a deeper interest and more earnest inquirers. Mr. Boardman writes:

"In making a comparison to-day between the present and past, I thought it worthy of observation, that although I have not half so many visitors at the zayat as formerly, those who do come stay longer, listen more attentively, and cavil less. Whether this is owing to any change in my mode of address, I cannot tell. Formerly it was my custom to begin my discourse by telling them of a Supreme God against whom they had sinned, and that therefore they stood in need of a Saviour. But the passage to the dear Saviour was so much disputed, that I could seldom introduce Him to advantage. I now introduce the Saviour first; tell of His glories, His compassion, His pardoning mercy, His sufferings and death in our stead, and propose to the people to choose whom they will worship, one who *can*, or one who *cannot*, save them from sin. They do not pretend that Gaudama or any other Buddh can save from sin. They trust entirely to their own good works. In their dreams they are floating by the buoyancy of their own meritorious deeds, over the ocean of existence to the opposite shore, annihilation, where existence itself is no more, and where happiness and misery cease with the final wreck of their being."

In the midst of all these labors, the gentle and severer discipline of a Father's love visited Boardman and his family. Sickness in themselves, and the removal of their little daughter, so tenderly loved as their first-born child, produced in them those peaceable fruits of righteousness, which sprang up richly to the praise and glory of their God. His labors were unwearied and greatly blessed, but already the hectic color, the brightening eye, the failing step, spoke of disease and death; yes, and of a glorious immortality. Besides his eldest child they had also lost an infant of a year old. Sorrow had indeed compassed them about, when fresh calamities came suddenly and unexpectedly upon them. On the night of the 9th August, 1829, they were roused from sleep by strange sounds, and rumors at first inexplicable, but they soon discovered that the province had risen in rebellion against the English Government, and that the Burmese rebels were flocking into the city. Col. Burney, who was Commissioner, was absent at Maulmain. The officer in command was dying, they had no English troops, and only about a hundred sepoys, so that their position was one of extreme danger. The little party of Europeans were, however, gathered together, and, after a most gallant stand of four or five days, were relieved by the arrival of Col. Burney in the English steamer. The vessel was immediately despatched for reinforcements, and Mrs. Burney and Mrs. Boardman and their children, were sent in her. But such was the energy shown by Col. Burney and his little band, that before the steamer returned with succor, Tavoy was again in our possession, and the leader of the revolt paid the penalty of his temerity. The mission house had been destroyed by the rebels, together with all his property, but after a hasty and refreshing visit to Maulmain, Mr. Boardman returned to renew his labors at Tavoy. The people received him gladly, and in his tours into the interior hundreds heard from him the word of life, and started off to communicate the good news to others, often accompanied by Ko-thah-byu.

Mrs. Boardman was indefatigable in the schools which she had established at Tavoy, and the influence of her Christian character was felt perceptibly in the mission. She was indeed one of whom it might be said, " She opened her mouth with wisdom, and in her tongue was the law of kindness :" and to this day there are those who remember with thankfulness, the holy counsels, the loving warnings, and the fervent prayers, with which she received them into the mission circle. At this time her health which was always feeble, had given away under repeated shocks, and it was thought desirable they should go to Maulmain for a season, and supply the vacancy produced by the absence of Mr. and Mrs. Wade at Rangoon. In writing to his mother, at this period Boardman says, " If you ask whether in these circumstances I regret having come to Burmah, I promptly answer, No ; only I regret that I came with no more of the Spirit of Christ, and with so much to require the chastising rod of divine mercy. To spread the gospel through Burmah is worth a thousand lives." How glorious is the power of that faith, which enables its possessor to contemplate death without a fear, and an exchange of worlds with joy! Again an infant son was removed by death, but, as in former cases, they yielded him up without a struggle to the divine will.

In December, 1830, we find them back at Tavoy, and Mrs. Boardman then writes: "God is displaying His power and grace among the poor Karens in a wonderful manner. Since our return from Maulmain we have had several companies out to hear the gospel. At one time upwards of forty came, and stayed four days; listening to the doctrines of the cross, with an attention and solemnity, that would have done credit to a Christian congregation. We have seen all who were baptized previously to our visit at Maulmain, and so far as we can learn they have conducted themselves in a manner worthy of the followers of Jesus. Perhaps you recollect a chieftain mentioned as an inquirer about two years ago. He came at first with the sorcerer who was in possession of the deified book, and not long after professed a firm belief in the doctrines of the cross, and requested baptism. Having given good evidence of his piety, he was baptized. Not long after, another respectable man among them named Moung Kyah, and his aged father-in-law followed his example. Their manner of life since has been such as to remind us forcibly of the apostles and primitive Christians. The chieftain's name is Moung So. He and Moung Kyah take such portions of scriptures as we have been able to give them, and go from house to house, from village to village, expounding the word, exhorting the people, and uniting with their exhortations frequent and fervent prayers; and God has blessed their labors."

But the time of departure was at hand. In trembling characters there was entered in Mr. Boardman's journal on Jan.

1, 1831, "I am travelling with hasty steps to my long home. My health, my life, and those of my family and friends, I commit to our gracious God for the ensuing year, praying that he will dispose of us all, as shall most promote His glory and the good of our souls." This was the last record made with his own hand. Mr. Mason, who had been designated by the Board in America to assist Mr. Boardman in his labors at Tavoy, arrived at the end of January, 1831, just in time to witness his triumphant death. He had determined once more to visit his beloved Karens in their jungle homes. The people had finished a zayat at the foot of the mountains, and they were to carry him there before he died. Mr. Mason accompanied them. They reached the place on the third day; it was upon the banks of a beautiful stream at the foot of a mountain range, and in that sweet solitude were assembled nearly one hundred Karens, more than half of whom were waiting for baptism. No wonder that the spirit of the dying missionary was stirred within him, that the vain hope was raised in those who loved him, that he might yet revive. Even Mrs. Boardman for a moment forgot her bitter griefs, in joy over repenting sinners. The failing breath soon warned them again that he was sinking, but when he was gently urged to return home, he replied, "What, if my poor unprofitable life be somewhat shortened by staying, ought I, on that account merely, to leave this interesting field? Should I not rather stay and assist in gathering in these dear scattered lambs of the fold?" Mrs. Boardman writes: "The chapel was large, and open on all sides except a small place built up for Mr. Mason, and a room not above five feet wide, and ten feet long, for the accommodation of Mr. Boardman and myself, with our little boy. The roof was so low that I could not stand upright, and it was but poorly enclosed, so that he was exposed to the burning rays of the sun by day, and to the cold wind and damp fog by night. But his mind was happy, and he would often say, ' If I live to see this one ingathering, I may well exclaim with happy Simeon, Lord, now lettest thou thy servant depart in peace, according to thy word; for mine eyes have seen thy salvation. How many ministers have wished they might die in their pulpits; and would not dying in a spot like this be even more blessed than dying in a pulpit at home? I feel it would.' " It was plainly perceptible that earthly desires had passed away, and that he was enjoying sweet foretastes of that rest into which he was soon to enter. On the Wednesday evening about thirty-four persons were baptized. Mr. Boardman was carried to the waterside, but the joyful sight was almost too much for his exhausted strength. On being taken back to the chapel, he expressed a wish to be present at the evening meal, and, as if gathering up his little remaining strength, he afterwards addressed his disciples who were present, about fifty in number, to the following effect: " When I am gone, remember what I have taught you, and O be careful to persevere unto the end, that when you die, we may meet one another in the presence of God, never more to part. Listen to the words of the new teachers, as you have done to mine. The female teacher will be much distressed: strive to lighten her burdens, and comfort her by your good conduct. Do not neglect prayer. The eternal God to whom you pray is unchangeable. Earthly teachers sicken and die, but God remains ever the same. Love the Lord Jesus Christ with all your hearts, and you will be safe forever."

Early in the morning the little mission-band left for home. The sufferings of the journey were increased by a severe storm of wind and rain, and they were thankful the next morning to leave the comfortless roof of a heathen Tavoyer, who had given them shelter for the night ; but on carrying the dying saint to the boat, his gentle spirit fled, and he stood before God " accepted in the beloved." The sorrowing Karens knelt down in prayer to God—that God of whom their departed teacher had taught them, and whose service was commended to them with his latest breath. We will not attempt to describe the sufferings of the widowed heart : God knew it, and it was He who sustained and comforted Sarah Boardman.

## CHAPTER III.

### CO-WORKERS.

> "O though oft-depressed and lonely,
> All my fears are laid aside,
> If I but remember only,
> Such as these have lived and died."
> 
> LONGFELLOW.

WE have been induced to linger over the pages of the preceding chapter, from the desire to mark not only the origin and commencement of the Karen Mission, but also the character of him who first labored amongst this people, and who left there "footprints on the sands of time." Well might Helen Mason write to her husband from Maulmain. "Your introduction to the mission will, I imagine, leave an impression upon your mind never to be effaced. Your visit to the jungle must have surpassed in interest, any previous event in your life. Were you not disposed to cry out as you stood by Boardman when dying, 'My Father, My Father! the chariots of Israel, and the horsemen thereof?' For it seems to me that his dying at mid-day in the field, must have been to you more like a translation, than dying." Mrs. Mason had been compelled by sickness to remain at Maulmain, while her husband proceeded to Tavoy; but two months after Boardman's death, we find them stemming the rough and stormy sea, on their way together to Tavoy. Landing in the evening, they found their way to Mrs. Boardman's frail bamboo dwelling, but the light of home shining pleasantly through the lattice-work, fell like sunshine on their hearts, and the air of neatness and order which reigned within, told of the character of the occupant. A cloud of sadness tinged the sweet expressive smile which greeted them, and as Sarah Boardman stood with her child beside her, it was impossible to forget that she was a widow, and he fatherless. Mrs. Mason found in Mrs. Boardman, the most perfect congeniality of sentiment and unity of action. They had come, not merely as wives, but as missionaries to Burmah; and this seems to have been one of the peculiar characteristics of the women of the American Missions. They have pre-eminently lived, and labored, and died, in seeking the salvation of the heathen, and it is impossible to remember the names of Judson, Boardman, Mason, Harris, Cummings, and Macomber, without emotions of the deepest admiration. True it is that the majority of them found early graves, but shall others therefore cease to labor? Shall survivors now cease to feel that responsibility for the salvation of the heathen which leads them to warn and entreat, to teach and exhort, with many prayers and tears? "Whenever a long unblest life of comparative uselessness is to be preferred to a short one filled with 'twice blessed' deeds, they may!" Till then, who shall stay their free-will efforts for the salvation of men? Shall we not rather pray that America may send forth a continued succession of her daughters, to labor for the extension of Christ's kingdom, and to emulate those who have gone before?

After her husband's death, Sarah Boardman came to the determination to labor on. She had sat down quietly with the cup which her Father had given her to drink, and which He had appointed for her sanctification; she found there was sweetness at the bottom, and she rose up better fitted for the work which was before her. The Masons had yet to acquire the language, and could do but little in the schools, or amongst the female converts. Here then was her special sphere of usefulness. From early dawn till late at night, she was occupied ; and yet so modest, so unobtrusive were her labors, that she passed on, her influence more felt than seen. Besides boarding and day-schools in Tavoy, village schools were also attempted. She says : " The superintendence of the food and clothing of both the boarding-schools, together with the care of five day-schools, under native teachers, devolves wholly on me. My day-schools are growing every week more and more interesting. We cannot, it is true, expect to see among them such progress, especially in Christianity, as our boarders make ; but they are constantly gaining religious knowledge, and will grow up with comparatively correct ideas. They, with their teachers, attend worship regularly on the Lord's-day. The day-schools are entirely supported at present by the Honorable Company's allowance ; and the Civil Commissioner Mr. Maingy appears much interested in their success."

That Mrs. Boardman was conducting Government Schools on the plan she mentions, was owing not to her superior tact, but to her quiet, unassuming manner ; which creating no alarm by ostentatious usefulness, gave her almost unbounded power, whenever she chose to exercise it. Although she was not aware of the fact, it was at that time far from the policy of the Bengal Government to allow the introduction of Christianity into their schools. There is a letter addressed to the Commissioner on the subject, a year after our present date, which, with his answer, will explain her position.

"*Tavoy, August 24th,* 1833.

"My dear Sir,

"Mr. Mason has handed me for perusal, the extract from your letter to Government, which you kindly sent him. I apprehend I have hitherto had wrong impressions in reference to the ground on which the Honorable Company patronize schools in their territories, and I hope you will allow me to say, that it would not accord with my feelings and sentiments, to banish religious instruction from the schools under my care. I think it desirable for the rising generation of this province to become acquainted with useful science; and the male part of the population with the English language. But it is infinitely more important that they receive into their hearts our holy religion, which is the source of so much happiness in this state, and imparts the hope of a glorious immortality in the world to come. Parents and guardians must know that there is more or less danger of children deserting the faith of their ancestors, if placed under the care of a foreign missionary; and the example of some of the pupils is calculated to increase such apprehensions. Mr. Boardman baptized into the Christian religion several of his scholars. One of the number is now a devoted preacher; and notwithstanding the decease of their beloved and revered teacher, they all, with one unhappy exception, remain firm in the Christian faith.

"The success of the Hindoo College, where religious instruction was interdicted, may perhaps be urged in favor of pursuing a similar course in schools here. The overthrow of a system so replete with cruel and impure rites as the Hindoo, or so degrading as the Mahomedan, *might* be a matter of joy, though no better religion were introduced in its stead. But the Burman system of morality is superior to that of the nations around them, and to the heathen of ancient times, and is surpassed only by the divine precepts of our blessed Saviour. Like all other merely *human* institutions, it is destitute of saving power: but its influence on the people, so far as it is felt, is salutary, and their moral character will, I should think, bear a comparison with that of any heathen nation in the world. The person who should spend his days in teaching them mere human science would, I imagine, (though he might undermine their false tenets) by neglecting to set before them brighter hopes, and purer principles, live to very little purpose. For myself, sure I am, I should at last suffer the overwhelming conviction of having labored in vain.

"With this view of things, you will not, my dear Sir, be surprised at my saying, it is impossible for me to pursue a course so utterly repugnant to my feelings and so contrary to my judgment, as to banish religious instruction from the schools in my charge. It is what, I am confident, you yourself would not wish; but I infer from a remark in your letter that such are the terms upon which Government afford patronage. It would be wrong to deceive the patrons of the school; and if my supposition is correct I can do no otherwise than request that the monthly allowance be withdrawn. It will assist in establishing schools at Maulmain, on a plan more consonant with the wishes of Government than mine have been. Meanwhile I trust I shall be able to represent the claims of my pupils in such a manner, as to obtain support and countenance from those who would wish the children to be taught the principles of the Christian faith.

"Allow me, my dear Sir, to subscribe myself,
"Yours, most respectfully,
"Sarah H. Boardman."

"My dear Madam,

"I cannot do otherwise than honor and respect the sentiments conveyed in your letter. You will, I hope, give me credit for sincerity, when I assure you, that in alluding to the system of instruction pursued by you, it has ever been a source of pride to me to point out the quiet way in which your scholars have been made acquainted with the Christian religion. My own Government in no way proscribes the teaching of Christianity. The observations in my official letter are intended to support what I have before brought to the notice of Government, that *all* are received who present themselves for instruction at your schools without any stipulation as to their becoming members of the Christian faith.

"I cannot express to you how your letter has distressed me. It has been a subject of consideration with me for some months past, how I could best succeed in establishing a College here, the scholars of which were to have been instructed on the same system which you have so successfully pursued.

"Believe me,
"Yours very faithfully,
"A. D. Maingy."

Mrs. Boardman's Christian fidelity and firmness were productive of great good: an appropriation being obtained from Government for schools throughout the provinces "to be conducted on the plan of Mrs. Boardman's schools at Tavoy." The plan was not fully carried out, for the teaching of Christianity was soon prohibited, though *she* was never interfered with, but was allowed to follow the dictates of her own conscience.

In addition to her other work, Mrs. Boardman commenced

the study of the Karen. In Burmese she was already well read. The glimpses of some of her jungle tours are very interesting, though they scarcely reach us from her own pen. At the end of three years of such labor Mrs. Boardman married Dr. Judson; one whom she emphatically describes to be "a complete assemblage of all that a woman's heart could wish to love and honor." This union was greatly blessed to their mutual help and comfort, and in leaving Tavoy Mrs. Judson entered upon a field of perhaps still higher and more enlarged usefulness; while in Mrs. Mason she left behind her a fellow-worker every way fitted to follow in her steps.

Helen Mason's motto was to "love and be silent;" but like the violet betrayed by its own fragrance, so her works follow her. The service which she had early chosen, was stedfastly pursued to the close of her life. Simple in her tastes and habits, she wished to live, so that the humblest contributors to Missions, could enter her house without feeling offended at anything that they might see. "We are," she would say, "the representatives to the heathen of a Saviour, who *chose* to be poor."

The most exquisite neatness pervaded her home, and regulated her dress, but the vase of flowers, and the few choice shells, gathered from the sea-shore, proved that she had a taste for the beautiful in nature and in art. "Let us give ourselves unreservedly to this glorious work," the work of winning souls to Christ: *this* was the constant utterance of her heart, as it was the absorbing aim of her life.

In the jungle tours with Mr. Mason, she had the happy art of gathering the women around her, and interesting them in the story of the Saviour's love. In town also she had a school of Karen girls, in whom she felt peculiar interest. Knowing that their good conduct, on their return to their mountain homes, might produce a favorable impression on the minds of the Karens who came to the school in future years, she would follow them to the hamlets, and many a happy meeting took place between the teacher and the pupils, who were all eager to do something for herself, or her babe. The married women too benefited by her precepts and example. In one of the sequestered glens was a woman of the name of Naughapo, signifying "Daughter of Goodness," who was a great favorite of Mrs. Mason, and shared largely in her instructions. She was the Dorcas of the glen, clothing the naked, feeding the hungry, soothing the afflicted, and often making her little dwelling the home of the poor, that they might enjoy the privilege of a neighboring school. Mrs. Mason was struck with the beauty of her peaceful home, evidently a spot which the Lord had blessed. It was on the declivity of a hill, overlooking a well stocked garden, and a mountain stream flowed murmuring past, pouring forth its eternal harmony. On asking Naughapo and her husband if God should call them from their garden to their grave, would they feel alarmed? they answered, "No, *we do not consider that anything we have is our own. All, all* is God's." The day before Mrs. Mason left, a box-wallah\* had called, with his tempting fabrics for sale; but though this good woman was in poor garments, she had but *one rupee* for purchasers, while on the following morning, she and her family put *thirteen rupees* into Mrs. Mason's hands, to be deposited in the mission treasury. She had not only learned that "godliness is profitable unto all things; having promise of the life that now is, and of that which is to come," but that "it is more blessed to give than to receive." Such was some of the fruit of Mrs. Mason's example and instruction. For the twelve pupils of her first

\* Pedlar.

Karen school, she ever felt a tender interest. She had asked God for all of them, and while thankful for the conversion of one, she could not rest without that of the whole. And what she asked she obtained; though the last of the number was not baptized until about ten years after the school was closed.

For many years Mrs. Mason also labored for the Burman children, and had six day-schools in Tavoy, containing about one hundred and forty children. She at first found it very difficult to meet a woman who could read, and still more so one who would be willing to read "Jesus Christ's books." At last one was found, and then another, and another, to assist in this work of love.

In the midst of all her earnest labors, she had to retrace her steps to America, and there to leave her beloved children to be trained by others. It was some years after this that in writing to a friend she said: "We have heard of the tortures of the Inquisition, but I do not know that any could exceed this *self-sacrifice*. When I was leaving my children, Lucy, who was old enough to understand something of her loss, clung around me, saying, 'Other little girls have their mothers: I want mine.'"

The following lines were wrung from that full heart during her return voyage in 1838.

> "Sleep, lov'd one, sleep! thy gentle rest,
>   Oh! how unlike to mine!
>   What would I give, could once my breast
>   But beat as light as thine.
>
> "Sweet flowret! might the storms of life
>   But spend their wrath on me;
>   Glad would I bear their wildest strife,
>   And smile to think of thee.

> "Heaven shield thee, tender little rose,
> As thy soft beauties spread;
> And temper every wind that blows
> To thy defenceless head."

One sunny evening, on Mr. Mason's return from a preaching excursion among the Burmans, the first object which arrested his attention upon entering his home was the fine form of a Sgau Chief, who seated like a child at Mrs. Mason's feet was earnestly imploring her to visit the Karens in his village and neighborhood. "We have heard of Christianity, and it seems to us something wonderful. We do not understand it: and yet it seems the thing we want. Come to our jungle homes, and preach to us on our native streams. Many will believe. I have a Burman wife, and I have daughters, and sons-in-law, and brothers, and nephews, all of whom will become Christians, as well as myself, as soon as we really understand." Many months passed away before they reached the Chief's dwelling, but he had obtained light and strength slowly, and was not one to turn back. It was five long years before he was clear entirely of the trammels of heathenism, and stood forth Christ's freed-man. For five years the missionary travelled through the region where he dwelt, but not a single soul was baptized: but from the time the Chieftain was made willing to give up all for Christ, he became one of the most efficient laborers in Mergui and Tavoy. Mainly through his efforts, all his own family, as well as all under his influence were made to feel the power of Christianity, and many were baptized. The last mention of the old man was, on his return from a visit to his brother. His tall form doubled like a leaf, was on the back of his grandson. His brother's dwelling was a long day's journey distant; and most of it had been performed in this manner. The lad was a fine intelligent Christian, and it would be difficult to know which most to admire, the willingness of the young man to perform such a fatiguing service, to carry the gospel to his uncle, or the zeal of the old Chief, who seemed to forget his aching bones, in the delight he felt at having once more exhorted his brother, and seen in him some evidences of divine grace. "*I can't die*," he said to Mr. Mason, while a gleam of youthful fire glowed through his feeble frame,—"*I can't die, till I see my brother converted.*"

Helen Mason was eminently a working Christian, and she continued so till the close of life. Sometimes she would half playfully remark, "I shall vanish away from you before long," and no doubt the gradual weakening of her strength was gently warning her that rest was at hand. There was no disease, it was simply exhaustion.

"I thought it likely I should *wear* out in this way," she said, "and therefore had clothes made for you and the children, that you might be well provided for, but prepared none for myself."

The most remarkable feature during her illness, was the calm and unruffled peace that *constantly* pervaded her mind. In dictating a letter to her aunt, she said, "From the commencement of my illness to the present time, my peace has been like a river; and the words of my Saviour have been verified to me, 'Peace I leave with you: my peace I give unto you!' At eighteen my spirits would have been more buoyant. Then I should have felt like mounting on the chariots of Aminadab; now

> 'This heavenly calm within the breast,
> Is the dear pledge of glorious rest.'"

She was never seen to weep but once during her whole sickness, and that was when her infant child was brought to her for the last time. Bursting into tears, she said, "Poor babe, you will never know a mother's love!" On one occasion, in speaking of the trials of their missionary life, she said: "Missionary work is hard work, and none ought ever to engage in it, that are not called to it. No, certainly, none ought ever to come, unless specially called."

On awaking one morning, she remarked: "Hitherto I have felt passive, but I awoke this morning with *strong* desires to depart. Do not call me back. It is much easier dying, than coming back to life again."

When her aching frame was turned in bed, she would often say, "Oh! that I had the wings of a dove; for then I would flee away and be at rest." Conversing during one of her last days, on the great work to be done for the heathen, she said, "Tell the native Christians, that I loved them to the *end*, and that had it been the will of God, I would have willingly stopped, and taught them longer. Tell them to *strive* to get to heaven; that the kingdom of heaven suffereth violence, and the violent take it by force!" "Tell them," she continued, stretching out her withered arm with an energy, such as she manifested on no other occasion, and in tones so loud and sonorous, that all were startled, "tell them to *lay hold* on eternal life." "Thus," says Mr. Mason, "she reached the goal of her mission path, and left us, like the disciples on Mount Olivet, looking up stedfastly towards heaven."

Let us pause for a moment to think of the character which has just passed under review. Helen Mason was not an ordinary Christian, and perhaps in the consideration of her life we may gain some lessons which may be useful to ourselves, for "none of us liveth to himself, and no man dieth to himself."

She was remarkable for great meekness and gentleness of spirit, which in the sight of God is of great price. Her husband never once in the whole course of their married life, saw her manifest any indication of anger, she was ever

> "Sweet in temper, face, and word,
> To please an ever-present Lord."

She was remarkable also for strong affections. We see this in the anguish she endured when called to separate from her children. The "fearful chasm" then made was filled by God Himself. "Previous to the decision in my mind to become a foreign missionary," she wrote, "I heard Dr. Griffin preach on the church being guilty of 'keeping back part of the price,' and often during my lonely voyage back did I inquire, 'Have I kept back anything?' If my heart clung to anything, it was to my children; yet I willingly gave them back to God, though the act lacerated my heart to the core."

She was one who sought to "*walk with God.*" This was the *habit* of her mind. In writing to her husband she says, "Pray much and often for me, that I may be able to 'abide in Christ,' to 'live in the Spirit,' and 'walk in the Spirit.'

> 'As pants the hart for cooling streams,
> When heated with the chase,
> So longs my soul, O God, for Thee,
> And thy refreshing grace.'

"I daily and hourly wish you the best blessings, and pray that you may have much communion with God. It was in the wilderness that Moses saw the burning bush; on Pisgah that he saw the promised land; and from mount Nebo that he went up to take possession of the heavenly Canaan. In each of these places we may suppose he had very intimate communion with God."

Into this spirit of communion, she herself drank deeply: she was eminently a woman of prayer. Here was her strength. Her husband writes, "Often, often, times without number, have I awoke in the silent watches of the night, and found that she had stolen from my side, and was holding earnest communion with God. Her silver whispers, her bosom swelling with suppressed 'groanings that could not be uttered,' would awe into stillness, lest a motion should indicate that her hallowed converse with the Holy One was observed. She struggled with the Angel of the Covenant and prevailed, and He blessed her."

In the little missionary cemetery near their house, Boardman had erected a small bamboo oratory, fitted with a chair, a table, and a Bible, to which he had retired " and had prayed into existence the Karen Mission." Here too Sarah Boardman had followed his example : and to this favorite retreat the steps of Helen Mason often resorted. There she " spent days in fasting and prayer ; communing with God, and feeding on Angel's food." There too she was " laid to rest like a weary babe upon its mother's bosom." It was meet that where she had so often agonized in prayer, she should be composed to her quiet sleep, and that her grave should be, where she had so often gone up to commune with God. Shall we say that this is an example beyond our imitation ? Far be it from us to say so, for the grace of Christ is all-sufficient. Helen Mason had no great gifts or talents peculiar to herself, but she had a heart which was consecrated to the love and service of God, that service which is perfect freedom. " Go ye and do likewise."

## CHAPTER IV.

### REGIONS BEYOND.

"He that goeth forth and weepeth, bearing precious seed, shall doubtless come again rejoicing, bringing his sheaves with him."—PSALM cxxvi. 6.

It was in the year 1830, that Ko-THAH-A, a Burman convert of Rangoon, appeared before Dr. Judson, and Mr. Wade at Maulmain. During the long dark period which had intervened since the war, and the expulsion of the missionaries from Burmah proper, Ko-Thah-a, in the midst of much peril and persecution, had endeavored to keep together the little church at Rangoon. He had now travelled to Maulmain to represent its suffering condition, to seek for advice and encouragement, and to receive from Judson and from Wade those wise and holy counsels, which he knew would be so freely given. Ko-Thah-a is first introduced to us by Dr. Judson as being a frequent visitor at the Rangoon mission house, and shortly afterwards as " giving good evidence of being a true disciple." He is described at the time as a respectable householder, rather above the middling class, about fifty years of age, unmarried, and living with his aged mother, who was dependent on him, in a small village called Nau-dau-gong, about half a mile from the mission. He had formerly been an officer under government, and had amassed considerable property, which he mostly spent in building pagodas, and making offerings. " But he obtained no satisfaction, found no resting place for his soul, until he became acquainted with the religion of Jesus. He now," wrote Dr. Judson, "rests in this religion, with conscious security; believes and loves all that he hears of it, and prays that he may become fully a true disciple of the Saviour." He was baptized in 1822, just before Dr. Judson's departure for Ava. His manner of application evinced his earnestness. "Early in the morning Moung Thâh-a came in, and taking Dr. Judson aside, knelt down, raised his folded hands in the attitude of reverence, and made a very pathetic and urgent application for immediate baptism. He stated that he had considered the Christian religion for above two years; that his mind was completely settled on every part; and that though he had been harassed with many fears, he was now resolved to enter the service of Jesus Christ, and remain faithful unto death, whatever the consequences in this world might be." The rite was administered the following day, August 20th, the new convert making the seventeenth Burman, who up to that time had publicly professed his faith in Christ in baptism.

He had spent a few months, at the end of the war, in 1826, at a large village in the neighborhood of Shwaydoung; and there devoting himself to the preaching of the word, had produced a very considerable excitement. Several professed to believe in the Christian religion; and three of the most promising received baptism at his hands. Others requested the same favor, but he became alarmed at his own temerity, and declined their repeated applications. On his return to Rangoon, he continued to disseminate the truth, but in a more cautious and covert manner. He had now come to Maulmain to inquire what he should do with those who wished to be baptized, and to get some instructions concerning his own duty.

Of his qualifications for the ministerial office, Dr. Judson wrote:—"He has been so evidently called of God to the ministry, that we have not felt at liberty to hesitate or deliberate about the matter. But, if it had been left to us to select one of all the converts to be the first Christian pastor among his countrymen, Ko-Thah-a is the man we should have chosen. His age, (fifty-seven,) his steadiness and weight of character, his attainments in Burman literature, which though not perhaps necessary, seem desirable in one who is taking up arms against the religion of his country, and his humble devotedness to the sacred work, all conspire to make us acquiesce with readiness and gratitude in the divine appointment." Succeeding years have shown that the "divine appointment" was not misapprehended.

Moung Ing, who was soon afterwards ordained, was associated with Ko-thah-a in the Rangoon pastorate. Their united labors were greatly blessed, and many who had been scattered during the raging of the war and the persecution which followed, returned to the flock, so that by the end of the year twenty were added to the church.

Early in 1830, Mr. and Mrs. Wade removed to Rangoon, where for several months they continued strengthening and confirming the disciples. They were followed by Dr. Judson, who had never ceased to feel an interest in the scene of his earliest labors. It was with some apprehension and fear, that they attempted again to establish the mission in this stronghold of idolatry, but the Governor was friendly, and although the subordinate officers kept up a continual surveillance, it did not deter the people from coming in large numbers for copies of the scriptures and tracts. The Burman troops who came in for enrolment or inspection, merchants, who travelled from different parts of the empire for the purposes of traffic, all had the opportunity of hearing of the true God; and though watched, and warned, multitudes visited the mission house saying, "We have heard the fame of this religion, and are come to get books." Thus was the word of life conveyed to many a far-off region. And in that great day when the Lord shall make up His jewels, perhaps it may be found that many hidden ones dwelt in those mountains, who, unknown to man, were well known to that Saviour God, who had sent His word and Spirit to enlighten them, and to guide their feet into the way of peace.

In the beginning of the summer of 1830 Dr. Judson determined to make a tour up the Irrawaddy, for the purpose of visiting the towns, and villages on its banks. Taking with him Moung Ing, and some other native Christians, he embarked upon those bright waters, upon which he had so often sailed, in safety and in peril, in joy and grief. Wherever he landed he commanded attention, and the people flocked around with eagerness to listen. In this way he pushed up to Prome, a large city midway between Rangoon and Ava. Here he remained for a time the guest of the only European inhabitant, but at last received permission to occupy an old zayat, standing near a pagoda; and those who visited the idol temple listened to the earnest teachings of the Christian missionary. Here he spoke of Christ to the votaries of Gaudama, but when a spirit of inquiry was roused, and crowds flocked to hear or to cavil, and the hopes of the missionary were raised, they suddenly ceased to come, and it was not until after his return to Rangoon, that Dr. Judson discovered that the Emperor annoyed at his having ventured so far into the interior had given orders for his return. The intelligence that such an order had been given, was sufficient to account for the absence of the inquirers.

On Dr. Judson's return to Rangoon he resolved to give himself with more earnestness than ever to the completion of that great work, the translation into Burman of the entire Scriptures. The early morning hour, the lonely lamp burning still at midnight, testified to his unwearied diligence. Denying himself the cheering influence of Christian converse, he confined himself almost entirely to his solitary task. His praise was not of man but of God. It was not, however, till the 31st of January, 1834, that these noble labors were brought to their completion. They had been prosecuted through the changes of a most eventful life, often under the pressure of sickness and of sorrow. How full of affecting interest and sublimity is the scene presented to the mind by the simple touching postscript to his letter home, dated January 31st, 1834. "Thanks be to God, I can *now* say I have attained. I have knelt down before Him, with the last leaf in my hand, and, imploring His forgiveness for all the sins which have polluted my labors in this department and His aid in future efforts to remove the errors and imperfections which necessarily cleave to the work, I have commended it to His mercy and grace, I have dedicated it to His glory. May He make His own inspired word, now complete in the Burman tongue, the grand instrument of filling all Burmah with songs of praise to our great God and Saviour Jesus Christ. Amen."

In the beginning of the year 1831, the great Buddhist Festival was celebrated with unusual pomp in the magnificent Shway Dagong Pagoda at Rangoon, and from the countless multitudes who were gathered from the most distant parts of the empire, Dr. Judson had an excellent opportunity of judging how far an interest had been awakened by the labors of past years, and by the circulation of books and tracts, through the land. From every province of the interior, from the frontiers of Cathay, and even from the borders of China and Siam, numbers visited Dr. Judson, saying, "We hear that there is an eternal hell,—we are afraid of it. Do give us a writing that will tell us how to escape it." Others, perhaps from the very opposite quarter of the empire, would say, " Sir, we have seen a writing that tells us of an eternal God : are you the man that gives away such writings ? If so give us one, for we want to know the truth." Others, living nearer at hand, had heard of the name of Jesus, and asked, " Are you Jesus Christ's man ? Give us a writing that tells about Jesus Christ." The numbers who came in this way, to inquire after the truth, were estimated by Dr. Judson at not less than six thousand, to each of whom was given some book, or tract, or portion of Scripture, which might reveal to them the way of life.

In the summer of 1831, it was found necessary for Mr. and Mrs. Wade, who were again at Maulmain, to try a change of climate. The health of the former had long been failing. Dr. Judson had therefore to return to Maulmain to take charge of the mission during their absence. His heart was cheered with the progress that had been made, and by the accession to the missionary band of Mr. Kincaid, who, with Mr. and Mrs. Bennett, had recently arrived there. The missionaries had extended their labors far into the surrounding jungles, and a most interesting settlement had been formed for the Karen Christians, called Wadesville, in commemoration of the devoted missionary who first preached the gospel there.

Mr. Wade's health was so far improved by the voyage to sea, that he returned for a season to Mergui, a city on the Tenasserim coast, about a hundred and fifty miles south of Tavoy. Accompanied by Mrs. Wade he visited the Karen villages of Mergui with the gospel, and a more interesting reception than was given them, it would be difficult to find on record. They were met by an intelligent chief, now a pillar in the church, and were led into the village on their arrival, by several young women, whom he had invited amongst others for the purpose of singing a hymn, of which the first verse in the chorus was—

> " The Lord his messengers doth send,
> And he himself will quickly come ;
> The priests of Buddh, whose reign is short,
> Must leave the place to make the room."

After a residence of six months they were sent to Rangoon, leaving Ko Ing pastor of the church at Mergui, but the following year Mr. Wade's health was so completely exhausted, that they were compelled to seek its restoration in their native land.

We shall now endeavor to trace out some of the early labors of that intrepid missionary, Mr. Kincaid. We find him in the early part of 1832 at Rangoon, and at its close surrounded by inquirers from all parts of the country. Some confessed their belief in the Great God, others that they had long studied the books, and had been thinking of Christianity. " It is wonderful," they would exclaim : " a great light that is visiting the world." In the beginning of 1833, three Burmans were baptized, and others desired baptism ; many more were known to be secret believers, but from fear of persecution were kept back. Some of those who frequented the zayat had often said to Mr. Kincaid, " Why do you not go to Ava and to all the great cities of the Empire ? Many have heard of the new religion and the books, and wish to understand them." The reiterated inquiry, produced the desire to unfurl the standard of the cross in that city in which it had once been trampled under foot ; and having, after some difficulty, obtained a pass, Mr. Kincaid started for Ava, accompanied by his wife and her sister, on the 6th April, 1833. Three native assistants followed them, with large supplies of tracts and portions of the Scriptures. The passage up the river was not without its dangers, but everywhere they found a spirit of inquiry amongst the people, and traces of the influence which had been exerted by native Christians and Christian books.

Arrived at Ava, they were met at once with difficulties. The Government, on the most trifling pretences, refused them a shelter; but, on the British Resident representing that Mrs. Kincaid and her sister were British subjects, they were immediately provided with a house in the city. "Here," writes Mr. Kincaid, "the very thing that ought to rejoice my heart often troubles me; it is the numbers that are flocking to the verandah to read and hear the word of God. If I would I could not resist the tide that is setting in. Our verandah is pretty well filled during the day, and sometimes forty or fifty come in at a time." He was treated with great courtesy by the officers of the Government, and invited to visit the Prince Mekhara, who was a man of some education, and could speak English. The King also expressed some curiosity about the art of printing, one of the printers with a press was sent to Ava, and much interest was excited by the books printed in the Burman tongue. Two persons also were baptized. One was a priest of considerable learning, who had long been a most popular expounder of Buddhism in the city.

. The exhibition of excitement and curiosity regarding the truths of Christianity which marked this period, was very remarkable. "It seemed like the waking up of the popular mind to the light of Christian truth; the commencement of a mighty and speedy revolution in the religion of the country." It could scarcely be expected that the great enemy would allow such a state of things to continue, without some effort to maintain his hold over the minds of men. In 1835, a violent persecution broke out in Rangoon. The first victim was Ko Sanlone, a man of deep piety, great intelligence, and bold and active zeal in the service of Christ. He was one who had accompanied Mr. Kincaid to Ava, and since his return to Rangoon had been amongst the few who had dared openly to distribute books, and to lift up a voice for God and His cause, beneath the frowning despotism of a Burman Court. He was at last seized, thrown into prison, beaten, loaded with chains, and compelled to cruel labor. His faith never wavered under the storm of persecution, but only shone forth the more brightly through the dark cloud. Whether before the tribunal of Burman magistrates, or under the lashes of the persecutors, or in the loathsome dungeon, he bore all with the meek and holy fortitude of the Christian martyr. Though repeatedly threatened with death, unless he would abjure the faith and worship Gaudama, he trusted unwaveringly in God, and exhibited a noble pattern of the Christian character. After a time he was released from prison, but his entire property was confiscated, and he was forbidden on pain of death to resume his labors in the mission. But he had fought a good fight, he had finished his course, he had kept the faith, and now the angel call had come; he was to hear those gracious words: "Come, thou blessed of my Father, inherit the kingdom prepared for you before the foundation of the world." He died deeply mourned by the missionaries with whom he had labored.

The persecutions were not confined to Rangoon. The Karens who were scattered up and down a little stream known by the name of "The Karen Brook," in the district of Maubee, were subjected to fines and heavy taxations, while they refused to worship the Nats, or to acknowledge Gaudama. These converts were the fruit of the unwearied labors of Ko-thah-byu. It was in the spring of 1833, that this excellent native preacher went up to Rangoon with Mr. and Mrs. Bennett; and such was the blessing resting upon his work in the Karen villages, that in writing to Mr. Judson at the close of the rains, Mr. Bennett says, "We are in distress, and send to you for relief. For the last several days, our house and Ko-thah-byu's have been thronged; men, women, and children, all anxiously inquiring about the religion of Jesus. They are all anxious for schools, and offer to build zayats for preaching, if any one will come and teach them. There are many who already keep the Lord's day, read our tracts, and endeavor to instruct one another as best they can. They daily read the tracts, and all get together in their families, and sing and pray to the God who rules in heaven. They declare they have left off drinking spirits, and as far as they understand, endeavor to practise according to the requirements of Scripture. What shall we do? Ko-thah-byu is only one among a thousand. He cannot preach the gospel, and teach these people to 'read in their own tongue' the precious truths of God's word, at the same time. We want one man to go to Bassein, another to go up to Prome and along the river, another to Maubee and its vicinity, towards old Pegu, all these to preach the gospel; and we certainly need as many more school-masters. Can you send us any assistance? If so, do; for Christ and his cause require it. . There surely is the sound of rain, I would say 'of much rain.' Oh! could we go amongst these people as freely and easily as in the provinces, I have no doubt hundreds would be added to the Lord. I think the Karens here superior to those in the provinces, so far as I have seen; and could they be collected together, and civilized, and Christianized, they would be a lovely nation. When will this happy time arrive? Hasten it, Lord, in thine own time, for Jesus' sake."

It was in this interesting and hopeful field that trial now abounded, and some of the oppressed Christians had to fly, to escape the tyranny of their Burman persecutors. But they bore with them the faith they had embraced, and preached the Gospel in all the regions into which they fled. Ko-thah-byu was soon found with a portion of his scattered flock, telling the story of the cross and teaching the precepts of Christ, in districts hitherto unvisited.

At Rangoon all labor was for a time suspended; but when Mr. and Mrs. Vinton went up at the end of 1836, and, with Mr. Abbott and Mr. Howard, made a tour up the Irrawaddy and into the district of Maubee, they met large numbers, who, notwithstanding the severity of the trials to which they had been subjected, had embraced Christianity, and had been long waiting for baptism. In the course of that journey alone one hundred and seventy-three were baptized nearly all of whom had received the truth from the preaching of Ko-thah-byu.

Mr. Kincaid, who was at this time at Ava, had among the small congregation of believers under his care, a young Burman of rank, whose sister was maid of honor to the Queen. Hearing that her brother had renounced idolatry, she used every effort to persuade him to return to the faith of his fathers; but finding all her attempts were fruitless as long as he remained under Christian influence, she obtained for him through the Queen an appointment under Government in the province of Bassein. It was with deep sorrow that he left his home and Christian brethren, for a province five hundred miles distant, where he could have little hope of finding any who, like himself, knew and loved the God of Israel. He was scarcely, however, installed as Governor of the Karens in Bassein, when the Burmese officials brought before him some men from the jungles, whom they charged with worshipping a strange God. "What God?" was his first question. "They call him the eternal God!" was the reply, and great was their astonishment when the new Governor instead of ordering them away to punishment, commanded that they should be set free, and the Karen Christians returned to their homes unmolested, and in peace. When the rumor spread abroad that the new Governor not only tolerated the religion of Jesus, but kept His day and observed His laws, there could no longer be any doubt that he was a Christian. Persecutions on account of religion were at an end; during the two years of his mild rule at Bassein, the word of God spread and prevailed, and at the end of that time, two thousand persons were reported by the native preachers as converted souls.

So diversified and wide spread were the labors of the missionaries at this period, that it is impossible, in a work of this kind, to give more than a passing glance at all. Dr. Judson was pursuing his labors at Maulmain; and the Wades, who had returned from America, were now stationed at Tavoy, and together with the Masons carrying on their indefatigable work of teaching, preaching, and translations. Mrs. Judson at this period gave great attention to the Peguans, a race who are entirely distinct from the Burmans in everything but their religion. They were numerous in the neighborhood of Maulmain, and as they mingled with the congregations of Burmans or Karens, had often awakened an interest in the hearts of the missionaries. Nothing however had been especially attempted for them, until Mrs. Judson, with her accustomed energy and zeal devoted herself to acquiring their language and translated into it several tracts, a compilation of her own of the Life of Christ, and a considerable portion of the New Testament. On the arrival of Mr. Haswell in 1836, who had been appointed to take charge of the Malaing mission, she surrendered to him her labor and the fruits it was already promising, and returned to the appropriate duties of her station, having performed a task of great difficulty and importance, which no other member of the mission was then able to accomplish.

In the commencement of 1837, we find that Mr. Kincaid had been strengthened at Ava by the arrival of Mr. and Mrs. Simons, and Mr. and Mrs. Webb. Certainly no place in the empire offered greater facilities for the prosecution of their great work than the capital itself. As the centre of authority, and the residence of the Emperor, it was resorted to from every quarter of the realm by persons of influence, as well as by the princes and their retainers, and the merchants and traders who brought their produce from every corner of the land.

Mr. Kincaid had become acquainted with several who had travelled to Ava in the train of some Shan princes. These people occupy the provinces on the northern frontier of Burmah. Having carefully inquired from them the position of their country, he conceived the idea that it would be possible by this route to gain access to China, and by this means not only to convey the gospel to the Shans, but to that great nation also. For the purpose of ascertaining how far his views were correct, and to become acquainted with the people of the northern provinces, he determined with the approval of his brethren to visit the frontier of Assam. On the 27th January, 1837, accompanied by four native Christians, he embarked on the Irrawaddy in a boat despatched on the public service by Col. Burney, who was then the English Resident at Ava.

After a twenty-two days' passage, through a country of great natural beauty, they reached the city of Mogaung, distant three hundred and fifty miles from the capital. Here beneath the shadow of the Himalaya mountains, rising as the natural barrier between the countries, lay the vast wilderness which separates Burmah from Hindustan. During his stay in the city he made several excursions into the valley, but from the difficulty of obtaining either men or provisions to enable him to pursue his journey further, he was compelled very reluctantly to return to Ava. The country was now in a state of civil war, and overrun with hordes of banditti eager for the lives and property of those who fell into their hands. On his way down the river Mr. Kincaid was attacked and captured by one of these marauding parties. He was bound and carried off to their village. Here a guard of about five and twenty men formed in a ring was set around him. Every morning a portion of the band departed on some expedition of cruelty and wrong, and returned in the evening to exhibit their prisoners and their spoil. Many were the frightful scenes to which Mr. Kincaid was witness. Just outside the ring by which he was enclosed, met the council of chiefs, before whom the prisoners were brought up. Their great difficulty seemed to be to know how to dispose of him. If they killed him, it was argued that search would be made, and reparation demanded for the life of the "white foreigner." If they released him, he would tell of the deeds he had witnessed and of the treatment to which he had been subject, and again nothing but difficulty and danger would ensue. In this way their counsels were divided, and day after day passed by, and found them undecided, and life or death trembled in the balance. Mean while God was working out a way of deliverance. In the number of the guard was a young Cathay chief, who viewed the captive with compassion. Probably he had heard him tell the wondrous story which had attracted so many listeners. The face, at all events, was familiar to Mr. Kincaid, and there was a look of pity in those dark eyes which awakened hope, and spoke of sympathy. One day, when unobserved by the others, he slipped his brawny hand into that of the captive, and deposited a small silver coin. The impulse was to decline the proffered kindness, but the quick "Hush!" in the Burman tongue, "you may want it," silenced him. That evening the Chiefs assembled as usual, and amongst the prisoners brought before them, was a Burman woman carrying an infant in her arms, and followed by a young girl, her daughter, and two other little ones. There was a nobility in her step, and a lofty courage on her brow, which seemed for a moment to awe into silence the persecutors. She was interrogated as to where her property and her jewels were concealed, and threatened with death if she would not confess, but she was immovable, and was ordered to receive the lash. In vain were the cries of the frantic children who clung around her, or the supplication and entreaties of the elder girl; there was no heart to pity there. The back was uncovered, the massive hair fell heavily over one shoulder, and the executioner with a heavy bamboo cane did his work. Stroke after stroke descended. The lips moved not: no cry was uttered; but a cloud passed over the upturned face, and she sank to the ground motionless: all was over! The captive, who had watched that scene till reason reeled, and the brain was fired, was only brought to consciousness by finding that the strong arms were pinioned, and he sank back in the agony of despair. That night when all were sleeping round him, the young Cathay chief loosened his bonds, and, stealing gently through the dusky forms, Mr. Kincaid was once more a free man breathing the free air of heaven. His journey onward was most perilous; hiding by day, he had to travel on by night, and when pressed by hunger, waiting at the wells in the early morn-

4*

ing, until the women came to draw water, he would throw himself on their compassion, and was seldom refused the nourishment which enabled him to pursue his journey. In this way, after innumerable dangers, from which the hand of God alone delivered him, he reached the capital in safety. He found it in confusion and alarm, and threatened with the horrors of a civil war. Prince Tharawaddy had dethroned the King his brother, and was investing the city. The missionaries vainly hoped that the new King might be more favorable to their views; but in their first interview, he strictly prohibited the work in which they were engaged; and, seeing no hope of pursuing it in the present excited state of the country, they retired for a season to Maulmain.

## CHAPTER V.

### ARRACAN.

"Tell them that near your idol dome,
There dwells a lonely man,
Who bade ye take this message home,
"Six men for Arracan."—THURBY.

BEFORE proceeding, we must endeavor to take a brief survey of the Mission in ARRACAN. This province is bounded on the north by Chittagong, on the east by the Yoma mountains, while on the south and west, it is washed by the waters of the Bay of Bengal. It belonged formerly to the Burman Empire, but was ceded to the British Government in 1826.

Mr. and Mrs. Comstock were the first of the American Mission who established themselves in Arracan, at Kyouk Phyoo, a town near the northern extremity of Ramree Island. This was in the year 1835. Preaching and schools were commenced, and the people listened with interest and curiosity. In consequence of the ill-health of some, and the death of others who joined the mission, it passed through a series of most trying vicissitudes for the first five years, when, in 1840, it was strengthened by the arrival of Mr. Kincaid and Mr. Abbott from Burmah. They had been compelled to leave their field of labor there, in consequence of the persecutions to which their presence subjected the converts, but they determined nevertheless to keep up communication with their suffering flocks: Mr. Kincaid with Ava, and Mr. Abbott with the scattered disciples in the districts of Bassein and Rangoon.

After visiting the missionaries at Ramree, Mr. Kincaid went to Akyab. Here, since the year 1826, Mr. Fink of the Serampore Baptist Mission had been laboring, and both here and at Cruda little churches had been formed. When however the stations supported by the Serampore Mission were made over to the Baptist Missionary Society, it was resolved that Akyab should be given up to the American Mission, and Mr. Kincaid took charge of it on their behalf in 1840. Mr. Abbott at the same time selected Sandoway as being favorably placed for opening up communication with the Karens, who dwelt beyond the mountains of Arracan on the neighboring districts of Burmah Proper.

Ko-thah-byu and his family had accompanied Mr. Abbott to Sandoway; and it was here, just as he had commenced to reap the fruit of his few months' labor in a little village in which he was located, that he was summoned to his eternal rest. He had suffered much of late years from rheumatism, and was often unable to walk or to rise; but a violent cold settling in inflammation of the lungs, soon hurried him to the grave. He came to die near Mr. Abbott, and had " no fears :" " As it pleases God," was the frame of his spirit. "No mound marks his grave, no storied urn his resting place; but the eternal mountains are his monument; and the Christian villages that clothe their sides, are his epitaph." In his beloved work he was unceasingly active even to the close of life, and seemed incapable of fatigue. " It was the death of Christ as a substitute," he used to say, with peculiar emphasis, " that laid the foundation of our hopes. It is because He stood in our place and suffered the penalty due to our crimes, that we, who believe in Him, may now be saved." This great truth he used to bring into almost every sermon; so that those who were converted through his instrumentality, had usually a thorough knowledge of the doctrine of justification by faith. His success as an evangelist was most remarkable. "Perhaps not one in a thousand from the days of the Apostles to the present time, of those who may have devoted their whole lives exclusively to this work, have been the instrument of converting as many individuals as this simple hearted Karen." But it may be asked, how was it that a man of such inferior power should have been such a Boanerges, as a preacher of the gospel? His strength was in *prayer*. He was pre-eminently a man of prayer. "Of myself I am nothing, and can do nothing. In the name of the Lord, I can do all things." It was this feeling of self-distrust, combined with simple faith in the promise, that drew him to the mercy-seat, and kept him there. When not employed in preaching he spent his time almost exclusively in prayer and reading. "It was," says one who knew him well, "his practice, to read and pray aloud, though in a low tone of voice; so that I have known him spend whole days in this way. After evening worship he would commence again; and continue until nine, ten, and even eleven o'clock at night, when he would retire; but not spend the whole night in sleep. At the time I knew him, he used seldom to spend a night without praying as many as three times, or at least as often as he awoke; and I have heard it said of him that he has occasionally spent whole nights in prayer to God." Is it then a matter of wonder that such a man should be honored of his God; that he should have souls given him for his hire; that he should preach with demonstration of the Spirit and with power?

"In 1828 he was the first Karen Christian. In 1840, when he died, there were officially reported as members of Christian congregations in Pegu, above one thousand two hundred and seventy individuals of that oppressed and despised race."

On arriving at Sandoway Mr. Abbott sent out two native assistants to the Karens to tell them of his arrival, and to invite them to visit him. They were also commissioned to search for the young men who had been studying with Mr. Abbott at Rangoon, and to beg them to come and continue their studies at Sandoway. The news soon spread that the teacher had arrived, and was located on the other side of the mountains, and within their reach; and although the passes were guarded by Burmans, many escaped their watchful vigilance, and flocked over the mountains, some for books, some for baptism, and others desiring to remain and study with their beloved teacher. Many of the converts from Maubee, Pautanau, and even from the neighborhood of Rangoon found access to the missionary, and from them he was able to gain intelligence of others, and from time to time to hear of the wonderful progress of the gospel amongst the people. Many of the assistants believed that at that time there could not have been less than four thousand Christians in Burmah Proper; and although persecutions abounded, grace to endure abounded also, and fines and imprisonment were borne meekly and patiently for the sake of Him who had borne so much for them.

The Burman Magistrates began to find that the work was beyond their control, and in some instances said, "Let them worship their God, if they pay their taxes and obey the laws." This policy was followed to prevent the Karens emigrating in a body into the British Provinces.

In a tour made by Mr. Abbott in January, 1841, he met large numbers of Karens who had come from the Burman side of the mountains, who told him of the sufferings they had endured for reading the "white book." He was surprised at the amount of knowledge and intelligence which they possessed, and within a month he baptized fifty-seven persons, who gave every evidence of true conversion. In the following year still more fruit was found, churches formed, assistants placed over them, and nearly 300 admitted into the church by baptism. In this manner Mr. Abbott saw the cause to which he was devoted, everywhere triumphant, and though obliged to conduct the mission unassisted and alone, he beheld over the fields which it occupied a whole people turning to God. Within the period of five years three thousand were baptized.

During the cold season of 1842–43, in consequence of a royal order to exterminate the white people, and the religion of the foreigners, the persecution of the Karen Christians raged with unmitigated fury. In their homes and in their places of worship whole families were seized, and often cruelly beaten; while mothers separated from their children, were driven like sheep to prison, where they remained until they could satisfy the rapacity of the Burman officers. Mr. Abbott in writing of them says: "The noble, fearless testimony which those prisoners bear to the truth, has given their cause notoriety and character. The common people throughout the country generally look upon the new religion with interest at least, and *whisper* their sympathies with its suffering votaries."

So severe were the trials of this period that hundreds left the fields they could no longer cultivate, and fled across the mountains into Arracan. Whole villages would follow their pastor, bringing their buffaloes, and any small articles they could carry. Their condition was most pitiable, and met with generous sympathy, not only from the missionaries, but from the British residents in the province. Captain Phayre, the Assistant Commissioner, supplied them with food, and gave them one year to repay his loans without interest. And now, though in part dependent, they were at least secure, and enjoyed the priceless privilege of "Freedom to worship God." But their trials had not ended here. In the hot season which succeeded their arrival, the cholera laid waste the country, and so panic-stricken were these suffering people, that many fled to the mountains, and others to the jungle, where they perished uncared for, by the very pestilence they sought to escape.

The anxieties and labors of Mr. Abbott told heavily upon him. In the summer of 1844, both his children were taken from him, and in the January following, after a short illness, Mrs. Abbott followed them to their early grave.

Mrs. Abbott had been unwearied in her efforts for the salvation of the Burmese, with whose language she had become well acquainted. Taking her seat in the verandah of her house fronting the wayside, with a bundle of tracts and Scriptures, she would read and explain to all who might be disposed to listen. Occasionally a large group would sit in silence for hours, and some received into their hearts that truth which was able to save their souls. But her work was ended; the Master's call had come; and Mr. Abbott left alone, shattered in health and spirits, was compelled to return for a season to America.

Contemporaneously with this work at Sandoway, was the labor of Mr. Kincaid, at Akyab. He found on going there in 1840, the remnant of a little church, numbering thirteen members which had been gathered by Mr. Fink. They had been so long without any pastoral care, that even the first principles of the gospel were beginning to fade from their minds, and to have little influence over their lives. They were soon, however, gathered together for instruction and prayer; and the missionary, ere long, had the joy of finding himself surrounded with intelligent listeners, some eagerly inquiring to be more perfectly instructed in the way of life. Among the number was a man of superior learning, who, not many years before, had been sent by the King of Ava as a Buddhist missionary to Arracan, to explain the sacred books to the priests and people. Several persons were at this time baptized, and trial and persecution followed; but notwithstanding this, the church grew, and another was planted at Cruda an out-station five days' journey from Akyab.

In the beginning of 1841, Mr. Kincaid was visited by several people belonging to a tribe called the Kemmees, a race inhabiting the mountains, and similar in habits and appearance to the Karens. One of chiefs also visited the white teacher. He was at the head of several subordinate clans, and was known as the "mountain chief." They listened with but little interest to the teacher's words, and left, apparently unaffected by the great truths they had heard.

Not many months had passed away after this visit, when Mr. Kincaid was surprised by receiving a letter signed by "Chetza, the mountain chief," and thirteen other chieftains, stating that they had considered the new religion, and as their people were ignorant, they desired that the teacher would come, that they might "know the true God, and be taught the true book." The letter also contained the names of two hundred and seventy children, whom they would place at school, if he would come to their mountains. So eager was desire for instruction that this request was soon followed by a visit from the chief in person, who, followed by a large retinue, came to the mission-house just as Mr. Kincaid and Mr. Stilson were about starting for their villages.

Great was their joy at finding their request complied with. They hastened back to prepare, and when the missionaries reached their mountain homes, they found, to their surprise, not only a zayat erected for their accommodation, but many little articles which the observant eyes of the people had noticed in the mission house at Akyab, and which they had procured for the comfort and convenience of their welcome guests. The chief offered to build a house for the missionaries, if they would but remain; but this was impossible, and a few occasional visits were all that could be accomplished; sickness again interrupted this interesting work, and Mr. and Mrs. Kincaid were obliged for a time to visit America, leaving Mr. Stilson at Akyab.

Dark clouds were beginning to break over the Arracan mission. Since 1840 Mr. and Mrs. Comstock had been laboring with no common zeal at Ramree. He was a man of superior education, and of the noblest qualities of character, distinguished for his wisdom, earnestness, and zeal. Mr. Kincaid took home the Comstocks' two elder children, and while staying with them before embarking, Mr. Comstock used all his powers to impress Mr. Kincaid with the importance of urging upon the church the duty of sending out more missionaries to Arracan. So deep rooted was this desire in his heart, that even when parting with his beloved children, it burst forth in that long remembered message to the American churches: "Remember, brother, six men for Arracan!" It was on these few words, that the following verses were written.

> He sa'd,—My brother when you stand
>    Beyond the raging deep,
> In that delightful, happy land,
>    Where all our fathers sleep;
>
> When you shall hear their Sabbath bell
>    Call out their happy throngs,
> And hear the organ's solemn swell,
>    And Zion's sacred songs:

Tell them a herald, far away,
  Where midnight broods o'er man,
Bade you this solemn message say,
  "Six men for Arracan."

While in that happy land of theirs,
  They feast on blessings given,
And genial suns and healthful airs,
  Come speeding fresh from heaven;

Tell them, that near yon idol dome,
  There dwells a lonely man,
Who bade you take this message home,
  "Six men for Arracan."

Sweet home,—ah, yes! I know how sweet,
  Within my country, thou,
I've known what heart-felt pleasures meet,
  I've felt—and feel them now.

Well, in those lovely scenes of bliss,
  Where childhood's joys began,
I'd have you, brother, tell them this,
  "Six men for Arracan."

Oh! when the saint lies down to die,
  And friendship round him stands,
And faith directs his tearless eye,
  To fairer, happier lands—

How calm he bids poor earth adieu
  With all most dear below!
The spirit sees sweet home in view,
  And plumes her wings to go;

Stop dying saint—O! linger yet,
  And cast one thought on man—
Be this the last that you forget—
  "Six men for Arracan."

In the beginning of 1843, Mrs. Comstock fell a victim to an epidemic then prevailing; her two little ones soon sank under the same disease, and at the end of 1844, Comstock himself followed them, to his great reward. His loss to the mission was irreparable: his sound discretion, and deep devotion of spirit being felt throughout; but " shall not the Judge of all the earth do right ?" Thus, one after another of the missionaries, who for nine years had been laboring in Arracan, disappeared from the field, until Mr. and Mrs. Stilson in 1845, found themselves the solitary workers in that mission which had so justly created the highest hopes, and which apparently only needed additional laborers to ensure for it the noblest results.

We add now a brief review of the state of the missions at the other stations about this period. We find at Maulmain, in 1840, Dr. Judson, Messrs. Howard, Stevens, Osgood, and Simons, in connection with the Burman department, and Mr. Vinton with the Karen. The wives of the missionaries were more or less actively engaged in the schools, either for the Karens or Burmans. At Amherst, Mr. Haswell was still preaching to Talaings, or Peguans, or translating the New Testament into their language, while Mrs. Haswell pursued her work in the schools. Around Maulmain were several smaller stations for the Karens, superintended by the missionaries, but primarily under the charge of native assistants.

At Tavoy, although there was a small Burman church, the chief labors of the missionaries were amongst the Karens. Mr. and Mrs. Wade, and Mr. and Mrs. Mason, were now the only missionaries at this station, the Bennetts having had to revisit America. The churches at the out-stations round Tavoy, eight in all, numbered four hundred and seventy-three members. In connection with this branch of the mission was the important station of Mergui, under the care of Mr. Ingalls and Mr. Brayton, who with their families had been laboring there since 1839. Here too were out-stations, and little flocks of Christians gathered from among the heathen into the fold of God; and here, silently, earnestly, faithfully, had the work of God been carried on.

At the close of 1842 six churches were connected with this station, embracing 190 members. Mr. Ingalls and Mr. Brayton, besides preaching the gospel, devoted themselves to improving the special and domestic condition of the Karens, helping them to establish themselves in permanent homes, and thus to break off their wandering habits, which were so injurious to their civilization and spiritual improvement. The fact that there were Christian teachers at Mergui, became known to the Karens in the jungles east of Tenasserim, and many of these came in to see and hear for themselves. Thus the work of God grew; a new impulse was given to the cause of education; the social position of the Karens was elevated; and some of them were appointed to offices of trust.

At Maulmain Dr. Judson still devoted his principal attention to a careful revision of the Burman Bible, at the same time preaching to the Burman church, and superintending the labors of the native preachers, who were employed among the Burman population of the town and the neighboring villages. Mr. Stevens superintended the theological school, besides being pastor of the church of Pwo Karens at Dongyan; and Mr. Howard and Mr. Simons took the English services, and had charge of other schools at Maulmain. This disposition of their labors left none free to give his undivided attention to preaching the gospel to the Burmans, and was, we believe, a subject of regret. The Karen missionaries, on the contrary, from the peculiar character of the people, and the circumstances in which they were placed, were able not only to superintend the schools, and translate and prepare books, but to give a large portion of their time and attention to their chosen work of preaching the gospel. The dry season of each year was spent in visiting the villages in the jungle for this special work, while in the rainy season they resided in town, teaching the schools, writing for the press, and preaching on the Sabbath and on other days of the week. This constant proclamation of the gospel by the preacher's own voice, has undoubtedly been the instrument blessed of God above all others to the conversion of this people : a fact which every year's experience more fully illustrates. The universal cry with them appears to be " How beautiful upon the mountains are the feet of him that bringeth good tidings, that publisheth peace ; that bringeth good tidings of good ; that publisheth salvation."

## CHAPTER VI.

### THE JUDSONS.

> " All flesh must come
> To the cold tomb;
> Only the ashes of the just
> Smell sweet and blossom in the dust."

In 1841 Dr. Judson's health became seriously impaired, while that of Mrs. Judson and the children was also failing, and a voyage to sea became imperatively necessary. They left Maulmain in June and arrived in Calcutta in the following month; but while waiting for a vessel to take them to the Isle of France, the youngest child Henry was suddenly removed from them, and now sleeps beside Carey, Marshman, and Ward, in the burying-place at Serampore. The voyage to the Isle of France recruited their failing health and spirits, and they returned to Maulmain in December.

Dr. Judson immediately entered upon a work he had long been meditating, the preparation of a dictionary in English and Burman for the purpose of facilitating the acquisition of both these languages. In writing of this, he says : " Several years were spent in translating the Bible, and several more in revising it, and carrying the last edition through the press: after which, in May last, I commenced a dictionary of the language, a work which I had resolved and re-resolved never to touch. But it is not in man that walketh to direct his steps. The Board and my brethren repeatedly urged me to prepare a dictionary, the one printed in 1826 being exceedingly imperfect; and as Burmah continued shut against our labors, and there were several missionaries in this place, I concluded that I could do no better than to comply. We are apt to magnify the importance of any undertaking in which we are warmly engaged. Perhaps it is from the influence of that principle, that, notwithstanding my long-cherished aversion to the work, I have come to think it important; and that, having seen the accomplishment of two objects on which I set my heart, when I first came out to the East,—the establishment of a church of converted natives, and the translation of the Bible into their language,—I now beguile my daily toil with the prospect of compassing a third which may be compared to a causeway, designed to facilitate the transmission of all knowledge, religious and scientific, from one people to the other."

Mrs. Judson's pen was at this time not idle, but was also adding to the store of Burman literature, notwithstanding the many duties which crowded round her. With her "whatsoever her hand found to do" was done earnestly and with a ready will. It mattered not whether in the Karen wilderness surrounded by many a listener, or teaching the infant at her knee, or bending over her translations, or whispering those words which were to cheer her husband's heart, whether teaching, counselling, or praying,—all was done as to the Lord, and to the glory of His great name. Some of the literary performances of this closing part of her life are thus briefly mentioned by Dr. Judson:—"Her translation of the Pilgrim's Progress, Part I. into Burmese, is one of the best pieces of composition which we have yet published: her translation of Mr. Boardman's 'Dying Father's Advice,' has become one of our standard tracts: and her Hymns in Burmese, about twenty in number, are probably the best in our chapel Hymn-book, a work which she was appointed by the mission to edit. Besides these works she published four volumes of Scripture Questions, which are in constant use in our Sabbath-schools. It has been remarked that the translation of the Pilgrim's Progress into an Eastern tongue, is 'a work worth living for, if it were one's only performance.' It was indeed a laborious work, under the circumstances exceedingly laborious; and is performed as only one who knew and loved the language as she did, assisted by her native genius, could perform it. She also contributed some valuable articles to the Burmese newspaper; and in the absence of Mr. Stevens, its excellent and able conductor, she was two or three times called upon to take the editorial charge of it. Her Sabbath cards with the breathings of her devotional and poetic spirit yet warm upon their surface, (her last dying gift to the Burman church,) are still circulated from hand to hand: her Scripture Questions furnish hundreds of bewildered minds with the clue to many a fountain, flowing over with the fresh waters of truth and wisdom, and her sweet hymns are heard wherever the living God is worshipped in Burmah."

She avoided society, because it interfered with important pursuits, but she still had warm friends beyond the pleasant missionary circle. Their sympathy and love were not, however, her sweetest reward. In April, 1844, she thus writes: —"The state of religion is now very interesting in the Burman church. It would do your heart good to look in upon our little circle of praying Burman females; so humble, so devout, so willing to confess their faults to God and before one another, that I sometimes think Christians in a Christian land might well copy them. I think they do strive to walk in the footsteps of our blessed Saviour. The study of the Scriptures and social prayer seem to be greatly blessed to their souls. Some of them have formed themselves into a Bible class, and meet with me once a week for the purpose of studying the Scriptures. They are now examining the 'Life of Christ,' with questions which I prepared on the work some years ago. I think it does my own soul good, thus to ponder over the life of our blessed Lord. This Bible class has increased from about five to upwards of fifteen within the last month, and I see no signs of the members diminishing. Some of them are quite elderly women with grey hair. You would be pleased to see them with their spectacles on, sitting in a circle, reading the life of our Lord Jesus Christ, and conversing with each other respecting their duty. One of them, upwards of seventy years old, amused me a few days ago, by saying she was the same age as my little daughter Abby Ann. I asked her what she meant by that. She replied that she was converted the year Abby Ann was born, and it was not till then that she began to live."

In one of her last letters she says, "It is nineteen years last month since I bade adieu to my native land; and I can say, with unfeigned gratitude to God, that amid all the vicissitudes through which I have been called to pass, I have never for one moment regretted that I had entered the missionary field. We are not weary of our work; it is in our hearts to live and die among these people. I feel conscious of being a most unworthy and unprofitable servant, and I often wonder that my life has been spared, while so many, to human view so much more competent than myself, have been cut down. Even so, Father, for so it seemeth good in thy sight."

The disease, from which she had long suffered, had at last taken so firm a hold, that they were compelled to contemplate a voyage to America as the only hope of prolonging a life inexpressibly valuable. Followed by many a tearful eye and prayerful heart, they set sail on the 26th April, 1845, taking the three elder children, while the three little ones were left behind. the youngest only three and a half months old. "We left them," as Dr. Judson touchingly expressed it, "cast upon the waters, in the hope of finding them, after many days." On arriving at Port Louis, the health of Mrs. Judson appeared so decidedly to improve, that Dr. Judson determined to return to Maulmain, and to leave her and the children to prosecute their voyage to America alone.

It was in anticipation of this separation that Mrs. Judson penned the following lines: the last ever written by her trembling hand.

> "We part on this green islet, love,
> Thou for the eastern main,
> I for the setting sun, love—
> Oh, when to meet again?
>
> My heart is sad for thee, love,
> For lone thy way will be;
> And oft thy tears will fall, love,
> For thy children and for me.
>
> The music of thy daughter's voice
> Thou'lt miss for many a year;
> And the merry shout of thine elder boys
> Thou'lt list in vain to hear.
>
> When we knelt to see our Henry die
> And heard his last faint moan,
> Each wiped the tear from other's eye—
> Now each must weep alone.
>
> My tears fall fast for thee, love,
> How can I say, farewell?
> But go ;—thy God be with thee, love,
> Thy heart's deep grief to quell!

Yet my spirit clings to thine, love,
Thy soul remains with me,
And oft we'll hold communion sweet
O'er the dark and distant sea.

And who can paint our mutual joy
When, all our wanderings o'er,
We both shall clasp our infants three,
At home, on Burmah's shore.

But higher shall our raptures glow
On yon celestial plain,
When the loved and parted here below,
Meet ne'er to part again.

Then gird thine armor on, love,
Nor faint thou by the way,
Till Budh shall fall, and Burmah's sons
Shall own Messiah's sway."

The anticipated sacrifice was not permitted. The revival was deceptive, and together they again set sail " for the setting sun," in hope that life would be granted; but still strength declined until they reached St. Helena, when she gently passed away on the 1st of September, 1845. Dr. Judson says, " Heaven seems nearer and eternity sweeter, when I think of her and other dear friends who have gone before. . . . . . . . . . . They had prepared the grave in a beautiful shady spot contiguous to the grave of Mrs. Chater, a missionary from Ceylon, who had died in similar circumstances on her passage home. There I saw her safely deposited, and blessed God that her body had attained the repose of the grave, and the spirit the repose of paradise. . . . . For a few days in the solitude of my cabin, with my poor children crying round me, I could not help abandoning myself to heart-breaking sorrow. But the promises of the gospel came to my aid, and faith stretched her view to the bright world of eternal life, and anticipated a happy meeting with those beloved beings whose bodies are mouldering at Amherst and St. Helena."

Dr. Judson arrived at Boston on the 15th October, and was received by the whole Christian church with the expression of the warmest sympathy and attachment; but he shrunk from popular applause, and the more his brethren were disposed to exalt him, the more deeply did he seem to feel his own deficiency, and the more humble was his prostration at the foot of the cross. He still suffered so much from the complaint in his throat he was quite unable to address large audiences, but the impression left upon the minds of those who did hear him, was that to him, " to live was Christ, to die was gain." It it was quite evident that although interested in all that he saw in his own country, his heart was in Burmah, and that he longed to resume his quiet labors there for the salvation of the heathen. He married Miss Chubbuck, distinguished for her literary talents, and sailing from America on the 11th July, 1846, arrived at Maulmain on the 30th November following. They were accompanied by several new missionaries ; Mr. and Mrs. Harris, who were appointed to the Karen department of the mission at Maulmain, and subsequently to Shwaygyeen ; Mr. and Mrs. Beecher, who were destined for Arracan ; and Miss Lillybridge who was to be a teacher in the Burman school at Maulmain. During the absence of Dr. Judson many changes had occurred. Mrs. Helen Mason and Mrs. Ingalls had been removed by death ; and Mr. Ingalls had gone to Akyab to fill the vacancy that had been made by the removal of Mr. Stilson to Maulmain. At Akyab Mr. Ingalls had commenced the work of preaching. His house was thronged by visitors from morning till night: Some came expressly to hear the gospel, some to dispute and oppose. A chapel was built close upon the public streets, and the word, notwithstanding the hardness of the hearts of the people, took effect. Within two months, fifteen converts were baptized at Akyab, among whom were five Kemmees, the first-fruits among that people. The principal employment of Mr. Ingalls and his assistants was "preaching the word," and after a residence of fourteen years in Burmah, Mr. Ingalls reported he had never seen the prospects so encouraging. He says :

"The work is going on among the Kemmees, and souls are being converted. I have twenty here in a day-school. The Kemmee chief, with many of his tribe, dressed in their rude clothes, came with a long petition, saying, 'Come and preach to us, and tell us of Him who came to save us.' Glory be to God, even with the Arracanese, these hard people, are seeking the way to heaven. I preach until my lungs are almost worn out. Karens have come to my school from Sandoway, as their teacher (Mr. Abbott) has gone to America. Cholera has now come, and our Christians are being called home. Several have died. One poor man, as his limbs became cold in death, reached me his only rupee, and said, 'Teacher, put this in for the building of our chapel.' And then he closed his eyes.........Baptized some to-day and buried some. I have no fears for those in the grave, but I have anxieties for the others, for their temptations are great in this place." Early in the year 1850, Mr. Ingalls had to abandon this interesting work for a season, and to return to America.

On Dr. Judson's return to Maulmain, he found all the departments of labor there well supplied. In Rangoon there was not a single missionary nor in all Burmah proper, and he therefore determined, if possible, to find an entrance and shelter there for himself and his family, and once more to attempt to gather the little flock together. A large dilapidated house in a street of Mussulmans was at last obtained, his family were around him and the dictionary re-commenced. At their first communion, ten Burmans, one Karen, and two foreigners were present. In writing home at this time, Dr. Judson says: "I have just returned from baptizing a Burman convert, in the same tank of water where I baptized the first Burman convert Moung Nau, twenty-eight years ago. The present administration of Government, though rather more friendly to foreigners, is more rigidly intolerant than that of the late King Tharawaddy; any known attempt at proselyting would be instantly amenable at the criminal tribunal, and would probably be punished by the imprisonment or death of the proselyte, and the banishment of the missionary. The Governor of this place has received me favorably, not as a missionary, though he well knows from old acquaintance, that that is my character, but as a minister of a foreign religion, ministering to foreigners resident in that place, and a dictionary-maker, 'laboring to promote the welfare of both countries.' Our missionary efforts, therefore, being conducted in private, must necessarily be very limited. It is, however, a precious privilege to be allowed to welcome into a private room a small company, perhaps two or three individuals only, and pour the light of truth into their immortal souls; souls that, but for the efficacy of that light, would be covered with the gloom of darkness, darkness to be felt to all eternity."

Things were thus going on when Dr. Judson learned that a private order had been issued to watch the missionary's house, and apprehend any who might be liable to the charge of favoring "Jesus Christ's religion." This of course put a stop to any further effort, and Dr. Judson determined once more to visit Ava to solicit toleration from the Government.

But funds were wanting from the mission treasury, and the object had to be abandoned; he returned with his family to Maulmain, and employed himself without intermission upon the Burmese dictionary until the month of November, 1849. He was then seized with a violent cold, followed by an attack of fever of a much more serious character than any from which he had before suffered. A trip down the coast afforded partial relief; but he was again prostrated, and it was evident that his life was drawing to a close. We cannot forbear giving a few extracts from Mrs. Judson's account of his last days—but we earnestly recommend Dr. Wayland's Memoir of Dr. Judson, to the careful perusal of all those who have not yet read it. Mrs. Judson remarks, "Being accustomed to regard all the events of this life, however minute or painful, as ordered in wisdom, and tending to one great and glorious end, he lived in almost constant obedience to the apostolic injunction, 'Rejoice evermore!' He often told me, that although he had endured much personal suffering, and passed through many fearful trials in the course of his eventful life, a kind providence had also hedged him round with precious and peculiar blessings, so that his joys had far out-numbered his sorrows........As his health declined, his mental exercises at first seemed deepened; and he gave still larger portions of his time to prayer, conversing with the utmost freedom on his daily progress, and the extent of his self-conquest. Just before our trip to Mergui he looked up with sudden animation and said to me earnestly, 'I have gained the victory at last. I love every one of Christ's redeemed, as I believe He would have me love them, in the manner, though not probably to the same degree as we shall love one another in heaven; and gladly would I prefer the meanest of his creatures, who bears his name before myself.' This is said, in allusion to the text 'in honor preferring one another,' on which he had frequently dwelt with great emphasis........ From this time no other word would so well express his state of feeling as that one of his own choosing —*peace*. He had no particular exercises afterwards, but remained calm and serene, speaking of himself daily as a great sinner, who had been overwhelmed with benefits, and declaring that he had never, in all his life before, had such delightful views of the unfathomable love and infinite condescension of the Saviour as were now daily opening before him. 'Oh, the love of Christ! the love of Christ!' he would suddenly exclaim, while his eye kindled, and the tears chased each other down his cheeks, 'we cannot understand it now— but what a beautiful study for eternity!'"

After their return from Mergui, sea air and sea bathing were recommended, and they went for a month to Amherst, but he rapidly declined, and on returning to Maulmain a sea voyage was ordered as the only hope of recovery. Mrs. Judson, who was not in a state to accompany him, was anxious to ascertain before he left her, his own opinion with regard to his state. She says : " I could not bear him to go away without knowing how doubtful it was whether our next meeting would not be in eternity." The question was suggested : Is it your wish to recover ? "If it should be the will of God, yes. I should like to complete the dictionary on which I have bestowed so much labor, now that it is so nearly done ; for though it has not been a work that pleased my taste, or quite satisfied my feelings, I have never underrated its importance. Then after that, come all the plans we have formed. Oh, I feel as if I were only just beginning to be prepared for usefulness."

"It is the opinion of most of the mission," Mrs. Judson remarked, " that you will not recover." "I know it is," he replied ; " and I suppose they think me an old man, and

5*

imagine it is nothing for one like me to resign a life so full of trials. But I am not old, at least in that sense; you know I am not. Oh, no man ever left this world with more inviting prospects, with brighter hopes, with warmer feelings." ...... His face was perfectly calm, even while the tears broke away from the closed lids and rolled one after another down to the pillow. To some suggestions which his wife ventured to make, he replied, "It is not that, I know all that, and feel it in my inmost heart. Lying here on my bed when I could not talk, I had such views of the loving condescension of Christ, and the glories of heaven, as I believe are seldom granted to mortal man. It is not that I shrink from death, that I wish to live, neither is it because the ties that bind me here, though some of them are very sweet, bear any comparison with the drawings I at times feel towards heaven; but a few years would not be missed from my eternity of bliss, and I can well afford to spare them, both for your sake, and for the sake of the poor Burmans. I am not tired of my work, neither am I tired of the world; yet when Christ calls me home, I shall go with the gladness of a boy bounding away from his school. Perhaps I feel something like the young bride when she contemplates resigning the present associations of her childhood for a yet dearer home, though only a very little like her, for *there is no doubt resting on my future.*" "Then death would not take you by surprise, if it should come even before you got on board ship?" "Oh no," he said, "death will never take me by surprise, do not be afraid of that: I feel *so strong in Christ.* He has not led me so tenderly thus far, to forsake me at the very gate of heaven. No, no; I am willing to live a few years longer, if it should be so ordered; and if otherwise, I am willing and glad to die now. I leave myself entirely in the hands of God, to be disposed of according to His holy will."

And now came the final parting. He was carried to the ship, and left in charge of Mr. Ranney and one of the Burman converts, who were to accompany him; and little more than a week after he embarked, on the 12th April, 1849, he slept in Jesus.

During the last hour Mr. Ranney bent over him, and held his hand, while poor Panapah stood at a little distance weeping. The table had been spread in the cuddy as usual, and the officers did not know what was passing in the cabin, till summoned to dinner. Then they gathered about the door, and watched the closing scene with solemn reverence Now, thanks to a merciful God: his pains had left him; not a momentary spasm disturbed his placid face, nor did the contraction of a muscle denote the least degree of suffering; the agony of death was past, and his wearied spirit was turning to its rest in the bosom of the Saviour. From time to time he pressed the hand in which his own was resting, his clasp losing in force at each successive pressure; while his shortened breath—though there was no struggle, no gasping, as if it went and came with difficulty—gradually grew softer and fainter, until it died upon the air, and he was gone. Mr. Ranney closed his eyes, and composed the passive limbs; the ship's officers stole softly from the door, and the neglected meal was left upon the board untasted.

They lowered him to his ocean grave. And there they left him in his unquiet sepulchre: but it matters not, for while the unconscious clay is "drifting on the shifting currents of the restless main," "nothing can disturb the hallowed rest of the immortal spirit. Neither could he have a more fitting monument than the blue waves which visit every coast; for his warm sympathies went forth to the ends of the earth, and included the whole family of man."

Thus lived and died the " apostle of Burmah." " He mastered its language," said Dr. Mackay, one of the Calcutta missionaries who specially revered him, "he made it his own and smoothed its difficulties for his successors. He translated into the language of the people the whole word of God, with such skill, patience, and judgment, that his version bids fair, in the opinion of competent judges, to be the standard Bible of Burmah. He made the first Burman converts, and gathered together the first Burman congregation of Christians; and, with full assurance that the good seed had taken root, and would spring up vigorously in the land of his adoption, he died ' in his harness,' young in spirit, but ripe in years and honors. He stood out as the most remarkable man in the modern era of missions. Tried by every vicissitude of humanity, he came forth like pure gold: chained in a dungeon, and face to face with the executioner, or swimming on the topmost wave of popularity, the idol of all that was holy and good in his native land; in the extremes of household happiness, and household bereavements; driven again and again, as it seemed for ever, from the mission field, or rejoicing over his little flock and his completed Bible; in the pulpit, on the platform, or in cheerful social intercourse, Adoniram Judson was always true to his own high nature, combining the warm affections of a man, with the strength, simplicity, and directness of an apostle of the living God."

His uncompleted work of the dictionary was taken up by Mr. Stevens of the Maulmain mission, who, with great patience and perseverance, brought it to a conclusion in 1852, and thus completed a work which will be of lasting value to every student of Burmese.

## CHAPTER VII.

### NATIVE PREACHERS.

"He gave some ..... Evangelists."—Eph. iv. 2.

It will be well for us now to take a glance at the various mission stations, in order to trace the progress that, under the divine blessing, was being made in one of the most interesting departments of labor. In all was felt the increasing value of the Native Assistants and pastors. Some are mentioned in reports from different quarters in terms of the highest commendation.

The nomination of pastors to the office was generally effected in the following manner. A number of baptized Christians, living in the same village or vicinity, would select from among their own number a man to conduct public worship and discharge pastoral duties, and call him "teacher." Almost invariably he proved to be the best adapted for the work, by age, intelligence, and piety. Without further formalities, this band of Christians was called a church, and the man their pastor. The pastor generally pursued a course of study with the missionaries, during which period his character and qualifications became known; and if approved, he would be appointed an assistant. The standard of moral purity among the Christians is very high, and in two instances, individuals have been cut off from communion and fellowship, by the unanimous vote of the native assistants themselves. The readiness with which ministerial support has been supplied by the native churches is most encouraging, as also the manner in which the pastoral relationship has been in general sustained.

Writing from Sandoway in 1351, Mr. Beecher says of the "Great Plains:" "This church has been greatly afflicted in the sudden death of its pastor, Wah Dee, while on a preaching tour in Burmah. His memory was held in most affectionate remembrance. Wah Dee, though dead, 'has become a sweet smelling savor,' was the remark of the aged headman of the village. A great improvement had been made during the past three years in his village. The houses arranged in rows and built with care,—the ground under and around, free from rubbish and often swept,—the little plots of vegetables well cultivated and fruitful,—the thriving nurseries, the streets wide and straight and mostly bordered with fruit trees and flowers, whose fragrance filled the air, all done by Wah Dee, all planned and directed by Wah Dee, altogether formed a spot lovely and pleasant. The outward condition of the people was a fair representation of their spiritual state. Their many and severe afflictions, (for many have befallen them,) have been sanctified to their growth in grace; and a degree of intelligence and spirituality are exhibited which far exceeded expectation. Arrangements are made to supply the place of the pastor by his son, a youth of great promise, the headman meanwhile continuing to aid in conducting worship and watching over the members."

Again, writing of Thay Rau, he says: "The people of this village have exhibited much of Christian enterprise in building it, and are advancing in civilization as well as Christianity. Four years previously, the place was a dense wilderness, but the rice field has appeared instead of the jungle; and where, a few years since, roamed herds of wild elephant, Christians now walk in company to the house of God. The prosperous appearance of the people is here also attributable in a marked degree to pastoral influence. No native preacher has a greater or better influence abroad, and none is more beloved and respected at home. As we passed by or entered his room from day to day, and saw Tway Poh,—the *Rev.* Tway Poh we should say, for no minister was ever more worthy of the title than he, sitting by his table, reading and studying, or conversing with those who sought his advice, we often wished that our brethren and sisters who feel such an interest in this people, could experience the delight that we did, as the expression came involuntarily to our lips, How much like a pastor in his study at home! Let the prayers of Christians ascend to the great Head of the church, that he will raise up from among this people many such pastors as Tway Poh."

In the early part of 1851, Mr. Van Meter gave a most interesting account of one of the annual associations, or meetings of the churches in the jungles at Thay Rau. Mr. and Mrs. Beecher had started in another boat to accompany him, but a violent storm prevented their accomplishing their object. Mr. Van Meter mentions the order and solemnity which pervaded the meeting, and the feeling of extraordinary interest with which he listened to the preaching from day to day of the native pastors.

The details of their missionary labors and the blessing which had followed, were very striking. Tha Bwa had been the means of the conversion of a whole village, which at once asked for a teacher, and promised to build him a house to live in. On hearing this, one of the young men who had just commenced preaching, begged and obtained permission to go and labor among the people. The interest excited by these services was deep and solemn, there was no restlessness, and during the closing prayer, there was such a marked silence, that it was evident all hearts were engaged. Just as Mr. Van Meter was preparing to depart, a note was received from the Commissioner, informing them of warlike preparation in Burmah. There was universal alarm among the Karens, and before midnight the whole company were prepared to separate. It was a solemn parting. Would they ever meet again on earth? Would they ever reach their homes at all? These were thoughts which the circumstance too readily suggested, but the eye of faith could look beyond the present time, and pierce the clouds which for a moment hid the bright future from their sight.

In this year we have a very interesting account of the conversion and baptism of the first of the Khyen tribe. Mr. Knapp, who was now laboring amongst the Kemmees, mentions a visit from a Khyen woman, who having been long a slave in Burmah, had at length obtained her liberty, and had made the home of her old age among the Kemmees. The Burman disciples had taken great pains in explaining to her the way of life by Jesus Christ, and she proved her sincerity by her earnest desire " to put her sins all away, and to be Jesus Christ's disciple." When she came to Mr. Knapp she could scarcely speak from emotion, the tears trickled down her aged face, " I am in a dark wild land," she said, " but I don't want to live so. I want *light*. I want to put my trust in Jesus, and to be his disciple. I want to be baptized. Mr. Knapp writes, " On Sunday morning I had the privilege of baptizing the Khyen woman ; she gave such evidence of faith and repentance, as satisfied all the Burman disciples who were with me; indeed all the evidence that could be hoped for. She calmly trusts in Christ, and now rejoices in hope of the glory of God."

How marked are the dealings of providence in this woman's history! Brought up a wild Khyen, carried by a band of robbers into slavery, by which means she became familiar with the Burman language, liberated by some means and brought among this Kemmee people, she now hears, in the Burman tongue, the glad tidings of salvation, believes, and is saved! Thus, 'the wrath of man shall praise Him.' After her baptism she was constantly at the meetings and engaged in prayer of her own accord; was anxious to learn to count the days that she might keep the Sabbath holy, and seemed very desirous to lead others, especially women, to Christ; and said she wished she could live within one hour or one day of the teacher, that she could hear more of the gospel, for it made her heart glad. May the great Shepherd keep her!

Not less interesting was the work that went on at this period in Tavoy and Mergui. The native assistants and pastors labored with earnestness and devotion of spirit, and were taught to endure hardness as good soldiers of Christ. One, in writing to his brethren to encourage and stimulate their zeal, says:

"When we travel among the unconverted, sometimes we are starved, and sometimes we are sick, and then our hearts are troubled. Why is it so? Because we lack love. Brethren! We ought to think of the work of the Lord Jesus, who possessed love. How did he show his love, the greatest possible exhibition of love? By his sufferings. Now he hungered forty days, and anon he suffered pain till the perspiration rolled from him like drops of blood, and in his final exhibition of love he suffered death. All his sufferings were for our sins. Our Lord's love extended to the sacrifice of his life. Now we ought to contemplate these things minutely, definitely, and tread in his footsteps all our lives. We should consider that he loved us unto death, and thus be led to love each other. We ought, each and every one of us, to arm ourselves in the Lord with the doing of his work and prayer. The Holy Scriptures say, 'The righteous man's supplication from the heart overcometh much.' Now we must go among the heathen, and as the disciples prayed and exhorted on the day of Pentecost, and the Holy Spirit was poured out, converting three thousand persons, so let us call out aloud and in earnest, like the apostles of old, that the people may become Christians."

Mr. Thomas, who with his wife had not long arrived in the country, gives a vivid description of his first impressions, on visiting the jungle. "The tour has been most refreshing to our souls. During the seven months since we arrived in Tavoy, we had been cooped up in this city, where the multitudes seem as mad upon their idols as if no missionary had ever visited these shores. But in visiting the jungles, we passed from the sight of idols and the tumult of their worshippers into quiet Christian villages: where, instead of gorgeous kyoungs, we found modest Christian chapels, in which, instead of idols and altars strewn with tinsel offerings or smoking with incense, are roughly-wrought tables bearing the Holy Bible and hymn book. Instead of being tormented by the dismal sound of instruments in honor of Gaudama, we joined a happy people in their songs of praise to Christ. I do bless God that I have witnessed the fulfilment of this his gracious promise, 'The wilderness and solitary place shall be glad for them, and the desert shall rejoice and blossom as the rose.' The most interesting feature of our tour was the Association of the churches of the Tavoy and Mergui provinces, at Ongpong. There the native Christians met, mingled their greetings and songs of praise, and joined in spirited discussions on subjects most intimately connected with the interests of the Redeemer's kingdom in these provinces. In all their exercises nothing but a spirit of love and harmony was manifest. What hath God wrought!"

At this Association the following resolutions were submitted by the Karen Christians for their mutual adoption. They were believed to have originated with the natives themselves, and what is here given is a literal translation. Another resolution pledges Christian parents to discourage the marriage of their children before they arrive at mature age. The contrary practice which did prevail, was most injurious.

"' 1. We will avoid that superstitious forsaking of property [such as quitting a house because a person has died in it, and a thousand things of that kind,] which was practised by our ancestors, but is contrary to the Scriptures.

"' 2. We will avoid all vain oaths, particularly such as refer to the name of God.

"' 3. We will avoid all attempts to frighten our children into obedience by telling them what is not true [as, that some fearful thing will happen to them, a tiger will bite them, &c.]; also, we will endeavor to avoid all kinds of deception, and lying words.

"' 4. We will avoid all kinds of vain and foolish songs, such as the heathen use, to excite their passions.

"' 5. We will avoid all kinds of personal contests, as wrestling, betting, &c.

"' 6. We will avoid all charms and amulets and all those supposed medicines which the heathen regard as securities against superstitious ills; tattooing, &c.

"' Avoiding all these, we will endeavor strictly to obey the commandments and doctrines of the Holy Scriptures. And every custom or practice which we find contrary to the Holy Scriptures, whatever it may be, we will be contrary unto it, and carefully avoid it. Whatever cannot be found in the Holy Scriptures shall not be reduced to practice.'

"In regard to public worship;

"'1. When we assemble for worship in the sanctuary, we will sit down in silence and wait for the communication of the word of God from the teacher.

"'2. When the gong sounds to indicate the hour of worship, we will immediately drop all work or employment, and repair at once to the sanctuary or the house of prayer.

"'3. All kinds of worldly talk, as of buying and selling, seeking food, &c., we will avoid on the Sabbath in our meetings for the worship of God.

"'All these obligations we will be careful to observe as long as we live. We are, according to the Scriptures, children of the light, and we will walk in the light. We will faithfully watch, as the Scriptures have taught us. Everything which tends to debase us, everything which is unholy, everything which will grieve or hinder the Holy Spirit, everything which brings darkness upon the kingdom of God, we will avoid. We will never permit any of these to enter our practice.'"

The preceding sketches present a view of the mission as it appeared just before the outbreak of hostilities in Pegu.

At that time a fiery trial fell upon the infant churches of that province. The Christian Karens were known to bear no allegiance to Burmese rule, and were held responsible for the war. In many parts ruinous taxes were levied upon them, their worship was forbidden, and their chapels were destroyed. Many were imprisoned as hostages for peace, with the threat that on the first invasion by the English, they should all be put to death. The appearance of the English happily caused so dire a panic, that the prisoners escaped without harm, but after a little space the courage of their oppressors revived. Burman troops and hordes of lawless robbers, ravaged the country, burning and pillaging in all directions, and torturing and killing the defenceless villagers. Goaded by suffering to an unwonted degree of courage, the Karens prepared to repel force by force. They were disarmed by the Burmans at the commencement of hostilities, but they took the field with what weapons they could procure, obtained further supplies from the English, and acted with bravery and effect. In several skirmishes they defeated their enemies with inconsiderable loss to themselves; in some others they were less successful.

The occupation of Pegu by the English interposed only a partial check upon the ruinous disorder. The delay incident to military operations in such a country, gave time for fresh outbreaks of violence and rapine, some details of which are too terrible to relate, but the final expulsion of the Burmese force terminated this state of anarchy, and at last gave quiet to the land. Immediately on the establishment of the English at Bassein, the peculiar claims of the Karens to protection were regarded by the Commander. One of their own head men, known as the " Young Chief," was made their Chief Magistrate. A pious officer obtained from Maulmain a box of books to distribute among them; and Mr. Abbott, who had now returned from America, and Mr. Van Meter, embracing the earliest opportunity to visit them, arrived at Bassein on 12th July, 1852. They were received with demonstrations of joy by the Karens, and the news of their arrival brought numbers from all parts to see their teachers, many to see them for the first time. Soon after they landed, they had an interview with a company of native preachers, who gave a minute account of their sufferings and necessities. The following account of the martyrdom, during the war, of one of their pastors, written in Burmese by a Burmese doctor, an eye-witness and a heathen, is most affecting.

"Thagua, pastor of the White Book people in the vicinity of Bassein, was taken by the Burman Magistrate, on the accusation of having called in the English to take their country. They seized him and his son and struck him thirty lashes on his way to prison. The son they struck twenty-five lashes. A nephew also was beaten. They took him to the Governor and paid 30 Rs. to the ruler. Now these Burmans were agreed in killing all the disciples, but waited a little to get money. They said to the Governor, These white book men will come and kill you as they did the chiefs in Rangoon. The Governor then said, 'Seize them!' So they seized the pastor and forty of his people, and hooked them together with iron hooks. Then they liberated the old men, and told them to go and get 130 Rs. and they should be free again. The elders did so, and paid the 130 Rs., but the Burman Kala did not free them, but hooked them again. The next day he dragged out Thagua the pastor, and struck him twice, then pressed him between bamboo, then tied him by the neck to a mango tree, his hands tied behind to the tree. Thagua cried out, 'My lord, my lord, do you kill me?' Kala answered: 'Give me 170 Rs. and you shall be free.'

"Thagua replied: 'I have no silver, my lord.'

"The Magistrate answered: 'The disciples give you 100 Rs. per year.'

"'No, my lord. They never gave me so much.'

"Then said Kala to the disciples: 'Give his ransom, and take your leader, and all shall be peace. If not, we will slaughter him.'

"The disciples said: 'My lord, if his life may be spared we will give the money.' The 170 Rs. were given, but still they did not free him. Then Kala led them all back to the village of Pataw, and gave the pastor into the hands of the Judge. The Judge reviled him, saying:

"'If your God is Almighty bid him take you out of these hooks.'

"Thagua replied; 'If the Eternal God does not now save me from your hands, he will save me eternally in the world to come.' The Judge asked, 'How do you know that?'

"Thagua replied: 'God's Holy Book tells me so, and it is true.'

"The Judge replied: 'Yes, you teach the people this book, and because you are talented and cunning the white men come and take our country.'

"Then the Judge himself fell upon him, mad with rage, and beat him with the elbow severely, then hooked him with five pairs of hooks, and ordered him back to prison.

"Three days after, the Judge again dragged up Thagua and said: 'Your God you say can save you. Read his book before me now.'

"Thagua replied: 'Though I read you will not believe, but persecute me still. But the Eternal God, my Judge and your Judge, the Lord Jesus Christ, he will save me.'

"'Command Him then to save you from my hands now!' said the Burman.

"The chief Judge then beat him with a cudgel as large as his wrist thirty blows, then ordered him back to prison with very little rice. Two days after Kala went to this Judge, and Thagua asked him, 'My lord, what do you?'

"'Kill you every one,' he replied, and kicked him as a horse kicks.

"Then said Thagua: 'We cannot live,' and dropped his head.

"Then said Kala to the Judge:

"'Kill these men, and I will give you a viss of silver.'

"'If I kill them I cannot endure the punishment, (as the consequence,)' said the Judge, but took the silver.

"A day or two after, Kala went and gave him fifty rupees more, but the Judge said: 'If you will marry your daughter to my son I will kill them.'

"Then Kala replied: 'Brother, I will marry them.'

"Then the Judge said: 'If I do not destroy them the white people will come and take our lands and kill us every one.' Then he scourged pastor Thagua three times.

"Thagua said: 'If because I worship God you torture me, kill me at once I entreat you.'

"They then took him, struck him sixty times, fastened him to a cross, shot him, embowelled him, and cut him in three pieces."

But besides these atrocities, they had to tell of the ravages of cholera, by which many had been swept away, of whom five were preachers. One of them was Myat Kyau, the first Karen ordained to the ministry, who had been deputed at a time when no European missionary could enter the country to organize the disciples in Burmah proper into churches, and baptized in his first tour fifty persons; the number that afterwards received the rite at his hands appears to have been little short of one thousand.

Some Burman kyoungs at Bassein having been fitted up for a chapel, a school and a mission house, the missionaries were literally thronged with visitors for several weeks. There was no lack of persons anxious to become pupils in the schools; the difficulty was to select from the mass the limited number it was practicable to receive. The companies that came daily were of all classes, Sgaus and Pwos, heathen and christian, members of churches, and disciples who had embraced the truth but had never been baptized, because no ordained minister, foreign or native, had visited them. All equally regarded the foreign teachers as their friends; the heathen, on being questioned, declared that they had continued such only because they had no teacher. Thus there was no want of work to be done, and that of the most delightful kind, teaching those who were thirsting for instruction in the truths and duties of Christianity.

The prostration of Mr. Abbott's health in September which enforced his removal, together with the tumultuous state of the country, demanded the dismissal of the school. The Karens took leave of their beloved teacher with inexpressible grief, " sorrowing most of all for the foreboding that they should see his face no more." Mr. Van Meter was left alone for some time, when Mr. Beecher joined him. The succeeding months were months of terror to the people, and of anxiety and unremitting labor to the missionaries. But with the return of peace came the returning prospect of engaging anew in the quiet exercise of their duties.

In 1852, we find mention of the death at Maulmain of the Burman convert MYAT KYAU,* the first Talaing preacher of the gospel. He came to the grave at the advanced age of seventy-six, full of years and of grace, after a long and stedfast course of usefulness. By birth he was a Buddhist, and connected with persons of rank and influence amongst his countrymen, his brother being the Governor of Shwaygyeen under the Burman Government, and himself the Collector of taxes among the Karens of the Shwaygyeen districts.

Being a man of superior intellect and education, and having a very thoughtful and inquiring mind, he searched deeply into the claims of Buddhism, and came to the conviction that the religion of his fathers was a baseless fabric. There

* Mentioned in Mrs. Wade's letter.

can be little doubt that his intercourse with the Karens had made him acquainted with their traditions of an Eternal God, the Creator of all things, not liable to change, decay, death or annihilation, and probably these wonderful traditions had shaken his false confidences, and raised the spirit of inquiry in his mind. From that time he began his search after truth, but it was many a weary year before the true light shone upon his path. He, at this time, became acquainted with a Brahmin ascetic, and, being struck with his supposed sanctity and devotion, became his disciple and follower, and for two or three years, practised various austerities. As the real character of the Gooroo developed before him, and he became convinced that his teacher was but a polluted and sinful man like himself, he fled from him in disgust and disappointment, and returned to his family and friends. But his spirit was not at rest. Like Noah's dove he could find no place for the sole of his foot. "There must be a revealed religion," he said; "O that I knew where I might find it," was the language of his heart.

In this state of mind he entered a Muhammedan mosque, and heard of " one God and Muhammad his prophet." The idea of one eternal, unchangeable, omniscient Being, the Creator of all things, struck his mind. It was a ray of light shining in through the dark clouds of heathenism which surrounded him. The same idea he had conceived from the traditions of the Karens, but they had no sacred writings, they could give no account of this great Being, and no instruction as to the worship he expected from his creatures. It was with intense interest that he listened to the Koran, expecting to find in it some revelation of the way in which he might obtain divine light and favor, but he was disappointed, it was not there, and the only spark of light which was reflected from the Koran was this: 'There is one God.'

He returned from the mosque dissatisfied, but determined to follow on to know the Lord, whose goings forth had been prepared as the morning. He was leading his servant by a way he knew not to the true refuge of his soul.

He was next attracted by a Roman Catholic chapel and attended the services. There for the first time he heard the name of Christ as the Saviour of men, but was also directed to pray to the Virgin Mary and to worship her as the mother of God, and to seek the intercession of Peter and an endless succession of saints. This appeared to him to be but another form of heathenism. The worship of the Virgin was particularly offensive, and he said, "If I must worship a human being as God, I would rather worship Gaudama, a man, than this woman. And as for Roman images, I cannot see that they have any more claim to divine honors than Burman images."

A long period of darkness and distress succeeded, and Myat Kyau almost despaired of ever finding that divine knowledge which he so earnestly sought. In 1824-7 he and his family came to Maulmain in consequence of the war, and it was from similar causes that Dr. Judson and Mr. Wade came there also. Myat Kyau and his brother the late Governor of Shwaygyeen took up their abode not far from the zayat at which Dr. Judson was accustomed to preach. His brother was at this time one of the chief men in the employ of the English Government. He took but little notice of the foreigners or their teaching, but Myat Kyau, on the contrary was found at the zayat amongst the most interested of the inquirers. The previous discipline through which God had brought him, had prepared his mind for a ready reception of the great truths of the gospel, and when he heard that Jesus said, "If any man thirst let him come unto me and drink," his thirsty soul, which had long panted for this water of life, drank, and drank freely. Day after day he was at the zayat from morning till night. One prejudice after another melted away, cloud after cloud dispersed, until the Sun of righteousness arose with healing in his wings, and he stood forth a new creature in a new world. The Holy Spirit had convinced him of sin, righteousness and judgment, and of the love and power and grace of Christ as the Saviour of sinners.

It needed no power of eloquence to arouse him, or of arguments to persuade him. The pearl of great price was within his reach, and he resolved to part with all to obtain it. He soon found that nothing less would do. His family, who had observed the change that was taking place were roused to the most determined opposition and hatred of the truth. His brother told him plainly that he would disown him, his wife that she would abandon him if he were baptized, his two sons and an adopted son that they would no longer call him father. None of these things moved him, or caused him for one moment to waver in his determination to follow Christ.

Wife and children were dear as a right hand or a right eye; but Christ was infinitely dearer. He was all his salvation and all his desire. "If friends forsake me because I adhere to Christ," he said, "I cannot discard Him for their sake. His is the only name given under heaven among men whereby we must be saved. I will persuade them if possible to become His disciples. I will pray for them. Perhaps God will give them light to see their need of Christ; but if not, they must take their own course; I cannot follow them in the way which leads to eternal death."

For several months the trial was indeed severe, and he had to endure all the anguish of spirit of one cast out and forsaken by those so dear to him, but the Lord stood by to strengthen and sustain him, and he found in Jesus the friend that sticketh closer than a brother. His heart yearned for his beloved wife and children, and he never ceased to plead with God until she and one of his sons, and his adopted son were not only reconciled to his profession of Christianity, but became themselves followers of the lowly Jesus.

Immediately after his own conversion, Myat Kyau, commenced earnestly laboring for the salvation of others, and it became evident to Dr. Judson and Dr. Wade that he was eminently fitted to be a true helper in their work. From that time forth he continued to testify the gospel of the grace of God to his countrymen during a long course of years, with unabating energy and zeal, until total blindness and the infirmities of age entirely disabled him. Many were the fruits of his labors, not only among the Burmans and Talaings, but also among the Karens. His labors were not confined to Maulmain, but almost every village and hamlet in the province heard the gospel from his lips. For several years he accompanied Dr. Wade in his excursions among the villages, performing the double service of assistant, and steersman of the boat, nor did he ever shrink from performing the smallest service which could render him more efficient in their minsionary tours.

He was prominently instrumental in bringing the Karens to the notice of the missionary. His office as Collector of Customs amongst them had made him familiar with their character and language, and as they travelled among the Burmans and Talaings, and observed their bigotry and blindness, he would often reiterate, " The Karens are not like the Buddhists; they have no idols, no priests, and if the teacher would go and preach to them, great numbers would listen and believe the gospel." He so constantly reverted to this, that it led to Dr. Wade's visit to Dongyan, which we have already noticed in our earlier pages. After a lapse of twenty years, in visiting this station again, Dr. Wade found the man and his wife in whose house they had staid, both living; both had become Christians with ten out of their eleven children. In the village was a flourishing church of eighty-six members. The old man and his wife had long been a father and mother in Israel, and spoke with affectionate remembrance of Myat Kyau and of his first visit among them.

When Dr. Wade was pursuing the important task of reducing the Karen language to writing, he received much assistance from Myat Kyau, more especially in his earnest prayers for wisdom from above to assist in accomplishing a work which, to his mind, seemed beyond the power of human wisdom.

Myat Kyau was pre-eminently a man of prayer. When travelling by boat as he held the helm he would constantly be chanting words of prayer and praise. When they stopped for the tide or to cook, and were again prepared to move on, he was frequently missing, so frequently that it led to an inquiry into the cause, when it was found that he had gone to some retired spot for prayer. Sometimes he was known to have continued whole nights in prayer without being aware of the lapse of time, till the cock-crowing reminded him that day was breaking. He continued to go daily to the zayat to preach some time after he had lost his sight, getting a child to lead him, and at length, when he was disabled from the increasing infirmities of age, he would sit in his verandah testifying to the love and faithfulness of God his Saviour to all whom he could induce to listen.

His liberality abounded to the last, even out of his deep poverty. His allowance as an assistant had ceased, and as he had only saved a hundred and fifty rupees, the interes ot which was all his support, he was often reduced to extreme poverty. It so grieved Dr. Wade to see the good old man struggling with want in his last days, and unable to procure the commonest necessaries of life, that he obtained some means for his relief, for which he manifested the deepest thankfulness. Notwithstanding his great poverty he would give four annas per month out of his pittance, for the support of a native preacher employed by the church. His wife told him one day, when the subscription list came round, that they were so poor he had better save the four annas for his own use. "No," he replied, "I can bear retrenchment on my daily food, but I cannot be deprived of the luxury of giving something to sustain the cause of Christ." And he continued to give his mite to the last. Such was the beautiful consistency of his Christian character that from his baptism to his death, both the missionaries and his fellow disciples testify that he ever walked worthy of his high calling, "in good report and evil report." For the last two years of his life he was very feeble, and totally blind, yet every communion Sabbath found him at his place commemorating the dying love of Christ his Saviour.

During his last days the powers of nature were so exhausted that he could say but little, but his heart responded to the mention of that Name which is above every other name, and it was evident he united in prayer, after it was thought he had ceased to be conscious. He had no fear of death, but longed to depart and be with Christ, and with teacher Judson and his fellow-disciples who had gone before, and the whole assembly of the glorified. As long as he could speak he ceased not to warn and exhort, especially his sons, who had both turned aside from the right way, and "though dead he yet speaketh."

A large concourse of all classes, both Christian and heathen, attended his funeral, and followed his remains to their last resting place. Truly "the memory of the just is blessed."

## CHAPTER VIII.

### THE ANNEXATION OF PEGU.

"The Most High ruleth in the kingdom of men, and giveth it to whomsoever He will."—DAN. iv. 32.

In March, 1851, Mr. Kincaid and Dr. Dawson proceeded to Rangoon, and having effected an arrangement for a temporary residence, removed their families thither in the following April, proposing to ascend to Ava at the close of the rainy season. On their first arrival, all seemed dark and dreary. Many had said, "You are going into the lion's mouth, what good can you expect to do under a government so relentless and bitter towards foreigners?" And the worst fears of the timid seemed to be but too well-founded. Mr. Kincaid was declared a prisoner, and forbidden to speak, or to walk beyond the limits of his own dwelling, without the surveillance of a Burman officer. Such was the state of things in April. Notwithstanding these hostile orders, the missionaries commenced dispensing medicines, and instructing all who came to the mission house; and on the 3rd of May, a royal message from the Court of Ava reached them, bidding them welcome, and expresing the hope that they would remain in the empire. From that time they labored without molestation; hundreds thronged to hear the word of God, and several distinguished and influential priests occasionally visited them. No doubt this fact imparted to the most timid a feeling of security in resorting to the missionary teachers. One day a Poongyee or priest, of considerable influence, called at the mission house with a number of his pupils or noviciates. When the time had arrived for the preaching to commence, he was invited to sit down, but politely asking to be excused, he expressed a wish that the young priests might go up and listen, saying, that he would wait for them below, where he was sitting. Opening a Bible which was handed to him, he promised to read it till the service was ended. Ko En, the native preacher, conducted the service, and preached nearly an hour; while the young Poongyees sat patient and attentive listeners. When Dr. Dawson returned to the priest, the latter was asked to give back the copy of the Bible he had been reading. When told that the Governor had forbidden them to give away books, but that he might read it as long as liked, he took up a volume of tracts that was on the mat before him, and running his eye over some of its pages, he said there were some things he wished to copy, and he wanted to know if they would lend it. "Certainly," was Dr. Dawson's reply. Apparently much gratified, he rolled it up in a handkerchief, and gave it to one of his attendants to carry to the kyoung. He then urged the missionaries to pay a visit to his monastery. His readiness to send his pupils, to listen to the preaching of the gospel, was a remarkable proof of liberality in a Buddhist priest, who lived under the very shadow of the great Shway Dagon Pagoda.

When the Christian Karens heard that the missionaries were at Rangoon, they soon came in little companies to visit them, and were incessantly in prayer that they might not be driven from the country again. Many touching notices of them occur in the journals of Mr. Kincaid and Dr. Dawson. One writes: "I feel ashamed when I look on this people so full of faith and stedfastness; so certain that a day of deliverance is at hand, that the empire of darkness will be overturned. The seal of God is on this people. Everywhere among them there is a spirit of inquiry, and the Lord is raising up men of strong faith for the work of the ministry. While the Burmans are groping their way amidst the darkness of Pantheism, and are toiling under the weight of a superstition more degrading than Popery, the Karens are inquiring for God's book, and the God of the Bible is their refuge."

As we have seen, some of the principal Poongyees of the place visited the mission house, sometimes for medicine, sometimes for a friendly call. The kindly disposition thus exhibited encouraged the missionaries to visit them at their monasteries. There they conversed fully on all subjects, freely admitting that in regard to "worldly knowledge," meaning the arts and sciences, the white race possessed a decided superiority, but that in "heavenly knowledge" they considered they had the advantage.

At the request of one of these men, who had been afflicted with hypertropsy of the nose for many years, Dr. Dawson went to visit him. A young Poongyee was sent to conduct him to the kyoung. After rounding more than half the base of the hill on which stands the Shwhay Dagon, or Golden Pagoda, the path stretched along between two tanks beautifully fringed with tufts of luxuriant grass, then winding round rather a bold eminence capped by a pagoda, it led into a grove of jack, mango, and palm trees, in the midst of which was situated the kyoung or monastery.

Ascending the steps, Dr. Dawson was ushered into a large hall, at the further end of which sat the chief Poongyee on his cushioned seat upon the floor. Behind him was a screen that concealed from view an assemblage of fancy idols, miniature pagodas, and gilt boxes containing the sacred books, and other valued articles. After conversing for a short time about his illness, the Poongyee expressed a wish to hear something of the cities, towns, and buildings, the manners and customs of the people in the "big island of America." Dr. Dawson endeavored to convey to him some correct idea of the continent, its relative size, its geographical position, and the time it would take to reach it, &c. Its happy and prosperous condition was traced to the Bible. A medical college was described, the mode and object of teaching, and the fact that thousands of lives are saved by skill and care ; and above all the goodness of God was descanted on, as bestowing the blessing of a pure religion, the highest and richest gift of all. The Poongyee now thought it his turn to speak, and began by saying there was not much difference between his religion and our religion when closely compared. "O yes, all possible difference as there is betweeen darkness and noon day," was the answer ; "how many gods have you ?" " A great many." " Your Betegat says twenty-eight." " Yes, the Hindoos or Brahmins have many millions, and we have many also." " Where are they all ?" "Some are now existing in other worlds, and many have gone to nigban"—(annihilation). " How many gods have you had in this world ?" " Four ; one more is yet to appear." " The difference now between Christianity and Buddhism on this one point is, that while you have many gods, the Christian religion teaches us that there is but one living and true God, without beginning and without end ; not subject to sickness, old age, or death, like the gods worshipped by the Burmans." On inquiring if he were not the head man of the monastery, he replied in the affirmative. "Well, it is a good thing to have authority somewhere. Suppose there were fifty head men in this kyoung. You tell the boys to do one thing, and another head man commands a different thing, and each one something still different from the rest. How would you all get on here?" He smiled and said, "That would be a bad business: all would be confusion." He felt himself in a dilemma, and flew off to the doctrine of merit: "Do good, and you will get good; do evil, and you will receive evil." He expatiated on the merit to be obtained by feeding the poor, giving medicine to the sick, building monasteries for the Poongyees, and bringing them offerings. "The religion of Jesus," the missionary remarked, "requires Christians to do good unto all men. If a servant simply does what his master has told him to do, to whom is it right to give the honor?" His answer was "to the master." "Certainly, that is a just conclusion. When a follower of Christ gives his property to support any worthy object, he does it not to obtain personal honor or praise, but to glorify God." Nodding his head very significantly, he said these were strange things, and *might* be true. It was growing late, and the missionary retraced his steps homeward.

In October 1851, Mr. Vinton paid a visit to Rangoon, and had the opportunity of seeing many of the Karen Christians and inquirers from different parts of the country. Sometimes fifty at a time would be present at the mission house. Nearly all the assistants came in for advice and instruction, and the earnestness with which they entreated that a teacher might remain at Rangoon, was very affecting, and proved what great importance they attached to it. The missionaries meanwhile were not without their difficulties. When books were sent from Maulmain they were stopped at the Custom House, and notwithstanding Mr. Kincaid's courage and perseverance, it was not without considerable difficulty that a portion were passed through at last. But a remarkable era was at hand in the mission's history: the Burman yoke was to be broken, and free course given to the preaching and progress of the living word of the living God.

One Sabbath afternoon at the end of November, 1851, a report spread rapidly through the city that an English steamer, and three men-of-war, were off the mouth of the river. The Governor despatched two boats one after the other to ascertain the truth of the report. All was activity and bustle on the part of the authorities, and of earnest anxious consultation in the little groups of terror-stricken people. It was not long before all doubts were at an end. Two armed steamers were measuring the waters, putting down buoys and towing up a fifty-gun ship. The excitement was very great. The Governor called in two or three thousand men, and began to arm them with old rusty muskets; the greater part of the night was spent in dragging worthless guns to the heights of the Shway Dagon Pagoda, and gathering there the treasure, and other property of the State. The Governor threatened to set the city on fire, and to seize the Europeans as hostages; all, therefore, were intent upon securing papers and property from the destruction that awaited them. It was near midnight when Mr. Kincaid and Dr. Dawson were sent for by the Governor, but they had scarcely set off when the order was countermanded. Capt. Crisp, an English merchant, was sent on board the frigate to inquire the object of its coming up the river. An order was issued by the Governor that any one, foreigner, or native, appearing on the wharves or river bank, should be beheaded. It was in vain that Mr. Kincaid remonstrated with the officers of Government, and suggested that there was every evidence that the ship had come on a peaceful mission, to prevent and not to make war. They felt it, but they could not but be conscious of the innumerable acts of injustice, and cruelty, which they had inflicted on all classes of the people, and they feared the time of retribution was at hand. At last the long-looked for ships made their appearance some miles below the city. The missionaries and their families went to the roof of their dwelling, from which they had a view of the river, and with emotions of joy and gratitude, saw the vessels come up and anchor before the oppressed city. They had seen and felt the insane and cruel tyranny of the Burman Government, and the presence of these ships spoke of peace, justice, and security. They could not forget the hundreds of Karens who had said to them: "God is our hope, and He will hear our prayers for deliverance." Commodore Lambert immediately sent a message to know at what hour the next day it would suit the Governor to receive a communication from him. The Governor wished to put it off till the day following. So all Wednesday was spent in busy preparations for an ostentatious display.

In the morning the Commodore sent Capt. Latter to request an interview with Mr. Kincaid, and for two hours he was detained, answering interrogatories in reference to the doings of the Burman Government towards British subjects. "Why have not these facts been sent to the Government at Calcutta?" said the Commodore. "From the terror under which all live;—the fact that the slightest whisper of dissatisfaction would only be visited by tenfold greater outrages, and even, as in many instances, with cruel tortures and death." "O this is dreadful!" he exclaimed. Capt. Crisp and Mr. Birrell, two English merchants were sent for. The statements elicited changed the current of affairs. The Commodore came to demand redress for outrages committed on Captains Shepherd and Lewis; but he now found that hundreds of British subjects had suffered as great, and many of them greater injuries, and that several had died under torture.

A deputation of four officers waited upon the Governor with the Commodore's letter in English and Burmese, and as soon as they left, Mr. Kincaid was sent for into the Viceroy's presence. He was deadly pale. His mind was so unbalanced that it overpowered his muscular system. His whole frame shook with emotion, his voice was feeble and tremulous, and Mr. Kincaid was almost disposed to pity the man who had no pity on the widow and the orphan.

Many hurried questions were then put, but the answers seemed to be scarcely comprehended. At length Mr. Kincaid was despatched with a message to the Commodore, but when half way there, he was again recalled, and ushered into a private room, where he found the Governor with some fifty chiefs around him. The Commodore's letter was again produced, and he was requested to say whether the translation was correct. After carefully reading it, he assured them it was.

"What does it mean ?" said the Governor. " I am accused of being a bad man, committing outrages on Her Britannic Majesty's subjects, and yet the letter does not specify in what way I have done this. Tell me what I should do ?"

"I am not competent," was the reply, " to advise in these matters."

" Do not tell me so," said the Governor, "you have more books and maps than all the other people in the city, and you know what the English want, and what I can do."

To get rid of his importunity, Mr. Kincaid replied : " You can write to the Commodore and ask for an explanation." This struck him favorably. Then he inquired whether the English had come for peace or war.

" For peace undoubtedly," was the reply. " If they had come for war instead of three ships, they would have had twenty-five or thirty." At last, Mr. Kincaid was released.

No person in Rangoon perhaps had spoken out from time to time so freely as he had, and yet he had often done violence to his better feelings by restraining his indignation when witnessing the enormities committed by order of this man. He had seen upwards of a hundred British subjects in prison, some of them in irons, not a few in the blocks. Several had been cruelly tortured, two had died under torture, one of them a woman. But justice had at last overtaken the wrongdoer. The administration of the Rangoon province was, however, no exception to the general management of affairs in Burmah. The whole system of the Government was bad. Each man had to pay a large sum for his appointment, and in order to keep it, had to make large annual offerings. This occasioned oppression and extortion in every form. Every officer was a slave to those above him, and a tyrant to all beneath him. The people were thus ground into the very dust. They prayed for a change of Government, and everywhere tyranny was triumphant and peace and security unknown.

After a few days, the Governor had, in some measure recovered from the panic into which he had been thrown, and commenced hostile preparations. He had collected from the neighboring villages about 10,000 men, and had invited to his aid a celebrated robber chief with all his followers, thus getting together all the desperate characters in the lower provinces. As yet the missionaries had felt safe in the old city, as the majority of the inhabitants were foreigners; but on the 4th and 5th of December, it was reported, that orders were issued to attack the foreigners, to kill and plunder them, and to burn the city.

Bodies of armed men of desperate character were constantly parading the streets, and Commodore Lambert invited the mission families to take refuge in one of his vessels.

As the ships of war were threatened with an attack by fire-rafts, it was thought better that they should go on board a merchant ship, and on the evening of the 5th, Mrs. Kincaid and Mrs. Dawson and the children, were placed in safety on board the *Duchess of Argyll.* Mr. Kincaid and Dr. Dawson still remained on shore, the latter to minister to the sick, and to attend to the few applicants who occasionally called at the Dispensary for relief.

A little after dark one evening, Mr. Kincaid, when passing along one of the principal streets, was suddenly seized by some eight or ten Burmans, who partly carried, partly dragged him into a dark narrow lane. There he was surrounded by forty or fifty armed men. A long and not very pleasant altercation succeeded, with threats on either side. They insisted on taking him to the Governor, while Mr. Kincaid was equally determined to go to the Custom House, and succeeded, though scarcely knowing how. A bundle of clothes which he had with him, was the excuse for this outrage. The Custom House officers interfered, and after a long dispute, the guards went off to the Governor for orders, and the Custom House officers hurried Mr. Kincaid to the ship.

The Governor of Dalla received orders from Ava to place his troops at the disposal of the viceroy of Rangoon, and accordingly 1500 men crossed the river early on the morning of the 19th, uttering the most savage yells. The only men, however, that the Governor could depend upon were the robbers and their chief. The Burman officers threatened the Karen Christians that they would put them into the forefront of the battle, if the English came on shore. The native churches sent messengers to the missionaries almost daily, to inquire how things were, and to let them know their position; few ventured to sleep in their houses for fear of robbers. The missionaries' hearts were full of sorrow for them, and they could only look up and commend them to the care of Him whose " eyes are upon the righteous and whose ears are open unto their cry."—The Burmans, heathen as well as Christian, sent messengers expressing the hope that the English would put an end to the tyranny under which they had so long suffered, and among the more than 10,000 disciples, as well as the hundreds of " almost-Christians," there was earnest prayer to Him who ruleth over all.

On the 1st January, 1852, dispatches arrived from Ava, making professions of peace and good will that for a time inspired hope that war might be honorably avoided, and the abuses of the Rangoon Government atoned for. The policy of the King appeared friendly, the Governor was removed from that office, and the viceroy of Shway Doung appointed his successor. But it was soon manifest that the pacific messages from the capital were only a device to gain time. The viceroy took no notice of Commodore Lambert, and forbade all communication between his vessels and the shore. The Commodore sent a deputation with a letter, but they were not permitted to enter the vice regal presence. They were openly insulted by the officers in attendance, and returned to the flag ship only to announce the failure of their errand. Upon this the foreign residents were summoned on board ship ; when Commodore Lambert stated, that all who claimed British protection must depart from the town within two hours. Dr. Dawson in writing, gave the following interesting account of the encounter of H. M.'s ships with the Burmese, and of their departure from Rangoon under the protection of the British flag.

"Mouth of the Rangoon River, January 13, 1852. —Since the despatch of my last letter, we have been called to pass through some most exciting and melancholy scenes, which happily fall but rarely in the path of missionary life.

The destiny of Burmah seems almost sealed. Soon perhaps, the sceptre will depart from the hands of her kings for ever! Her situation at present is exceedingly critical, and I feel more than I can express for her welfare.

"On the 4th instant the new viceroy appointed to the charge of all the lower provinces of Burmah, from Prome down to Martaban, made his grand entry into the town of Rangoon. As near as I could learn between twenty and thirty war-boats filled with armed men to the number of three or four thousand, accompanied him down the river as his personal escort. A guard of honor, consisting of three or four hundred men of the king's troops, was sent with him from Ava. During the journey down he gradually received additions, which swelled his retinue to a considerable force. His state-barge was decorated in the usual style of eastern splendor. On landing at the wharves he was welcomed with every demonstration of respect both by the government officials and the people. A long line of soldiers curiously dressed was paraded along the streets in the direction of government house, to receive him. Carpets were spread on the wharf for him to walk on till he ascended a buggy drawn by men, which had been provided to bear him to his new residence. A clusture of brahmins, each holding a 'horn of plenty,' awaited his arrival and pronounced their benedictions upon him.

"According to Burmese custom, or rather, a custom introduced by the late oppressive governor, hundreds of the inhabitants carried their offerings to his house to furnish the necessary provisions for his followers. Inquiring what they were, he declined receiving them, saying, 'he knew the people were very poor and could ill afford to spare such contributions.' By directing a discontinuance of the practice he won golden opinions among the masses. For two or three days a continuous stream of visitors crowded to his residence. They were of course mostly men in authority and their attendants, whose object was to pay their respects and receive commands.

"On the morning of the 6th, two days after his arrival, Mr. Edwards called on the viceroy with a message from Captain Latter, diplomatic assistant and Burmese translator to the embassy, to say that a deputation of British officers would wait on him during the course of the day. The viceroy replied that he declined seeing any officer but the Commodore. To this he strictly adhered. The deputation, composed of four officers from the *Fox*, and the *Hermes*, with Mr. Edwards as interpreter, waited on His Excellency, bearing with them a letter couched, it is said, in the most friendly terms. They reached government house soon after twelve o'clock. Messengers passed three or four times between the viceroy inside and the deputation, who were kept standing outside in a hot sun, when it was announced that His Excellency was asleep. The officers proposed to go in and sit for a short time, but admission was denied them; they could walk about outside if they chose. The officers retired to report the failure of their mission. The refusal to receive them was regarded as an insult to the deputation, to their flag, and to the British Government.

"A consultation was now held on board the frigate, and it was decided to have no further intercourse with the viceroy, unless he should first make an ample apology. Mr. Edwards was despatched on shore, to request the principal foreign merchants, the missionaries, and some others, to meet the Commodore on ship-board. In the mean time the English vessels lying in port, together with Chooliah, Arab, and Turkish vessels claiming British protection, were ordered to proceed down the river to sea. During the course of the evening most of them got under way and proceeded some distance below the town. On reaching the *Fox* we were informed that affairs were in such an unsatisfactory state, it was advisable we should all leave Rangoon without delay, and that the boats of the several armed vessels would be sent to the main wharf to protect us in getting away. No time was allowed the residents to remove their property. Thus to escape with our lives, most of us were compelled to sacrifice nearly everything. Except a few suits of clothes, our writing desks, and a small parcel of bedding, everything we owned is lost; furniture, valuable books, surgical instruments, medicines, crockery, kitchen utensils, saddlery, linen, all are gone. With the loss of all, we are thankful for our lives, that we are out of prison, and that our limbs are free of chains.

" As the *Duchess* did not go far below the town that night, information was brought to us about ten P. M., of the Commodore's intention to seize a ship called the *Ya-theé-náh-yaì-moon*, which signifies 'the most precious jewel of the ocean,'—belonging to the king of Burmah. This was decided on, we are told, by a council of war convened on the *Fox*. She was captured that night without firing a shot, the Burman crew offering no resistance. Knowing that such a step would render the Burmese provincial and city officers almost desperate,—for their heads would be in jeopardy under the displeasure of the king,—and that the property of foreigners would be more than ordinarily exposed to confiscation and destruction, I resolved, late as it was, to make an effort to procure some of our papers and letters which had been deposited for safe keeping in a strong godown at Mr. Birrel's house. Hiring a small canoe I pushed off for the shore and got to the godown by eleven o'clock. Though the moon shone out brightly, the whole town looked gloomy and deserted. Neither guard nor sentry challenged me in the adventure, though many entertained the opinion that to leave the vessel at such a time was exceedingly hazardous. Not being able to get keys of the buildings I was obliged to climb to the roof and enter the house through a trap-door at the top. With a lighted candle in one's hand this was somewhat difficult, but after some time I reached the box containing most of our private papers. The venture incurred some risk, but the object seemed worthy of an effort. While I was away at the godown four Burmans jumped into the canoe and paddled it off to the opposite side of the river. Providentially I was provided with another conveyance, by the timely arrival at the wharf of Captain Barker with one of the ship's boats. In the course of the night many women and children of Burmese extraction, connected with foreign traders, escaped in Chooliah vessels belonging to the Coromandel coast.

"About one o'clock the same night H. B. M. steam frigate *Hermes* passed down with the king's vessel in tow, and anchored below the Hasting sand, three miles from the town. At daylight the frigate *Fox* got under way, and drifting too near the Dalla shore grounded on a mud-bank, and was detained there till the next tide. While in that situation the governor of Dalla went on board to explain and intercede in behalf of the viceroy, though perhaps not officially authorized so to do. A similar visit had been made by other Burman officers and the royal interpreter the day before, during the interview of the merchants with the Commodore, but without success. Before seizing the king's vessel the Commodore had penned a note with the design of giving the viceroy an opportunity of apologizing for not receiving the deputation; and he would doubtless have sent it by the Burman officers, but unfortunately he had the impression that they would not dare to carry such a message to their governor. Subsequently one or two more endeavors were made by the deputy-governor of Rangoon and the governor of Dalla to reconcile matters. They went on board the flag ship, and the latter suggested that if the king's ship were delivered to him it would lead to his promotion to the post of governor of Rangoon, when he would grant ample redress for the injuries committed by the ex-governor. But the Commodore remained inflexible. His terms were that the viceroy should come in person, and on the deck of her majesty's frigate offer an apology to the officers who had been insulted. When this had been done he would be prepared to commence negotiations. These peaceful, though rigorous measures having failed, the Commodore determined to cut off all communication with the Burmans, and hasten to the mouth of the river with the 'prize' and all the armed vessels in company, pending a reference to the Supreme Government of India. A blockade of the Rangoon and Bassein rivers was proclaimed, and the brig *Serpent* of sixteen guns was ordered to a station at the entrance into the Bassein creek to intercept all suspicious looking boats.

"At this stage of the business the viceroy forwarded a letter addressed to the Governor-General of India, complaining that the officers of the deputation sent to him were at the time in a state of intoxication. The same evening, or the following day, another letter was received, intimating that if the king's ship was moved down the river with the other vessels, orders had been given to fire on the *Fox*. The Commodore expressed his regret to hear it ; he certainly would not fire unless he were first attacked, but if a single pistol were fired at the frigate, he would assuredly open upon them with his guns. Thus stood affairs between the parties before hostilities commenced.

"On the eastern and western banks of the river, about ten and twelve miles below Rangoon, are two substantial teak wood stockades, erected several years ago by direction to Tharrawady, the late king, who showed quite a spirit of enterprise in the public improvements he effected during his reign. To these stockades a few cannon and a number of jingalls were sent late one evening by the Rangoon officers, with a view to attack the men-of-war as they proceeded down the river. They were noticed as they passed our ship. About a dozen war-boats crowded with men were likewise stationed there. They took shelter up a creek behind the first fortification. How many men there were within the enclosures none but the Burmans themselves know. Probably there were three or four thousand, most of them provided with muskets, spears, and swords. On the summit of the palisades were guns in a position to command a section of the river. In two villages each contiguous to one of the stockades, the people were directed to arm themselves for the purpose of rescuing the captured ship of their sovereign. Such were the arrangements of the Burmese officers, who little understood the unequal contest in which they were about to engage.

"Early on the morning of Saturday, the tenth of January, the vessels commenced moving down with the tide. The steamer *Hermes* towed the flag ship as far as the upper stockade, and then went back to bring down the 'prize.' Things appeared somewhat warlike, and believing that the Burmans for once were going to be as good as their word, the *Fox* anchored directly abreast of the fortification, beat to quarters, and made ready to talk loud if first addressed from the shore. Besides several country craft, the *Mary Harrington, Falcon, Ararat,* and *Duchess of Argyll* were in the river. They had gained positions somewhat below the frigate, and were spectators of the painful scene which was then about opening. Our vessel anchored about midway between the two stockades, as the safest position, should the threatened outbreak occur.

"Just as our anchor had fairly taken the ground, the people of the village contiguous to the first fort were seen moving about quickly on the bank and looking earnestly up the stream. They were watching for 'the precious jewel of the ocean.' Many of them were observed in the war-boats hid under cover of the bank of the creek. Three or four of the boats now moved out of the creek and pushed up past the *Fox*, keeping in close to the shore. Some of the warriors were standing up, making a variety of antics and capers, and were heard singing a war-song. As the *Hermes* rounded a point in the river having the king's vessel in tow, the knot of watchmen on the bank disappeared to give the alarm to the boatmen and villagers.

"Just as the steamer came in front of the stockade, her bowsprit being on a line with that of the frigate, off went a flash and the report of a gun from the shore. Instantly many voices cried, 'They have fired!' Now commenced a murderous fire from the Commodore's vessel. The frigate was soon enveloped in smoke, her shot skimming the water and tearing up the bank. The stockade was shrouded in dust and smoke, and at times could scarcely be seen. The unfortunate Burmese kept up a spirited fire for nearly two hours, till they were literally cut to pieces, their boats abandoned, some of them drifting away and sinking, and their cannon dismounted and silenced. Both the steamers, the *Hermes* and *Phlegethon*, joined in the destructive work, and being able to run close in, played with deadly effect at the boats and up the creek, where hundreds of people were congregated. At one time during the hottest of the firing, the poor Burmese boatmen were observed hanging on by the side of their boats, all but their heads under water. Soon they rushed up the bank, wading through the mud and flying before the shot, which fell like hail around them. A line of persons on the margin of the creek was noticed through a glass busily engaged carrying off in scores the dead and dying.

"Having fired a number of times, the *Hermes* passed on her way, towing the Burmese vessel. A village close to where the *Duchess* lay fired one cannon and several muskets at the steamer as she passed, but this was soon checked. Having the king's ship in charge, the *Hermes* was a marked object on both sides of the river. When they got near the lower stockade, which is about two miles distant from the upper one, a fire was opened at long range, but did no harm to either vessel. Both the *Hermes* and the king's vessel, which was partly manned by hands from the frigate, kept up a steady fire for some time on this fortification, and then pushed down the stream to the mouth of the Bassein creek. Here they found the *Serpent*, and, anchoring the *Yá-thee-nah-ydi-moon* near the brig, the steamer returned to take the flag ship in tow. They did not leave, however, till all firing from both the stockades had ceased. The pinnace and launch of the *Fox*, which at one time were very much exposed, captured two or three deserted war-boats, and having pitched overboard all the weapons they could find in them, fired on them to destroy and sink them. Thus ended the melancholy battle of the stockades.

"On the side of the English not a single man was killed or wounded. A round shot struck a jolly-boat hanging at the stern of the *Fox*, and knocked a piece out of her bow. Another hit the counter of the frigate. Some musket balls hit her in different spots; but she sustained no further damage. A few musket balls, it is said, reached the two steamers, but did no injury to either of them.

"Among the poor Burmans, however, the slaughter, we have heard, was terrible. Three hundred were destroyed,—and who can portray the miseries of the wounded and the dying, the destitution of their widows and orphans? But I will not dwell upon this: it is more easily conjectured than described. After the battle a deputation with a flag of truce waited upon the Commodore, bearing a petition from the foreigners in prison at Rangoon, in which it was stated, that the viceroy was willing to accede to any terms in order to make peace. But it was too late. A report of the whole affair had been made to the Supreme Government of India, with whom the matter now rested."

Thus the missionaries were again for a season driven from Rangoon, and compelled to take refuge at Maulmain. It was not long, however, before active hostilities commenced between the British Government and the Burman. Martaban was taken on the 5th April. Rangoon was attacked on the 11th, and after a most desperate resistance of nearly four days, this devoted city fell before the British arms on the 14th of April, 1852. Mr. Kincaid had gone up with the fleet; and as soon as the Karen and Burmese Christians heard of his arrival they came flocking from their hiding places in the jungle to welcome him. Dr. Dawson and Mr. and Mrs. Vinton speedily joined Mr. Kincaid.

Not long after, Lord Dalhousie, who was then the Governor General of India, visited Rangoon, and we have an interesting account of the interview with which he favored the missionaries, from the graphic pen of Mr. Kincaid. He writes:—

"Rangoon, Aug. 8, 1852.—In my last I mentioned that Lord Dalhousie and suite were here. The day after his arrival one of his secretaries called on me and spent more than an hour, asking a great number of questions relative to the government, &c., of Burmah. On Saturday last, before he left, a line from one of his aide-de-camps informed me that the Governor General would see me and my associates at three o'clock. I went accordingly with Mr. Vinton and Dr. Dawson. His Lordship received us in the kindest manner, and at once began conversing on Burman affairs in a way that indicated great familiarity with the subject. He inquired about the three races, Karens, Talaings, and Burmans, the peculiarities of each, the number of native Christians, whether the government made no distinction between us and British subjects, whether I was acquainted with the present king, who were the leading spirits in the court of Ava, and what were the feelings of the people towards the English. He asked my opinion of the late viceroy, whether he came down with peaceful or with hostile intentions. To this last I replied 'Hostile, no doubt.'

"'How then,' he inquired, 'do you account for the pacific tone of the king's letter to me?'

"'It was to blind Commodore Lambert, and give the viceroy time to prepare for resistance.'

"'What are your reasons for thinking the viceroy's intentions hostile?'

"'He came down slowly, collecting men and money in all the towns along the river, and brought ten large boats loaded with powder. On his arrival he took no notice of Commodore Lambert. The very day that he made his public entry into the city he issued one of his most hostile orders, cutting off all intercourse between the shipping and the shore under penalty of death. When Mr. Edwards went with a message, one of the officers in the viceroy's compound drew a sword and threatened his life. When a deputation of four officers was sent, they were not allowed to enter the hall of audience, and were rudely treated by the officials. The viceroy's conduct was throughout consistent with the supposition that he came with hostile intentions.'

"The Governor-General inquired about the loss of my library, observing that it was a most happy circumstance we ourselves had not fallen into the hands of the viceroy. He spoke of our dispensary; said he had sanctioned the drawing of medicines for its use from the public stores; and added, 'If you will allow me, I will give a small donation to the dispensary.' About an hour after our return he sent 250 rupees. Before taking leave I said : ' We feel, in common with many others, that the well-being or otherwise of unborn millions depends very much on the decision to which your lordship shall come.' He replied with evident emotion : ' I feel it. Those who have not the responsibility may act hastily. I have come to a decision after long and careful examination.' When taking our leave he said, 'We may meet again.' Never will the impressions awakened by the interview be effaced from my mind."

On the 20th December following, we have an announcement of the ANNEXATION OF PEGU to British India, in the following letter from Dr. Dawson :—" At half past ten o'clock to-day the solemn act of dismembering the Burman Empire took place on board Her Britannic Majesty's ship *Fox*. The proclamation declaring the incorporation of the whole of the ancient kingdom of Pegu in the Empire of British India, was publicly read in the presence of a large company of naval and military officers, and a royal salute of twenty-one guns was fired in honor of the event. This year completes the century since it was conquered from the Talaings by the renowned Alompra, the hunter of the ' Moke-so-bo.'

It is a day of jubilee in Rangoon. The reign of terror ceases.

"Three millions of people have been emancipated from the dominion of the most heartless and oppressive Government that is to be found in Asia. The intelligence of annexation will awaken regret in none, except the King and Court of Ava. . . . . . Thus fields are opening on every side for the prosecution of evangelical labor, and how cheering it is to see men and means provided, as the providence of God bids us extend our borders. Before many years shall have passed, the whole kingdom of Burmah will be fully open to receive the gospel."

Another commencement had now been fairly made for the permanent occupation of Rangoon as a missionary station. Mr. Kincaid wrote, "The population of Rangoon and of all the villages in the neighborhood is rapidly increasing.

The principles of Christianity have taken deep root in the hearts of some twelve thousand, and through these a large amount of moral influence is brought to bear on some twenty thousand more. Our churches are found scattered all the way from the sea-shore to Prome. We have now at school in this city two hundred and fifty young persons preparing to go back to their villages, some to teach school, and others to labor as evangelists among their countrymen. About forty native preachers are now supported by the congregations over the country. I hope to see churches raised up along the whole line of this river to the Hukang Valley. Then we shall stand on the borders of Western China and on the upper waters of the Great Cambodia, and can reach by our books and our preaching untold millions in the centre of Eastern Asia. I almost wish that I had been born thirty years later in the Christian era, so as to see Christianity pouring its light over these vast regions."

The annexation of Pegu included the district of Bassein, and united in one continuous sea-board of British possession Arracan, Pegu and Tenasserim, commanding the entire outlets and deltas of the Irrawaddy, the Sitang, and the Salween. The British territory ran northward up the Irrawaddy to Meaday; and in addition to former stations, Toungoo, Shwaygyeen, Henthada, and Prome were occupied as mission stations.

## CHAPTER IX.

#### MATAH.

> "A little spot, enclosed by grace
> Out of the world's wide wilderness."—WATTS.

It is pleasant after the details of war and suffering in the preceding chapter, to turn to the peaceful labors of the missionaries in the TENASSERIM PROVINCES. Here they preached the word, taught their schools, pursued their translations, and took their jungle tours, none daring to make them afraid.

On the banks of the Tenasserim, surrounded by wooded hills, is situated one of the first Karen settlements, MATAH or the city of Love. Here, for many years, a little band of disciples has gathered together for the worship of the eternal God. They have been distinguished for their sobriety and industry; and the great change which has been effected in their social habits, proves that their hearts have been brought under the purifying and elevating power of the grace of God. One who visited them even in their early days said, "I am seated in a Christian village surrounded by a people that love as Christians, converse as Christians, act like Christians, and in my eyes look like Christians."

In 1846, one of the missionaries writing from Matah says: "The Christians here have just built themselves a spacious board chapel. It is, on the whole, the best chapel we have seen in the Karen jungles. It was built at the expense of the church, and considering the scarcity of paddy during the year, it was a great undertaking; for they have spent two hundred rupees for sawed timber. They have also furnished their pastor with food, and contributed forty-one rupees to the Tavoy Missionary Society. Here then we see what we desire to witness so much in every place; a church building its own place of worship, supporting its own ordained minister, and contributing to the spread of Christ's kingdom."

It would be interesting to trace how these people have been led on, preserved as a flock in the wilderness, fed and instructed by pastors raised up from amongst themselves, who have led them in the ways of peace and holiness, making their lovely glens and rocky mountains resound with the praises of their Redeemer God.

In 1852, we have the following interesting account of a Sabbath spent in Matah, and of a tour in the jungle from the pen of Mrs. E. Mason, the wife of Dr. Mason of Toungoo. She had left her husband at Tavoy pursuing his translations and missionary labors, and had travelled into the jungles accompanied by a few of the disciples, in the hope of inducing some of the girls from the Karen villages to come to her school in Tavoy. She writes to her husband:

"On reaching Matah, I fully proposed going on immediately to Longpung, to spend the Sabbath among the Shos; but I found the Sho preacher's wife here, and not a single boat to be found. All were gone to the fields, and the boats had gone with them to bring in the paddy, for it was harvest time. Moreover, the teacher's wife was very unwilling to let me go on; so I was for once obliged to yield to obstacles, very, *very* reluctantly, as I was anxious to hasten on my tour as rapidly as possible. But here I am in Matah, and a sweet and pleasant spot it is. I visited two Sho families and then returned to the chapel, it being very hot; and from the time I came in until just now, I have been constantly talking with

7*

visitors. They are very glad to see me; the Shos particularly keep close to me, some holding my dress, and some my feet, as if they felt I belonged to them, and they were afraid of losing me.

"After I had been here an hour, or perhaps two, who should come in but the Sho teacher, Klana, with a great paddy basket on his back and in his dirty field-dress. He had not, I imagine, heard of my arrival, and came along past the chapel. I was sitting in the door conversing with the sisters when they said, 'There is Klana.' The poor man was taken by surprise, and looked exceedingly mortified, but he set down his basket like a man, and came up smilingly. He is very pleasant, and I am sure I shall love both him and Kolapau very much." On Sunday evening she writes, "This has been a very happy day to me. I scarcely remember to have had more enjoyment than I have had to-day with the dear disciples of this jungle town. Last evening as soon as teacher Kolapau came back from Tavoy, he came to see that I was provided for, tired as he was; and in the evening they assembled for prayer. This morning at an early hour he came and rang the gong, when all that could came together for what I should call, a covenant meeting. After reading the Scriptures, and prayer, all related their feelings, and confessed their sins, and it was a very solemn and affecting season.

"All had something or other to confess, and Klana confessed that his heart still clung to the world. After all had spoken, I said a few words by way of encouragement, for I saw they were inclined to brood over their transgressions, which it seems to me is not the way to grow better. So I told them it was good to confess our sins one to another as the Bible commanded, and no one could say he was without sin, neither brother, nor sister, nor teacher, but after repenting of our sins, we should do as the apostle taught; '*leave* the things that were behind, and *press forward* to the mark of the prize of our high calling of God in Christ Jesus.'

"At the usual hour they came to worship, when teacher Kolapau preached to about a hundred attentive listeners; a very good assembly indeed at this season of the year, when the greater part are obliged to go very far away to harvest their fields. He preached an excellent discourse, standing like the teachers, and with a very dignified and impressive manner. I was quite amused at one little incident. While he was preaching very earnestly, suddenly he paused, and looking at a very respectable young man in the corner of the chapel said, 'Young man are you going to sleep? Look at me, and pay attention, and don't cover up your eyes again.' Then turning round he added, 'Don't one of you go to sleep : not a man, woman, or child !' I thought it would be well for some congregations at home, if they had pastor Kolapau in the desk, for I assure you no one so much as winked afterwards. The singing was very sweet, and the congregation generally clean and respectable, and every way it had the appearance of an enlightened Christian community, which speaks well for their teachers.

"After the close of the forenoon service I had a meeting with the females, when about fifty came together. After telling them of the good news I had often heard from the city of Matah, and how much it rejoiced the Christians in America, I read a portion of the 17th of John, and explained it to them, enlarging upon the duty of prayer, and the necessity of faith and obedience, in order to secure answers to our prayers; and drew their thoughts to the comforting assurance, that however poor might be their abodes here, they had the promise of a place in the 'Father's house above.'

"They seemed to understand me generally, and what the

Sgaus did not comprehend, Klana's wife interpreted. I prayed with them, and felt perfectly free, and unembarrassed; which I think was a particular blessing from God, because it is so long since I had the Shos about me, that I had greatly feared I should not recall the language, and had been making it a subject of prayer for some days. It was a very pleasant interview; and I trust not wholly unprofitable. At the close of this meeting I had the children together, about twenty, I believe, with whom I prayed and conversed for some little time, trying to stir them up to seek the Saviour with all their hearts. A few of them were disciples, and some were not.

"In the afternoon the gong again called the assembly together, for the study of the Bible; when teacher Kolapau took the Sgaus, and gave me the Shos. They read and themselves explained the 15th of John; which was selected because of some remarks made by them before. I feel it will not be a lost day to them. They seemed to have their thoughts somewhat quickened, and their aspirations after Christ increased.

"One man told me afterwards that he was one of teacher Mason's pupils, (as indeed nearly all the Sho men were,) and that he had not been happy since he ceased preaching. He said he knew but little, but he remembered that you told him once in a letter, that if a man waited to learn all the word of God, before he preached, he would die before he got through, without preaching at all. He said his wife had often urged him to come to you to attend to his Master's business; and he felt that he had buried his talent and was like the dried up branch. He formerly preached some years, but for the last three years he has been making paddy. He may perhaps conclude to dig up his talent, and go with me to town, and go to work again.

"In the evening the people came together again for a short season, when Kolapau explained the Scriptures, and one of the brethren prayed. It has been a most delightful day, and I feel my own soul refreshed more than I ever did amidst the privileges of our own native land. I am very glad now that I was obliged to remain over the Sabbath though the fact that the little church at Longpung do not return to worship on the Lord's day nor the teacher remain to look them up, only proves the necessity of earnest self-denying efforts in their behalf. I fancy the people are a little crooked, and the teacher disheartened; but he is going with me to visit the unconverted hamlets, so I have refrained from asking any questions, or saying anything about his feelings, hoping he will be warmed up by the Holy Spirit's influence, so as to commence again with renewed strength.

"The people here, especially the old disciples, (who almost all say you baptized them,) ask many questions about you, and always mention your name with a smile upon their lips, which shows that you still have a place in their hearts. They also mention their other teachers with interest, and I fancy from the way they speak, that Brother Thomas is fast winning their affections.

"This morning at an early hour I left Matah and came by boat up to Longpung. We were about six hours coming up, and what a mad stream it is! I think we came over five or six rapids where the waters rushed down with great fury. The men were obliged to work the skiffs with poles most of the way, although the skiffs were extremely small and light, only broad enough for one to sit comfortably on a seat. We had three skiffs, and there being but two men in one of them, they dropped behind and we were obliged to send back for them. I saw some of the richest arbors of creepers above the bank of the river that I could ever imagine. Old decayed heartless trunks some thirty or forty feet high, others ten or fifteen, scattered here and there, often a dozen within a few rods of each other, were completely shrouded with creepers in richest green, and sometimes, the old trunk being very large, it was a lovely sight. Others were lofty trees with huge branches; every inch of them covered with parasites hanging in garlands from every branchlet, and stretching from bough to bough in the most graceful manner possible. The scenery was simply one dense jungle of a great variety of trees, among which were interspersed the bamboo and wild plantain; and until the sun broke through the thick fog, the forest on either side was studded with the large delicate blossoms of a plant which, as they vanished with the morning dew, seemed like fairies gazing and laughing at each other.

"I found at Longpung a pretty new chapel, very small, but large enough for the place, and quite comfortable, except that there was no side to the front, and the roof being very low it was exceedingly hot during the day. The Christians appeared very happy to see me. I spent about three hours conversing with them on the interests of our Redeemer's kingdom, and found them very firm, faithful, working Christians. What I imagined yesterday I was glad to find not true. Brother Thomas could not desire more devoted disciples than this little band seem to be. There are but four or five houses, and the church members twelve or more. The teacher Klana I am much delighted with. I do not think he had been in the paddy field, as I supposed when I wrote on Saturday; he probably went down to Matah, because his people were watching their fields, which they say they must do, and they keep the Sabbath there. Do you remember a young lad whom you baptized with a throng of

Karens beside a stretch of sand between Longpung and Chongquait before Matah was founded? There was one whose name was Klana, and he is now the pastor, the honored and beloved pastor of this little vine in Longpung. He used to follow you in your perilous excursions up and down these rapids to the head of the Tennasserim, and now he is my guide over a portion of the same way. He is accompanied by his little son, a very clever boy, who bids fair to take the place of his father some twenty years hence.

"After a season of prayer with the Christians of Longpung, I came up to Chongquait. The stream grew more and more dangerous, and the men were frequently obliged to wade up to their loins and drag the skiff over the stones and rocks. I saw beside the stream a cave which gives the name to the Christian village, but I did not stay to enter it. I am now in a bong edifice in the midst of the village, a comfortable new temple which the people have built in obedience to the priest, who lives here and still rules over this village. Indeed he drew all the inhabitants away from Longpung up to this place fearing they might forsake him. There are however, two disciples here, and others who listen with interest.

I went into one house this evening and was immediately followed by a company of woman and girls and one young man, who listened very attentively to the truths of the gospel. I talked to them about half an hour, and so did Klana, and on our return we stopped to converse with some young men who had taken their stations by the way. We were followed to the temple by two or three men, and during evening worship several women and children came to hear the singing. Two or three are thinking a little of going down to school.

"Nov. 10th, 1852.

"This morning a young man came to see me, in whom I feel much interest. He is perhaps twenty-five years old, the son of the Bong-ko* of this hamlet, a very intelligent youth, and as wild as clever. He, however, conversed on religion for some time with unusual interest and some degree of solemnity.

"I left him, and went out to visit the women who would not come to see me. Visited four or five houses and found willing listeners in them all. In one was the sister of one of the Longpung Christians, and an aged mother. She said her brother had often told her of Christ and the way of salvation, but she did not yet believe; she had lived thus long without the Saviour, and she thought she should die as she she had lived. Still she listened with attention, and treated me like an old friend. In the first house there were two women, and the mother I thought at first was very far from becoming a believer. She was lame, and sat beside her cooking box attending to the breakfast. I sat down on the mat and talked to her until her heart softened, and she told me she was a widow, and had never known happiness since her husband died. I told her that I too had been a widow, and could therefore sympathize with her in her sorrow. This seemed to win her confidence, and she then conversed freely. I should not be surprised to hear of her becoming a Christian ere many years pass by. The father of another family is the son also of the Bong-ko, and yet he seems to be just ready to become a Christian. His son has already learned to read a little, and has been to school one rains at Longpung. He followed me to-day to the next hamlet. I have visited six houses, and have spoken to twenty immortal beings at different places until they all understood that they

\* A wizard priest

were sinners, and what they must do to be saved. One woman said she believed, but could not refrain from getting angry, and that kept her from being a disciple. The Bong-ko's wife was also an interesting auditor, and one of his daughters.

"The Bong-ko himself I was very sorry not to see, but he had gone to town. He still tells the people that he can see into futurity, and they assemble at eve of full moon to worship at the Bong. On one side is an altar over the elevated part of the building, with seven bamboo candlesticks; and when they worship they light up seven tapers along the front, and place upon the altar rice, plantains, &c., and bow down to Arumadaya, who the Bong-ko teaches them to worship.

"I left Chongquait about nine this morning, and started again upon my journey, travelling over two very high mountains and up a path so steep, it was scarcely possible to be carried. Much of the way was almost perpendicular, and where it was not, it was through the bed of the river. On the side of the first mountain, we found a little hamlet of three houses, where we stopped and endeavored to tell them of the Saviour. One man was from Siam and listened with a good deal of interest. After Klana had spoken to him, he got up and brought a torch and laid it down beside him, saying, 'There, take this, you are going into a dark jungle where you cannot see'—showing that he wished to manifest a kind feeling. He was a very poor man, and lived in a dwelling scarcely large enough for two to turn in. I have no doubt that that torch was an acceptable offering to God; and I shall expect if ever I reach heaven to see that man there. His wife seemed to take no interest in the subject, but another of the villagers followed us to this place, and gave good attention to all that was said. Here we had the privilege of speaking to eight or ten persons, notwithstanding it was in the heat of the day.

"We next came to a single house cooped up in a deep glen, where I stopped to breakfast, and speak to the woman who sat there weaving. There was also a young man there who listened with attention, and followed us on to this place, which is also on the Chongquait river in a glen of the mountains below the Matah range. There are ten houses here; I have visited five or six, and spoken to the people. Found one woman sick and her infant also, and was able to administer some medicines which gave relief. In the evening we had an assembly of twelve or fourteen persons to evening worship. After I had spoken to them, Pastor Klana began and preached such a sermon as I have seldom heard, and indeed I think I never saw one equal him in preaching to the natives. He has such a peculiar tact, such an adaptation to circumstances as could not be excelled. He kept their attention riveted for a whole hour. Occasionally one or two of the assembly would burst out into a laugh, and indeed it was sometimes more than I could do to preserve my gravity, his illustrations were so peculiar, so interesting and pointed; but usually all were solemn and thoughtful. I fancy Klana is another Kothabyu in preaching; but he wants the teacher with him to keep up his courage. He is now out preaching again with great earnestness to a family near, although I should think he must be exhausted from this evening's services.

"We have taken possession of a large forsaken building where Klana's uncle once lived who was the High Priest of the glen and officiated at all the sacrifices, particularly at the Thako Mosha worship. When this official dies amongst the Karens, his dwelling is forsaken; and so we find this one, just as he left it, with his utensils, mats, &c., all left to decay, an offering probably to the Thako Mosha. It is not, however, particularly comfortable, as there is not a single place where I can screen myself from the cold damp night air, it being simply a floor and a roof, with a slight balustrade round a part of it.

"Palatot, Nov. 11th, 1852. Having visited another house this morning, I left Chongquait about eight o'clock, and after crossing Palatot river, ascended a very high mountain and through another glen to this place, south west of Matah.

"Our path for the greater part of the way was through pong (reedy grass) often much higher than the coolies' heads, and usually five or six feet high, so that I was but a dwarf in the path; it so covered the way, and it was so sharp and tangled, that my feet were cut and scratched, and my dress literally drenched with dew.

"At this hamlet I find seven houses, and have just been speaking for a little while with the women who came to see me, only four in number, the rest being in the fields helping to gather in the harvest. One of the women is a very interesting person, and all listened with fixed attention. Who can tell but some of them may be saved by what little they have heard to-day of Christ: and if only one, of how much more worth than the cost and trouble of this little tour! I cannot but feel that our Heavenly Father had some design for the good of this place; or I should not have felt so impelled to come at this season, though I would not for a moment imagine that anything I could do or say, would be blessed; did I not know that God often chooses the weak things of this world to advance His kingdom, and cause His glory to appear before the heathen.

"From Palatot we came to Palatoter, about two or three hours' travel. We stopped in a field to converse with a heathen mother, who was gathering chillies and black pepper, and soon after with another who sat in a booth by the way. Both were very attentive, and one seemed not far from the Saviour. We came on from this garden through the bed of Palatot river to Palatoter, where we found four houses, all of which I visited and had the privilege of speaking to sixteen souls, eight men and eight women, besides children. One man was from Siam, and never heard the gospel till he came to these regions. He is a very interesting man, and has a beautiful daughter, whom I tried hard to persuade to come down with me to school, but she does not yet feel the value of learning to read. This man wears large horn cylinders in his ears, about four inches in length, four in circumference, and made hollow. All the women in this region wear polished ebony knobs in their ears, often more than four inches in circumference, and formed like spouts, except that they present concave fronts which are used for mirrors, very different from those of Dongyan. Their jackets also are very different, and not half so elegant, being wrought only a little, and that with cotton, but the houses present a much more comfortable appearance than is usual, having roofed verandahs.

"The Siamese Karen says there are a great many Shos in Siam, and that they all worship Gyike, which I suppose is the Talaing for Gaudama. I find many in these parts who worship Gyike. Those who observe this mode of worship do not adhere to the Thako Mosha custom, nor feed the Nahts (evil spirits.) One man here reads Burmese, and has often heard the gospel; he does not oppose, but seems only to want the new heart. He seemed much pleased to see us, and immediately invited us up into his house. Another listened for an hour, I imagine, asked many questions, and really seemed like a brother, though he does not yet confess Christ. Probably his wife hinders him, as she seems to be more opposed than any one I have met, although her parents have both united with the Christians of Longpung. She sat down, however, and heard what I had to say with attention.

"From Palatoter to this village the road is much worse than any I have yet traversed. We reached this place about five o'clock P. M., having walked as fast as the way would allow without halting the whole way up to the Paletot river, which, though but a brook, is often quite deep. I was carried by two men through the deeper portions, and walked the remainder. When I reached this place the first woman I met invited me into her house, offered me beetlenut, and brought water and washed the blood from my feet with her own hands. Of course, I refused so much kindness, but she would not desist until I was made comfortable, and laid down in the best place in her dwelling. This woman and her husband are the followers of the Bougko, but she listened with polite attention to the truths of our religion, and appeared very friendly. When I sat down to dine she brought out a bunch of plantains, and seemed very anxious to assist me, though she does not confess any belief in the Saviour. She had a sick child to whom I administered medicine, which probably accounted in part for her kindness.

"At this hamlet there are but three houses, and we found but seven or eight persons. I have had conversations with all the women and children, and more or less with the men, on the interests of eternity. One family is related to one of the disciples at Longpung, and the man seems ready to believe; but does not repent of his sins so deeply as I wish to see him. His wife says she believes in Jesus Christ, but does not yet worship Him. She seems to think she will, at some time, become his disciple. Two of this woman's children have learnt to read at Longpung.

"This evening we have had worship with the family where we stop, and some of the neighbors who came in, and since worship, the head of the family has entered into an energetic discussion to prove that Arumadaya is the Christian's God, and the Airys our angels. He is a son of the Bong ko, and a very well informed man for a Karen. But pastor Klana was fully competent to meet all his arguments and difficulties. The discussion has been very interesting, and led to a declaration of all the fundamental principles of the Christian religion, and a complete refutation of the Bong ko creed.

"I was greatly rejoiced to hear this young man speak so well for his Master, indeed he was a very superior preacher. I have heard none superior to him, and I doubt much if any foreign teacher will ever master the language so as to preach with the ease, fluency, and cogency of argument that this man exhibits. He is also very amiable in his deportment, and engages every one's affections. He never speaks as if he were a superior, but with true oriental politeness he says to the young by way of apology for his earnestness, 'I believe I have lived more years than you, it is therefore proper I should tell you what I know.' To his equals he will say: 'I know very little, but what the teachers have told me I ought to tell you, so that we may all be saved;' and to his elders he says with Elihu, 'I am young, and ye are very old, yet suffer me a little, for I have yet to speak on God's behalf.' This courteous way of commencing his discourses engages all hearts, and as he always appeals to his audience, they of course assent, and then they must listen. I look upon this man as a real jewel to the mission; indeed both these pastors Klana and Kolapau are *gentlemen*, gentlemen in feeling and manners, and apparently devoted to the service of God, and it does one real good to hold communion with such hearts.

"The man to whom Klana has been preaching says, 'Formerly we were all under the power of the Nahts, but now we cast them off without fear.' As they had taken one step he thought they would continue to advance, until they would all worship the true God; but he thought it must be done step by step, as some argue for the inebriate; they must first worship the Bong or Gyike, and so ascend up to the God of all.

"Longpung, Nov. 12th, 1852.

"We left Kangta early this morning; crossed over Palatot river, and a pretty high hill, and soon entered Dauchong brook, and followed it up to its source, where we entered Beong stream, which we traced down to its mouth. The first stream was very narrow, but most of the way one or two feet deep, and often much deeper, flowing through a deep gorge, the mountains on either side being very lofty and covered with thick jungle. This stream was very muddy, and the rank grass and water-plants grew up close to the middle, so that there was no path whatever; and we were obliged to struggle up through the middle of the stream, sometimes over fishing dams and logs, for about three hours. After leaving this stream we had to climb the side of a hill, over immense fallen trees, and then make our way through a thick bamboo jungle, and then through a forest as difficult-of access as any mangrove swamp. We had to cut our way, I imagine, for about an hour in our wet clothes, and when we reached the chapel, our feet and limbs were still covered with leeches, swollen, torn and bleeding.

"From Chongquait round to Longpung by this route must be about twenty miles, and at this season the paths are so bad, when there are any, that I have not been able to use the cot twenty steps the whole day. This is the great obstacle to early travelling in the jungle, for I do not think there is any danger of sickness; but the paths and whole face of the country are as different in November, and in December and January, as the roads of a city and those of a rough upland village. This should be especially borne in mind by all tourists; or those who pass through the jungle later in the season may suppose that early travellers exaggerated the difficulties of the way. In December these streams, which are now swollen and rapid, will be dried up, or very low, and the whole country which is now covered with reeds and tall grasses will then be burnt over.

"At Longpung I visited three heathen women in as many different houses, had a season of worship with the disciples, and then came on to Matah, where I immediately went to see an aged infirm disciple, who is unable to leave his room. He was, I believe, one of the number baptized at Lockyien, and told me all about Mamma Mason's* living in the jungle a great many days in a booth, while they were building Matah, and how he afterwards carried leaves to help to build her a house. He related a great many other interesting things of days gone by. He is a firm believer, and evidently enjoys the presence of his Saviour. He has no fear of death, and seemed to feel deeply the goodness of God towards his countrymen, in delivering them from the Burmese and Siamese who so often devoured them.

"On returning to the chapel, the dear Christians thronged me, inquiring if any had believed. 'Did you see my daughter?' inquired an aged mother who was herself formerly a priestess of the Thako Mosha. 'Yes, I saw her.' 'Did she say she would be a disciple?' And when I was obliged to answer in the negative, she bowed down her hoary head and

* Dr. Mason's first wife, Mrs. Helen Mason.

wept! O if ever my heart sympathized with parents it was that evening, to see the anxiety depicted on every face, as they inquired after unconverted children and relatives.

"Early this morning I left Matah and have walked, I fancy, a good deal more than ha'f the way; as there were so few coolies, I could not otherwise hasten at all. On the way I noticed a large rock on the side of the mountain, piled up with small stones, and on asking how these stones came there, they told me of a custom that prevails among all the Burmese. Every one who passes picks up a stone and throws it on the cairn; if they fail to do it, they believe sickness and other ills will befall them. It seems to be a species of worship to the spirit of the mountain, and they say the custom is very ancient. I stopped to see if my coolies observed the tradition, and lo, each one as he passed, stooped down, and picked up a stone, and threw it on.

"During this tour I have had the privilege of seeing and conversing with about seventy Sho women, nearly as many men, and a good many children. It was not my object to speak to the men; but when they came to me, and sought instruction, I felt it would be sinful to withhold it because I was a woman. O that the Holy Spirit would deign to bless this small effort to the salvation of some precious souls; for this I scarcely dare to hope; yet with God all things are possible, and he can use even such unworthy services for his glory."

In this tour Mrs. Mason travelled with some of the disciples, or the Christian pastor Klana. She went a distance of nearly one hundred miles over upon the mountains toward Siam. She was gone twelve days from her home, visited in all seven hamlets, saw and conversed with about two hundred individuals, and walked two-thirds of the distance out and back again. Dr. Mason was at the time engaged in the translation of the Scriptures into the Sgau, and could not have accompanied her without stopping that important work; she therefore went forth alone, as many other females of this mission have been wont to do, carrying the story of the cross to these children of the forest, visiting them in their mountain homes, and pleading with them to turn from their dumb idols to serve the living God. Surely such labors will be owned by Him who will testify at last that, " they have done what they could."

## CHAPTER X.

### LOVELL INGALLS.

*Meek souls there are who little dream,
Their daily strife an angel's theme.*—KEBLE.

It was early in 1850 that Mr. Ingalls visited America, but though absent from the chosen scene of his labors, he was not unmindful of the service to which he had consecrated his life, and his heart yearned to return to the heathen. Writing to a friend he says: " This delightsome land can have no charm for me while so many of our race sit in darkness, and Christ's last command remains unfulfilled. I still feel that Burmah is my home, and I shall when recruited return to my post with more pleasure than I left it." While he was at home he married one who was in every way worthy of him, and who proved to be a helper indeed in all his future labors for the salvation of the Burmans. At the close of 1851, they proceeded to Arracan, and Mr. Ingalls recommenced his labors at Akyab. During his absence the church had become reduced in numbers and greatly afflicted by dissensions: but on his return the clouds were dissipated, and circumstances of an encouraging nature re-appeared. Preaching was constantly maintained in two different parts of the town, and numerous visitors listened attentively to the word. Mr. Ingalls filled the place of the pastor to the church, and gave himself to daily preaching in the zayat, and conversation with inquirers, both there, and at his own house, which was always open to visitors. His labors were much blessed, and could scarcely have been more judiciously directed.

In February 1852, Akyab was visited with cholera, which carried off not only Mrs. Moore, the wife of one of the missionaries, but Mr. Campbell of Kyouk-Phyoo. In the midst of these afflictions, they had the comfort of seeing that the word of God grew and increased. In October, Mr. Ingalls writes: "Several have been baptized lately. It is very interesting to witness these conversions from Buddhism: these proud Buddhists going joyfully forth from the camp of this world bearing its reproach. One young man said, 'I was so happy, I spent the whole night in prayer to my God.' I find I have baptized fifty-eight within a few years in this place, but many of them have joined the church above."

Southern Burmah, however, was Mr. Ingalls' earliest field of labor, and thither he ardently desired to return; and now that the way was open, in accordance with his own request, he was authorized to remove to one of the stations. At Rangoon, therefore, Mr. Ingalls took up his abode, the last and most successful scene of his labors. He says, in writing at this time: "I believe the Lord has work for us to do here More than seventy Burmans have been baptized during the last eight months, a larger number than were ever baptized in so short a period. With these converts we have spent much time, and have had reason to rejoice over them." Five places for daily preaching were established in the city, where numbers congregated every day and listened to the word of God. A spirit of inquiry prevailed, more general, more earnest, and leading to more decisive results than at any previous period of the Burman mission.

The following interesting case occurred not long after Mr. and Mrs. Ingalls' removal to Rangoon. The narrative was received from Mrs. Ingalls herself.

The Sabbath was over, the sun had dawned upon another week, and the labors of the missionaries had again commenced. Their dwelling was a very humble one; for they had but recently arrived in Rangoon, and houses of any kind or description were difficult to obtain. It was in the memorable year 1853, not long after the British arms had broken the Burman power in Pegu, and as soon as the British flag waved over Rangoon, the American missionaries, under its protection, commenced preaching the glories of the cross. Mr. and Mrs. Ingalls had taken possession of a small native house, with no flooring but the cold earth. It had two doors, one of which opened upon a broad verandah, facing the busy street. In this verandah, day by day, the missionary and his assistant took their seat, and with a few of their Bibles and tracts spread out before them, endeavored to attract the little groups of Burmans, who, from time to time passed to and fro. Sometimes a goodly number would stop, and enter into a lively discussion with the white teacher, and then again a solitary individual would alone remain to engage his deepest sympathy, or excite his ardent hopes. Thus day after day passed on.

The Sabbath was over; a new day had dawned; and the teachers were sitting in the verandah, when their attention was arrested by a thick-set, sturdy looking Burman entering the verandah, followed by four others. He was hot, dusty, and wearied, and had evidently travelled some distance: but throwing down the bundle at his back, he commenced at once in a loud decided tone. 'Well! I've come back! I want to be a Christian, I want to be baptized; and I've brought four more with me.' He spoke with such earnestness and rapidity, that it was only when the man paused, that Mr. Ingalls could say, 'Where did you hear of our religion? who are you?' He started as he replied, 'Why, doesn't the teacher know me? Don't you remember, I'm the blacksmith to whom you gave the Testament and the tracts two months ago? I've been reading them ever since. I took them to my village, and have been reading on; and now I know all about it, and I know Christ can save a poor sinner like me, and I want to be baptized.'

All this time he had been unrolling his bundle, and had taken out the precious Testament which had made him wise unto salvation. Mr. Ingalls made him sit down beside him, that he might inquire into the amount of his knowledge. Of his sincerity there could be no doubt, for, like the poor blind man in the gospel, he could say, 'Once I was blind, now I see.' He was greatly distressed when he found that it was *Monday*; for he had travelled without resting, in the hope of reaching the teacher on the Lord's day, the Christian's Sabbath. He then said, that when he returned to his own village, he had read and studied the book; that at first he was awed by the thought of the majesty and purity of the great God, and that he feared he would not look upon such a one as he was; but he read on—on—such wondrous things, and of the Lord Jesus calling and saving even poor fishermen (who are held in great contempt by the Burmans); and that gave him hope, and he thought he 'might even save a poor blacksmith!' His eye glistened as he added, 'O how I have read, read, blowing my bellows with one hand, while I have held my Testament with the other. I want to be baptized.'

How did the hearts of the missionaries rejoice, not only over this saved soul, but over those whom he had brought with him! He had truly gone forth bearing precious seed, and had come again rejoicing, bringing his sheaves with him.

After a few days of instruction and counsel and prayer, the poor blacksmith was baptized, and returned to his family and his native village; but there the fiery trial of persecution awaited him, and the headman of the village, after treating him with much severity, drove him from his home. He fled towards Ava, no doubt with the desire of carrying the gospel there, but his work was done, and having witnessed a good confession upon earth, he was called to enter into the presence of his Master in heaven.

This was the commencement of the work again in Rangoon, amongst the Burmans, and the following extracts will show how rapidly it advanced. Mr. Ingalls writes in March 1853: "We find much to do, churches to be planted, and pastors instructed and ordained. No church going bell gives the welcome to the sanctuary in this city; no crowds throng the streets, wending their way to the house of God! Rice has been scarce, and the merchants are filling their houses with it, while crowds of women and children are flocking to the sales. How great the contrast to the solemn silence and order that prevails in Christian lands! A little company of Burman Christians are congregated together; and save this little band, none know or love the Eternal God.

Shortly after we have recorded the baptism of a priest and nun. "It was pleasant to see this man throw off his yellow robes, and with a Christ-like simplicity obey the commands of Jesus; and then dress himself in the garments which are worn by the Burmans. The nun, too, seemed greatly rejoiced as she cast her eyes upon the water which was to give her the outward name of Christ's chosen.

"The great Pagoda was near us in all its golden glory, but its glory is nothing compared with the glorious scene of these happy converts! Thirty have lately put on Christ by baptism.

"One, an old man just on the borders of the grave, has greatly rejoiced our souls. Another has come a distance of some hundred miles, and tells us he has worshipped God seven years. He heard the gospel from a man who heard it from

Mr. Kincaid: so the seed springs up! Another man came into the verandah, and after sitting a while listening with deep attention, he got up, and coming very near me, said, 'Were you not here seventeen years ago?' I said, 'Yes.' 'Then,' he replied, 'you are the man who gave me that precious book, and taught me how to pray to a God in the heavens. I have tried to do so since, and now I must learn the whole of this blessed way.' He remained fifteen days, and was baptized, after which he left for his distant home. The book I had given him so long ago was a Testament."

Another narrative received from Mrs. Ingalls pointedly illustrates some of the Burman habits and customs.

"It was noon day. The sun was pouring down its scorching rays, making it one of the hot days of Burmah. The poor Burman dog had dug his bed under the shadow of a shrub, or beneath the ladder-steps. The house cat had left her wonted sunny bed, and sought a resting-place close by the water jar; and most of the natives had sought a shelter from the rays of the scorching sun. Even the parrot bird drooped its green wings, and clung to the very bottom of his cage for a shadow. At this hour a Burman man of about thirty-five years of age, might have been seen slowly plodding his way to the city. For a turban, he wore some four yards of the finest book muslin. His Polka jacket was of jaconet; and a piece of fine blue plaided silk was round his body and limbs, and was fastened in front by a loose knot, allowing the ends to hang down in a graceful fold. His feet were incased in green sandals, and he carried over his head a leaf umbrella. His outer appearance was that of a respectable Burman. He walked slowly along, seemingly unconscious of the excessive heat, though he was evidently suffering from it. He scarcely raised his eyes from beneath his knitted brow, and only paused a moment at the door of a hovel to relight his cigar, ere he entered the town.

"He passed on, but suddenly his footsteps were arrested by the hand of a familiar friend beckoning him to enter the zayat, (an open shed, erected for the shelter of travellers, and where the priests go to give religious instruction,) in which he was sitting. He hesitated a moment, and turning round gazed at the poor bamboo hovels which he had just passed, and then turning again, he ran his eye along the group of zayats and monasteries, and then lifting his eye to their graduated roofs, with their curious carvings, and glittering spires, gazed on the golden Pagoda in the centre, and the tall flag staffs, interspersed here and there, from which float the long gauze streamers, which point the people to the holy place. The ground round most of these places was the highest, and about them grew the lofty palm, the cocoa-nut and various fruit and flowering trees, which, from their variety of shade and form, gave the place a most beautiful appearance. The Burman seemed lost in thought as he compared the wretched bamboo hovels, and the splendor of the scene before him; and the call of his friend was unheeded.

"'Why do you not come and visit us? Are you becoming Jesus Christ's man?' The last words struck upon his ear, and he turned his feet to the zayat, assuring his friend he was not Jesus Christ's man. The yellow-robed priests relighted their cigars, which had wasted from their long slumbers, adjusted their pillows, and with their strings of black beads, which answer the purpose of rosaries, placed themselves in the attitude of listeners.

"The old Burman pushed the cup of water to the traveller, Moung Shway Pau, and then began his inquiries: 'Where have you been? Do you think the white foreigners will drive us from our home? And why have you not attended our feasts, and made offerings to the gods of late?' 'The bells are falling from the Pagoda,' answered Moung Shway Pau, dissembling as he spoke: 'and it needs regilding. The people are getting slack: I fear they are becoming heretics; for I hear the American teachers are daily receiving the calls of many of our people, and I often see them with those little books. One of the heretics passed here a few days since with a large bundle of tracts, and pressed *me* to take one; but I quickly told him I would not soil my hands with one of them. He attempted to leave one, but I told him I would make kites for the children of it. So he left, saying his God could open my heart without books.'

"Seven or eight of the priests had jealously watched the countenance of Moung Shway Pau, and conjectured that he knew more of those books than he admitted; so they drew near, and in their sacred language, Páli, expatiated long on the beauties of their religion. They pressed him to seek for merit, and told him if he would only replace one of those soiled book muslin streamers which floated from the flag staff, he would get great merit. As many times as it floated on the breeze, so many times he would be king of the earth. He could not conceal his contempt for this folly, and told them, yes, it was only the natural course of things: if he hung his head-dress on the staff, it would float if there was any breeze. Then adjusting his silken garment, and carefully concealing a small book which he had in the fold, he left; and a half hour's walk brought him to his abode.

"His sister unrolled a mat for him, and his nephew, a boy of six years old, with a good share of the milk of human kindness beaming from his eye, stumbled over the mat, spilling the cup of water which he was wishing to give his uncle. A smile lit up the face of Moung Shway Pau, as he picked up the little boy; but his brow instantly became knitted, and throwing himself upon his mat he pressed his aching head and sighed deeply. His sister Mah Doke brought in her vegetables, and began dressing them for the evening meal. As she glanced at her brother, she saw from the quick heaving of his bosom that he was troubled, and throwing down her knife, she was soon at his side, asking him if he was ill. He replied, no and yes, in the same breath: and then said he did not believe their god could save them from hell. Their religion was all, give, give; and he saw they would only receive poverty in return for all their gifts, and after death go down to hell. 'I wish to worship the God who can save me from hell.' 'What,' exclaimed the sister, her eye flashing with shame and anger, ' Will you leave the religion of your forefathers, for that of the foreigners? You will bring shame and disgrace upon your sister!' And she returned to her cooking.

"Moung Shway Pau now drew from the folds of his dress a small book, which he carefully opened, and began perusing with eagerness. It was the gospel of Luke the 9th chapter, 26th v. 'Whosoever shall be ashamed of me and of my words, of him shall the Son of Man be ashamed, when he shall come in his own glory, and in his Father's, and of the holy angels.'—The tears rushed to his eyes, and he smote his breast vehemently saying, ' I denied thee, was ashamed of thee at the kyoung, and I must go down to hell. I believe, O God, thou art the only true God! yet I denied thee there.'

"The shades of evening drew nigh, Moung Shway Pau's brother returned, and when the evening meal was finished, his sister told her husband that her brother had become a heretic. His brother-in-law, who was a learned man, lit his cigar, and with all the arguments at his command endeavored to prove that the system of idolatry was a good one. Moung

Shway Pau opened his book and read of the God who made the heaven and the earth and everything therein. 'This God can save us from hell,' continued Moung Shway Pau, but Gaudama our god, cannot. Gaudama does not exist, and even if he did he could not save us from hell, for in his own book he tells us, 'If you have sinned, you must endure it.'

" The brother-in-law admitted the truth of the statement, but said it was a shame to forsake the religion of their forefathers. 'Ah,' said Moung Shway Pau, 'your eyes are not opened to your great danger, the children of murderers and robbers ought surely not to follow in the footsteps of their parents? It would be a virtue in them to forsake those sins, and follow after the good and wise.' The noise of these discussions soon brought in the neighbors and friends; and Moung Shway Pau to his surprise found himself surrounded by some fifty persons. For a moment his whole frame shook with agitation, but in two or three more, he gathered courage, and with the light and instruction he had received he pictured forth the wisdom of the God who created the world, and filled it with its millions of beauties and delights. He told them that this God had bestowed all these blessings upon man: 'Yes,' said he, 'even upon us Burmans and Talaings, who have never once raised our hands in the attitude of praise and adoration, to the Giver of them all.' He tried also to tell them of Jesus Christ, God's only Son, but his views were not yet distinctly clear about the wonders of the cross and its agonies; yet enough was told to strike the hearts of one or two of the listeners, and they resolved to visit the foreign teachers and learn from them the wondrous story.

" Moung Shway Pau sought his mat, but it was not to sleep: his mind was too busy with the past and present. He recalled the days of boyhood, and those of riper years

Where was the wife of his youth? and the children she had borne him? His little ones were sleeping in the quiet grave; and she had been driven from his home; for he had brought another to share the place in his affections she had so long held alone. His sin rose up before him as a thick cloud, and he groaned and wept in the bitterness of his soul, crying 'God be merciful to me a sinner!' He spent the night in deep repentance before God, and only closed his eyes just as the sun began to shed its first feeble rays of light. He was, however, soon aroused from his slumbers by the shouts of the people, and the tramp of multitudes. It was the waning of the moon, the day of worship for the followers of Gaudama. Business had been suspended, and young and old were busy in paying homage at the temples of Gaudama, and presenting flowers. The people were dressed in their best attire, loaded with yellow cotton cloth and silk, and every now and then were borne upon the shoulders of men, small trees, with hundreds of branches from which hung handkerchiefs, pillows, mats, umbrellas, cups, flowers, fruits, and candles, offerings for the priests: the whole producing a bright and gorgeous scene. These days had been the delight of Moung Shway Pau, and he had been wont to exult with pride over all this display, when he compared it with the humble worship of the foreigners and the heretics, but now his heart sickened at the sight. He had firmly resolved to become a Christian, and as the sun arose he hastened to the foreign teachers to receive instruction, and to tell them of his wish to worship the Eternal God. The teacher's heart beat with joy as he heard the glad news. The native preachers were called together, they all sought the mercy seat. God was with them, and Moung Shway Pau became a rejoicing convert. As his heart overflowed with love instinctively the image of his injured wife rose before him, and he longed to tell her of the joys of salvation through a crucified Saviour. The following Sabbath he was baptized, and the Monday following went in search of his neglected wife. He found her, told her of his conversion, confessed his sin, and humbly besought her to return to his home. At last she yielded, and before the church they were again united. She is now seeking the favor of God, and soon it is hoped she will be numbered among his children."

Many interesting circumstances occurred about this period in the mission at Rangoon. A great field was opening before it, and the land seemed waiting to be taken possession of by the "King of kings." A convention of the missionaries had been held at Maulmain to meet a deputation from America, to consider the best mode of pursuing their operations for the future, and the stations they were to occupy in Burmah Proper. Soon after the return of Mr. Kincaid and Mr. Vinton from the convention, we find mention of the ordination of Mau Ya to the pastorate of the Karen church at Ya-the by the aged and revered Ko-Thah-a, the venerable pastor of the Rangoon Burmese church.

Ko-Thah-a had been three times imprisoned for the name of Christ, and through good report and evil report had for many years testified to the grace of God in that city. He is now in his eighty-fourth year; "a shock fully ripe." Though unable to preach to his people, his life shone with increasing lustre, and in his prayers there was such a remarkable unction, that they awakened feelings of the deepest emotion in almost every heart. His language was always pointed, and beautiful for its conciseness and brevity. He would often remark with thankfulness that he had been spared to see that time when the gospel could be preached with none to oppose, and like Simeon of old he was now ready to depart in peace, for his eyes had seen the Lord's salvation. We can scarcely imagine a more striking picture than this venerable man presiding at the ordination of Mau Ya, his fine eye beaming with intelligence and holy joy.

Mau Ya had been baptized about twenty years before, and had been an assistant preaching the gospel for nearly fifteen years. The church in their letter asking for his ordination, bore testimony to the uniformity of his Christian character, and ministerial faithfulness. He had endured suffering and reproach for the name of Christ; had been fined, whipped, imprisoned under sentence of death, and condemned to the worst of all kinds of slavery. He had been made a pagoda slave, and required to spend his life in the service of a god whom he knew to be no god. His business had been to keep the pagoda in repair. He was rescued from this dreadful state by the kind assistance of Col. Burney, who had been long and intimately acquainted with the Governor, and said to him that he should regard it as one of the greatest personal favors he could do him, if he would give Mau Ya his liberty. The Governor yielded, and he had already been the instrument in the hands of God of the conversion from heathenism of some scores, if not hundreds, of his countrymen. He was now an ordained preacher of the gospel of Christ, from whose labors the missionaries anticipated much for the final and permanent establishment of the Kingdom of Christ in that dark land.

Thus the work went on, and the people released from the bondage in which they had been held, rejoiced in the milder rule under which they lived. "Now we can breathe and dare to sleep; but before the English took possession, we could neither breathe nor sleep." One old man, after speaking of the oppressions under the Burmans and their deliverance by the English, exclaimed with much warmth, " O how I wish I could see the Queen of England, how *I would worship her!*"

When told that her Majesty would not be pleased with such worship he appeared unable at first to understand it, but after repeated explanation, he for the first time seemed to receive the idea of the existence of an Eternal God to whom worship should be paid alone. In December, 1855, Mrs. Ingalls writes:—" Agreeably to the promise I made you last mail, I will try and tell you of our last tour. We left Rangoon, Tuesday the 13th, and at sunset reached the village of Sike gu. We went ashore, and the first street led us to the idol-temple, or worship-place. 'There,' said the aged man, pointing to a small marble idol under a canopy of yellow and red paper, 'there is our god.' We asked him if that image could save them when they presented their offerings, or asked to be saved from hell, or perhaps to become gods ? He seemed startled at the question, and said he never thought of it before; but his fathers had worshipped these gods, and he must not forsake their customs. Mr. Ingalls told him of the God who made the heaven and earth, and all therein, and the way of salvation through Jesus Christ. He gave the most respectful attention, and followed us on to a crowd of people, who gathered themselves around us, while we told the men, women, and children, of Him who alone can save them from hell. At dark we went to our boat, and left a preacher on shore to explain more fully the way of salvation. As Mr. Ingalls was not well, I went ashore, and found a house spread with mats, and a basket for my seat. The man of the house had read some of our books, and his eyes seemed to be opened to the truth. The preacher I left on shore, and at midnight I still heard his voice at the house. Left early in the morning, and reached a village called The-lu. The shore was so muddy that the men went above their knees in getting ashore; so we did not venture into the village. The preacher gave a few books and talked with the people; and in the evening we left for the mouth of the river. We came to a large stream on our left; and, as the tide turned we entered it, and called at a large town named Th'co'pein—meaning, the place where the robbers used to assemble and repair, &c. We found the people all engaged in boat-racing, and, as the tide was against us we were obliged to remain. The preacher climbed up the bank, and found only two grown persons in the place, the rest being at the river, attending the racing. The racing was near us, and divided into two parties who separated, one on the right and the other on the left bank; as the men rowed, each party cheered them on by music and dancing, and the waving of flags by the young women. Forty rupees were the stimulus; and when one of the boats gained the reward, that party sent up loud cheers, and the boat returned, the rowers singing and dancing until they arrived; after which the company separated. As the winners passed by our boat, we found that they were many of them Karens. Soon other boats came; and when they found who we were, they strongly urged that we should visit their place. We had felt somewhat sad about our reaching this place at this very time; but we had committed our ways to God, knowing that He would guide us in the way we should go; and when this warm invitation came, we concluded to go to the Karen village, and return to Th'co'pein in the morning, when we hoped the people would resume their usual occupations, and be ready to receive us.

"We therefore left; and, at sun-down, entered the stream leading to the Karen village. At first it was broad, but, after a few rods, it became very narrow, and, as it was getting dark, we found we were obliged to go on, or remain where we were; for return we could not, the stream was so narrow. After a long and toilsome time of cutting down trees and large bushes that obstructed our way and nearly ruined our boat, we arrived at the first village, called Co Doung. The mosquitos came in by thousands, and Mr. Ingalls not being well, we had a most dreadful night. Daylight came, and we found we must go out of the stream, or remain another day for the tide; which we could not do and carry out our plans; besides, it was a dreadful place for one in feeble health. Our time being short, we went ashore, and found that most of the people here were Burman, the Karens living a long distance beyond. Some aged men came, and said they wished to hear about the God who we said had made the world. Mr. Ingalls told them of man's fall, and the story of redemption through Jesus Christ. Smiles and tears were mingled together as they listened. They asked how they must pray to God, and when Mr. Ingalls told them they listened as though their life depended upon those words. 'But,' said one of the old men, with sorrow, 'I fear we cannot remember those words.' We told them that the book we had given them would teach them; and they clasped it, even as some precious treasure. They said they should come to see us, and we expect to see them, for we believe their hearts have been touched. Some Karen girls came to see me; but when they saw Mr. Ingalls they ran under the house; fearing, they said, he had come to steal them. Mr. Ingalls told them that I was his wife; one of the girls then looked in my face, and said 'O yes; she has a white face: he will not want us.' After a few words of explanation they came about us, and listened well. They understood Burmese very well, and told me there was one Christian in their part of the village. We had a pleasant time at this place, and left, followed to our boat by very many, and, better than all, by the grateful blessings of the aged men. We felt deeply interested in them; for they were so sincere in all their questions, and seemed to feel that their God could not save them. We had a hard time in getting to them; but we left, thanking God that we had been permitted to tell these aged men of the way of salvation.

"At noon we returned to Th'co'pein, and found the people of that place, and hundreds from other villages, engaged in making offerings to the priests, and consecrating a dress for them. Two boats were fastened together, and over them a canopy of paper, cut and painted in fantastic forms, and the sides hung and looped with yellow satin, made from the sacred cloth. Some half dozen priests seated themselves under this canopy, and read from their Pali books: while the people sat in their boats around them; after which a man went to the priests and presented the sacred dress, and a few others followed with fruit and flowers, and the scene closed We felt cast down when we came to this place and found the people all engaged in their forms; but before we left we thanked God for sending us at this very time; for while they were consecrating the sacred dress, our boat was completely surrounded by large boats, filled with respectable men from other villages, who listened to us with deep interest, and many of them confessed they had no confidence in their religion. We gave some choice books, and told them what they must do to be saved. When we left we felt that we were short-sighted creatures, and that God knew how to order all things well. Hundreds had come to that place to worship things of man's invention; but God had looked with compassion upon them in the midst of their sins and opened a door of mercy for them. God is truly a Being of mercy and long-suffering. We received a warm invitation to visit the homes of some, which we hope to do at some future day.

"At sundown left this place, and came to another village, and before morning left for Rangoon. This has been a kind of exploring tour, and, as we cannot revisit them ourselves, we shall try and send preachers to these places. We have presented the cup of salvation to many hundreds, and it has universally been received with gladness. But they must have 'line upon line,' to enable them to understand all God's will. After getting our mail, and attending to home affairs, replenishing our stores a little, we left in the evening, for a trip up the Irrawadi and Bassein River.

"At midnight reached the village of Tet-thit; at eight in the morning, after a chat with the people, left; and at noon reached the village of Co-tu-yoh, a large flourishing town, where the river forks, and large towns are built upon the banks, numbering some five five thousand people. We went ashore, and found the head-man was an old friend of ours, who had often attended our Sabbath service, and had given fifteen rupees towards the Burman chapel. He received us most cordially, and we concluded to spend the Sabbath at his place. He told us we might have our service in his audience hall, and in the evening, as we went through the town, we heard the streets resounding with the call of the runner, warning them to come and hear of the God who made the world. On Sunday they rang the native bell, and we went to the house of the ruler, where we found two chairs for us, and mats spread for the people in his hall. The people soon came, and hundreds heard, for the first time, of Him, who alone is able to save them from hell. Many of them were the builders of the temple, and the strong men of the priest. They, too, listened with the most rapt attention: they came, no doubt, with an eye of curiosity, but they soon became deeply interested, and the truth seemed to sink deep into their hearts. Not only was the large hall filled, but the house was surrounded with men, women, and children, who were so eager to hear, that the ruler gave them permission to tear off the front of the house. As Mr. Ingalls stopped a moment in his remarks, we could not but call to mind God's mercy to Burmah. How changed the scene!"

It was early in 1856, that, in the midst of these interesting labors, the health of Mr. Ingalls, which had been long failing, rapidly declined. As the work increased, the hour of his release drew near. A short trip to Bengal was tried in the vain hope that a cessation from labor and a change of air and scene might recruit his failing strength. Mrs. Ingalls was left at Rangoon to do what she could for the Burman converts, as there was no other missionary in the Burman department then at Rangoon; but he so rapidly declined at Calcutta, that she was hastily summoned by the return steamer. Knowing his great anxiety to get back to the scene of his labors that he might die there, they embarked to return thither. He still hoped he had work to do for Burmah, and used to say; "I cannot leave until some one is willing to come and care for these souls as I have done. I left America to die on heathen ground; and I have never repented the course I have taken."

Just as the vessel was nearing Rangoon, on the 14th March, 1856, it was evident that he was sinking. Miss Vinton, who was with them, had sung to him,

"The morning light is breaking,
The darkness disappears."

The light of heaven had indeed broken upon his soul; the darkness and storms of this world had disappeared; and he entered into rest in the forty-eighth year of his age. After Mr. Ingalls' death, we received the following from his widow:—

"*Rangoon, Nov.* 8th, 1856.

'Your very kind letter of August last came safe, and I have to thank you for your kindness. I was then deciding about my return to America; and I thought I should call upon you as I passed through Calcutta, and therefore did not reply. It seemed my duty to go home with my little girl, and I had some fears regarding the work of a single lady in Burmah. I packed my trunk, and was ready to go by the return steamer; but the woes of the heathen and the tears of the Christians, have come before me with so much power, that I dare not go yet. My fatherless child is left with but few relatives, and none of this world's goods; and I felt it my duty to seek for her a home, and see that she was decently educated, so that she might care for herself if God called me away; but I feel the claims of these people so strong upon me, that I must remain a little longer, and trust God in regard to the future. I have therefore decided to remain another year. It has been a bitter struggle of duty; but if I can see my Heavenly Father is guiding, then I shall not fear to remain. I shall leave my present home in the city, and go to a part of the town called Kemendine. It is a new Burman field, and we may have some obstacles to obstruct us; but if God is with us, we shall not work in vain. I shall have two or three Burman preachers, with their wives, some Burman schools, and shall go out into the jungle in the dry season. I thank you for the interest you have manifested towards me, and also your dear husband; and now I ask, as a favor, that you will pray for a blessing to rest upon my work here. I have led a happy life in this country. We have had our clouds; but I think we have had more of the sunshine.

"My dear husband loved the people, and they loved him; so that we have always been surrounded by dear Christians and heathen who were listening to the words of our blessed gospel. My dear husband always wished me to spend my time among the people; so I have always been with him in his work, and heretofore have had but little time for sorrow. At times now I feel that my cup of sorrow is too bitter for me; but at other times God does not forsake me, and I see His love in all that He has done. My dear one was ripe for heaven, and God knew when to take him. Every day something comes up to remind me of my loss, and the struggle is a hard one. Companies of Burmans come in. They inquire for the teacher. It is a bitter task to try and tell them that he is gone, gone.; and it is not an easy thing for me to compose myself to tell them of his peaceful end, and remind them of his exhortations to them, and his prayers on their behalf. These are bitter trials; but God has blessed some of these meetings, and I know he will not leave me. My confidence in my Heavenly Father was never so firm as now. And then, too, the Christians are most kind to me, and even the heathen seem to wish to do something to cheer me. A large company came to see me a few days ago, having heard that I was going to America. One said, if I would stay he would do any thing for me. One said he would give me the posts for a house; another the boards for the floor; another the material for enclosing; and one poor man, who had nothing to give, held up his hands and said 'Here, mamma, is my gift: they are strong, and can help make the house, if you will only stay;' another that he would bring a boat and convey me to his place. So you will understand I do not feel alone with these poor Christians and heathen. My health, too, is good, and that of my little girl was never better; so I have blessings with all my trials."

And thus this mission has proceeded, "in deaths oft." Probably in no modern mission, save that of the Church Missionary Society in West Africa, has there been so large a number of deaths in proportion to the brethren employed.

The following is a list to the present time of those who counted not their lives dear unto them, but have finished their course with joy and the ministry which they received of the Lord Jesus, to testify the gospel of the grace of God. (Acts xx. 24.)

## DEATHS IN THE BURMAN AND KAREN MISSIONS.

| NAMES. | DEPARTMENT. | APPOINTM'T. | DEATH. |
|---|---|---|---|
| Rev. E. Wheelock, | Burman. | 1817. | 1819 At Sea. |
| Mrs. Price, | " | 1821. | 1822 " Rangoon. |
| Rev. J. Coleman, | " | 1817. | 1822 " Arracan. |
| Mrs. A. H. Judson, | " | 1812. | 1826 " Amherst. |
| Rev. J. D. Price, | " | 1820. | 1828 " Ava. |
| Rev. G. D. Boardman, | " | 1823. | 1831 " Tavoy. |
| Mrs. Kincaid, | " | 1830. | 1831 " Maulmain. |
| Miss Sarah Cummings, | " | 1832. | 1834 " |
| Mrs. C. R. M. Hall, | " | 1836. | 1837 " Arracan. |
| Rev. Levi Hall, | " | 1836. | 1837 " |
| Mrs. E. B. Osgood, | " | 1834. | 1840 " Maulmain. |
| Miss Eleanor Macomber, | Karen. | 1836. | 1841 " London. |
| Mrs. A. S. T. Hancock, | Burman. | 1831. | 1843 " Arracan. |
| Mrs. S. D. Comstock, | " | 1833. | 1843 " Maulmain. |
| Mrs. C. J. H. Simons, | " | 1832. | 1844 " Arracan. |
| Rev. G. S. Comstock, | " | 1833. | 1845 " |
| Rev. A. P. G. Abbott, | Karen. | 1834. | 1845 " St. Helena. |
| Mrs. S. B. Judson, | Burman. | 1823. | 1845 " Maulmain. |
| Mrs. M. D. Ingalls, | " | 1835. | 1846 " Tavoy. |
| Mrs. H. M. G. Mason, | Karen. | 1829. | 1846 " Maulmain. |
| Rev. E. B. Bullard, | " | 1843. | 1847 " Akyab. |
| Mrs. L. C. J. Moore, | Burman. | 1848. | 1849 " Akyab. |
| Rev. A. Judson, D.D. | " | 1812. | 1850 " Sea. |

## DEATHS IN THE BURMAN AND KAREN MISSIONS.—(Continued.)

| NAMES. | DEPARTMENT. | APPOINT'T. | DEATH. | |
|---|---|---|---|---|
| Mrs. E. R. K. Knapp, | Burman. | 1849. | 1852 | At Arracan. |
| Rev. H. M. Campbell, | " | 1851. | 1852 | " " |
| Mrs. L. B. Stilson, | " | 1835. | 1852 | " Maulmain. |
| Mrs. Nisbit, | " | 1852. | 1853 | " Sea. |
| Rev. H. E. Knapp, | " | 1849. | 1854 | " Arracan. |
| Mrs. Rose, | " | 1852. | 1853 | " Arracan. |
| Mrs. O. C. W. Harris, | Karen. | 1844. | 1854 | " Shwaygyeen. |
| Mrs. E. C. Judson, | Burman. | 1846. | 1855 | In America. |
| Rev. E. L. Abbott, | Karen. | 1835. | 1855 | " " |
| Mrs. M. F. Beecher, | " | 1848. | 1855 | At Sea. |
| Rev. L. Ingalls, | Burman. | 1835. | 1856 | " Rangoon. |
| Mrs. M. V. Harris, | Karen. | 1841. | 1856 | " Shwaygyeen. |
| Mrs. S. C. Bixby, | Burman. | 1852. | 1856 | In America. |
| Rev. Mr. and Mrs. Satterlee, | " | 1854. | 1856 | " Arracan. |
| Rev. J. Benjamin, | Karen. | 1848. | 1856 | " America. |
| Mrs. Ranney, | Burman. | 1843. | 1857 | " Rangoon. |
| Rev. D. Whitaker, | Karen. | 1852. | 1857 | " Maulmain. |
| Rev. J. H. Vinton, | " | 1832. | 1858 | " Rangoon. |

These are they that "offered themselves willingly among the people. Bless ye the Lord."—Judges v. 9.

## CHAPTER XI.

### TOUNGOO.

"How beautiful on the mountains are the feet of them that bring glad tidings."—Isaiah lii. 7.

Within a year after Pegu was annexed to the British Empire in India, Mr. Mason, who had been laboring since 1831 in the Tenasserim Provinces, became so enfeebled in health, that he was compelled to contemplate a return to America. On reaching Maulmain, however, he determined, before doing so, to visit Toungoo, the ancient capital of that kingdom. In the days of the Burmese Government, no Christian or Christian missionary had ever entered that territory, and the sound of the gospel had never reached the people's ears. It was justly thought that the present moment would be favorable to the introduction of Christianity, especially amongst the Karens, who associated with the rule of the White Foreigners a time of prosperity and peace and of enlightenment in the knowledge of the Eternal God.

While Dr. Mason's own mind was being pressed to go forth into this new field, Sau Quala, one of the best and wisest of the Karen pastors of Tavoy, was being led to consider its importance too, and he had determined to go up the next dry season to travel through the length and breadth of the land, saying, in the spirit of Caleb: "Let us go up at once, and possess it; for we are well able to overcome it."

Dr. and Mrs. Mason started on the 28th September, 1853,

upon their journey northward, and stepping into a large canoe, with a Karen Bible and nymn book, turned its head towards TOUNGOO. From Martaban, to Ava and the Himalaya, a range of granite mountains runs nearly north and south, between the waters of the Salween on the east, and of the Sitang and Irrawadi on the west. For fifteen miles, they had to stem the torrent of the Salween, which at this season pours down an immense volume of water. At noon they rested for refreshment under the shade of a large spreading acacia tree, of which upwards of ten species are known in Burmah, some with globular heads of flowers, some white and some yellow; some are immense creepers, while others are noble timber trees, rivalled by none except the teak. Twenty miles' progress up the Benling river brought them before Zaingyeik or "Foot of God" mountain, two or three thousand feet high. At the base of this mountain is the site of the most ancient city in Burmah, Thatmug. Mr. Whitaker, who visited the site of this old city, says: "There remain only the walls and pagodas; two of which are the largest I have ever seen."

The footsteps of recent and ruthless war could be traced here and there, in the desolated villages, as the travellers passed along; but occasionally their sadness was relieved by an application for a Christian book from some Burmans who, perhaps years before, had received a tract, and who were anxious to know more of the Eternal God, and the way of salvation. On the third day they passed the site of the old city of Benling, marked by a single palmyra palm, raising its majestic head amid surrounding desolation.

They rested on the Sabbath, in a gothic-looking temple on the banks of the stream, under the shade of a banyan, and there, with their Karen and Burmese Bibles and hymn book they sought to attract the passers-by, and to induce them to listen to the words of heavenly wisdom. Many a little group, during the day, drew near, and for the first time heard of Christ, the Saviour of sinners.

At dawn they were on their way again, and after pulling between high banks for a few miles, entered a large lake extending further than the eye could reach. The western boundary of the lake is only four or five miles from the banks of the Sitang, into which it opens by a narrow outlet. Here, at three miles' distance, the *bore* is heard roaring like the waves on the ocean shore. At the mouth of the river the tidal wave sometimes drives up a perpendicular wall of water twenty-seven feet high, engulfing everything before it. Two or three hundred British troops lost their lives there, and it is not unusual to hear of boats swamped, and all but life lost. The city of Sitang is but an inconsiderable village, though the residence of a king six or seven centuries ago. The valley was everywhere disturbed by robbers, who, although the people were disarmed, found no difficulty in procuring arms and ammunition themselves, and kept all within their reach in a state of terror and alarm. Dr. and Mrs. Mason, however, proceeded in safety, and at last reached Shwaygyeen, which is so beautifully situated, that it affords one of the most picturesque views that can be found, even in the east. It lies on the forks of the Toungoo and Shwaygyeen rivers, with the mountains close behind, and is one of the most convenient stations for a Karen missionary of all towns in Burmah. The Karen settlements commence at half an hour's distance from the city, and continue, at short intervals, in untold numbers, north, south, and east. At this station Mr. and Mrs. Harris, from the time of the annexation, carried on their earnest self-denying labors. They and their four children had gone up to the place in a country boat rowed by Karen disciples. It was on a Saturday night they anchored, and the next morning, finding an empty shed, they assembled to worship God, and there, for the first time, the glorious gospel was proclaimed at Shwaygyeen. At that time no Christian hearts beat there; but now, scattered up and down the hills, are hundreds of baptized believers. Mrs. Harris was a woman of no ordinary powers, and seems to have had a good knowledge of the language. She had schools for the children, and taught the men and women to read with great success. She was at last struck with fever and dysentery. On asking the doctor what he thought of her case, he said, " I would not say there is *no hope.*" " No hope !" she replied, " you know I am not afraid to die." In speaking afterwards to her, her husband told her that nature must fail, if the disease was not checked. She then said, " Well, I have tried to show these Karens how a Christian should *live*, and now I hope to show them how a Christian can *die*. I had hoped to take my dear children home to America some day, but now you must do it, and I shall go to my dear mother; (her mother had died a trimuphant death not long before.) I shall need no outfit, and the voyage will be short." She did all she could to comfort her husband to the last; and had the Karens constantly with her, exhorting them to follow Christ, that they might reign with him.

To relieve her husband she had everything prepared, even to her coffin. To her dear children she said, " Don't think of your mother as *there*," pointing to the earth; " but think of her as before the throne of God and of the Lamb !" Having chosen her grave clothes and dressed herself in them, her spirit fled. Mr. Harris had to bury her himself, with the aid of the Christians. A little spot was chosen close to the grave of those brave British soldiers who had fallen in the service of their country; and as they laid her there the thought arose, how far brighter was the crown of glory which she won in the service of the King of kings, than the crown of victory won by those brave men, in the service of their earthly king. Almost her last words to her husband were, "*Remember*, do *all* you can for Shwaygyeen." So strong in death was her desire that Christ should be known, and loved, and served by the people for whom she had lived and died.

But to return. After nineteen days of travelling Dr. and Mrs. Mason came in sight of the walls of Toungoo, looming up from a forest of palm trees. The city is a rectangle, a mile from north to south, and a mile and a half from east to west. It stands on a plain, a quarter of a mile west of the Sitang river, which is there about four hundred yards wide, and deep enough for the navigation of large boats at all seasons. The walls of the city were built twenty-five feet high, with towers and battlements which have been destroyed; the walls themselves are still in good preservation, and the earth has been heaped up on the inside, so as to form a beautiful promenade all round the city. Here the chain of mountains on the east, which approached within a few miles of the river, is seen in all its glorious sublimity, pile upon pile until they rise to a height of eight or ten thousand feet. The distant western horizon is bounded by the Prome mountains, and by the valley of the Irrawaddy.

The position of Toungoo as a missionary centre, appears to be one of considerable importance. Burmans, Shans, Kyens, and Toungoos gather within its walls; and around are various tribes of Karens, two or three of which were before unknown. This station appears to be likely to rise in importance; and the hope is cherished that from it many will go forth to be lights in the surrounding darkness, and perhaps to be the heralds of salvation even into China and Siam.

The province of Toungoo was formerly ruled by an independent king; but about 1612 it became a dependency of Ava, and gave the title of Prince of Toungoo to a member of the royal family, until it was annexed to our empire in 1852. The missionaries having settled themselves within the city, many gathered round to see and hear. Dr. Mason's health was enfeebled and exhausted, but this made him only more anxious to work while it was day. Mrs. Mason gathered together a little school, and at the end of a week sent out a Karen tract, "The Sayings of the Elders," which Dr. Mason had prepared some years before. It embodied the biblical traditions of the Karens; and on the front page was written, "The Eternal God's commands come back to the Karens. Learn to read them." This little messenger was given to one who was told to show it to all who would listen upon the mountains; and no doubt the prayer of faith ascended, that God would make it successful. Some three weeks after, a chief with about forty followers presented himself in front of the verandah. Being seated, he began carefully to unroll some plaintain leaves, which he had in his hand, and which evidently contained something that he esteemed most precious. Leaf after leaf was laid aside, until at last the little tract appeared, which he reverently presented to Mrs. Mason, begging her to explain its contents. How gladly was he instructed, not only in that, but the Karen Bible! With wonder and astonishment he listened to the word of God in his own mother-tongue; and taking the book in his hand, he bowed three times before it, and saying, "Surely it is a spirit, for it speaks Karen." This chief and his attendants were present on the arrival of a letter from the churches of Tavoy; and their delight was inexpressible when they learned that they had brethren far away, who could read the Spirit-book, and write letters. Hearing that a Karen teacher was coming to visit them, they all exclaimed, "Send him to us!

send him to us! we'll feed him, we'll clothe him, we'll build a house for him, we'll take care of him;" but the old chief pressed before the others and begged that his name might be put down first. He is now not only a believer himself, but has several flourishing Christian churches among his people: nor have the tribe ever once offered to demons since the little messenger was sent among them.

It was not long after this interview, that a party of strange-looking Karens looked in through the door of the missionary's dwelling. They were altogether unlike any that had been seen before. Their leader was a tall finely-formed man, with an expressive countenance, and dressed in the picturesque costume of the Taubeah tribe. A curious basket was thrown over his shoulder, and a long bamboo spear served him both as a weapon and a staff. He was attended by eight or ten men evidently inferior to himself, who, with restless eye, seemed ever on the alert for the coming foe. They were from the lofty mountain to the east of Toungoo, and had come to see the Christian teachers, and to hear their words. The Chief was immediately asked whom he worshipped?

"Thako Mosha," he replied. This mythical being receives divine homage from every tribe of the Karens, but under different names, and it is probably Indra, whose worship is so popular amongst the Hindus. Whatever it be, the rites connected with it have a most tenacious hold of these nations, and present the greatest obstacles to their conversion. It seems an easy thing to induce Karens to say they will worship the living God, because they believe their ancestors worshipped him; but say to them, "You must not practise the Thako Mosha's rites," and they instantly dissent, especially the elders, who declare that if their children fail to observe them, the most terrible judgments will follow, and no persuasion can prevent them; nothing but the enlightening Spirit of God.

There is a place in the Toungoo mountains which is celebrated throughout this region and Tenasserim as the residence of this Thako Mosha. It is the Olympus of the Karens, and shoots up in two lofty points some seven thousand feet from the plain. Between these is a sacred pool, of whose magical virtues the country is full of legends, and here the Karens go up once a year to worship and make offerings to this great Thako Mosha, or great spirit, which dwells upon the summit watching over the actions of men. The Taubeah chief came from this mountain, and worshipped this being. He was asked if his people did so too; and if he believed it was this spirit that made the world? "No; L'Ouah Do," was his immediate reply. Ouah is the appellation given by all the Karens to the Eternal God, but with different adjectives attached.

A Sgau Karen would say G'cha Ouah, Lord God: a Pwo Karen might say this, but would be just as likely to say Moung Ouah, the Honorable God, particularly if not acquainted with the Christians. A Mona Karen would say, Ouah Pado, the Great God; and a Taubeah would say L'Ouah Do, also the Great God. To one acquainted with letters these local differences would present no difficulty; but to say to a Taubeah, 'G'cha Guah has commanded this or that, and he is unaffected by what you say; but change it to 'L'Ouah Do,' and the smile of interest shows that thought is awakened.

The Taubeah chieftain proved to be a minstrel, and recited three or four lines of genuine Karen poetry concerning the deity, of which the following is a literal translation:—

> "God made the earth, God made the sky,
> All creatures that walk, and all that fly,
> God made the trees, He made the sea,
> God made man, and all things that be."

Music ever has a charm; but nothing could have been more pleasant to the missionary's ear than the chief's wild chanting of his eloquent psalm of the great Creator. The more they knew of this man, the more the interest in him was increased, especially when he said that his young wife and child had been torn from him by the Burmans, and sold into slavery.

One day he asked the missionaries if they had come to remain. On being told that they would not go further at present, and having satisfied himself that no Burman was near, he began improvising, alluding to the Burman chiefs who were stockading near Toungoo. His measure was irregular and hurried, but the purport was as follows:—

>"Teachers! 'tis now a sorry day;
> These wicked chiefs all in array,
> Up in the north with great display,
> For boldest strife and bloody fray,
> The English power defy.
>
> "Say they, 'The conqueror yet shall bend,
> For all our loss shall make amend,
> Our border we will stout defend,
> And ever down our troops will send,
> Their strength again we'll try.'
>
> "So, teacher, rest; in Toungoo stay,
> Nor from the town stray far away,
> For scarcely yet dare we to pray,
> Or e'en to sing a heart-felt lay,
> Our foes are ever nigh.
>
> "Oh! we Karens could tell a tale
> Would make the pale man grow more pale;
> How sisters' shriek and brothers' wail,
> Are mingled on the sighing gale
> With the mother's piercing cry!"

Here the chief paused, and leant his head upon his staff, as if his heart was too full of painful memories. He had, however, touched in the breasts of those who listened a chord which responded with deepest sympathy, and they were henceforth friends. Many Taubeahs visited the missionaries during the time of their brief sojourn in Toungoo, and in none did they feel a more prayerful earnest interest than in the unfortunate minstrel. But the missionaries' labors were not exclusively confined to the Karens.

The following account of an interview which Mrs. Mason had with one of the former Governor's wives shortly after the arrival at Toungoo, will not be uninteresting. We give it in her own words:—"Fancy a Tonngoo lady, some sixty years of age, her silvery white hair smoothly combed up from an ample forehead, her lustrous eyes keenly glancing from beneath highly arched eyebrows, her fingers adorned with the nine magical stones of Burmah, her feet slipped loosely into scarlet sandals, her person attired in a pink and white silk robe, woven in small checks, open after the Burman fashion, with a crimson cincture concealing the bust. Over this a delicate lawn jacket open in front, and above all, gracefully flowing over the left shoulder, a richly-wrought white lace scarf. Imagine such a figure, and you have before you a Woonkadau of Toungoo, or a Governor's lady as she appeared when she paid me a visit with her suite, soon after our arrival. Having ordered mats to be spread, I took a low seat beside her, and inquired : 'Does the Woonkadau wish to hear of Jesus Christ?' She replied, 'I have come to hear.' Turning to an attendant I said 'How old is the Woonkadau?' 'I have lived sixty-five years,' was her own reply. 'Indeed! the great mother is as old as my grandmother. I am but a child in years beside her ; nevertheless God has shown me the true way to happiness'

"' Let us hear! let us hear!' said the attendants: so I endeavored to tell them slowly and solemnly of man's sinful state—of their individual sins—of Christ's atonement—of the comfort here, and everlasting bliss attendant upon receiving it, and the danger of rejecting it, pointing out to them distinctly the great difference between salvation by Christ, and the annihilation promised in their sacred books. The Woonkadau was a very understanding woman, and so were four or five others in her train, one of whom could read very well.

"'I am afraid you will not like my words,' I remarked, 'you will not like to hear that it is sinful to offer adoration to the idols, and Poongyees; but I must tell you, because God says so.' She smiled and replied:

"'You are a woman, the same as myself, only you have more knowledge; and what you say are not your own words, but God's words, we must receive them as God's words.' They all assented to the truth, but I fear only from true eastern politeness, as they did not seem at all affected; and as it was towards noon, she asked permission to retire, as it was her hour for sleep. After this interview, I used often to send her books and messages, and on sending her the 'Life of Christ' in Burmese, she was greatly pleased, and returned many salaams, saying she had long wished to see such a book, and would give attention to the paragraphs I had marked for her.

"In the Woonkadau's train was a pretty young Burmese, very graceful and lovely in her manners. She looked intelligent but said little: one of her companions observed: 'You say, God made us all, and loves us all; if this be true, why has He made you white and me brown? No, no,' she continued with a bitter smile, 'He does not love the Burmans; He's the God of the English, not the God of the Burmans.' 'You plant a garden,' I replied, 'you put in tuberoses, balsams, oleanders : you are very fond of your flowers, for you planted them yourself, so you carefully tend them, water them, dig about them, get rich soil for them, and watch with an admiring interest to see the blossoms open.'

"'Yes, yes.'

"'By and bye a companion comes in, and begins to carry off all the red and yellow flowers, "Stop stop!" you cry, "you are spoiling my garden." "No, no," she says, "you only want the white ones, I'll have all the others."'

"'She should not have them.'

"'Just so. The world is God's garden, and the people His flowers : white and yellow.' But Mahnaht (the devil) comes in with his legion, and pulls them here—there—armful after armful, saying, 'I'll have all the red, and all the yellow, to keep my fires burning.' But God says, 'No! You shall not destroy my flowers.' They were pleased with the simile, as orientals always are with anything like a parable."

"Nearly all the Menkadaus, or gentlemen's wives in and around the city," Mrs. Mason wrote at that period, "have visited us at different times, and one is a person of uncommon talents. She can read fluently, and the people say she knows more of Burman books than any man in the place, except two or three priests. This is a very rare case, for we have seen only a few women in Toungoo who could read at all. I feel much interest in this person, and much time has been spent in instructing her, perhaps more so, because she is, for a heathen, a really loveable woman, soft and winning in her manners and has a particularly sweet pleasant voice. She visits us frequently, reads our books, and says she is considering the Christian system ; but does not yet believe. Her husband is from Ava, a tall noble man ; but not friendly to our religion. This woman has a pretty daughter whom she has taught to read, and whom she wishes to place with me for instruction, and I cannot but hope they will some day become true disciples.

"One day she was stumbling on the doctrine of the Trinity. She was advised to let it alone until she had learned more of the character of Christ's life and doctrine, but she would dwell on that, and remarked,—

"'I can understand all the rest, but this point is inexplicable.'

"Having in vain tried to illustrate the subject, she was asked, if she did not love her husband? 'Certainly, and obey him too, usually.'

"'What, without understanding all his thoughts, or seeing into his heart?'

"'Ah, I see,' she replied; 'you mean we should be content to serve God without understanding Him.'

"'His own Son died for you; what husband would love like that?'

"'True, true.'

"'Would you feel any happier if you could look into the Eternal God as you can look into your idols of papiér maché?'

"'No,'—after a pause, 'I—I don't think I should; he would not seem so *great*.'

"'You think it hard,' it was observed another day, ' to give up what you call merit?'

"'Yes,' she said, ' I have done a good deal in my life for Pagodas, and monasteries, and it is very hard,—*very* hard.'

"Ah, dear friends, if you could be here on the spot to realize these things. I do not know how you would feel, but I know how I feel, and that I cannot stay the tears, as this gifted woman sits before me, bound in the iron fetters of Buddhism, which are from childhood tightening, tightening, and are still drawing, drawing almost irresistibly, down to eternal woe.

"Another Menkadau, an elderly lady, is perhaps equally intelligent, but very different. She has a great intellect, understands almost before the words are spoken; and will often turn round, and expound to the others: taking care, however, to give it as the sentiment of the teacher, not as her own.

"Many attempt to make out that Christianity and Buddhism are the same; and some of these women appear really inclined to believe Jesus Christ to be Arumaday, the anticipated Buddh; but this old lady saw the difference at once. 'They are not alike,' she remarked one day with emphasis, 'not alike; they are like this,' holding up her hands in opposite directions. Nothing could be more correct; though not one in fifty will acknowledge it.

"One day, several Mathoolaus or nuns came to see us, some of the first in the place. They asked for offerings. We had to tell them, as the Apostle did the poor lame man at the temple, that silver and gold we had none; and gave them Mrs. Ann Judson's catechism, and read to them from the Scriptures, after which they departed respectfully, and apparently very much pleased. One of the number could read; and I believe she is the only one who can, among the whole fifteen Mathoolaus of Toungoo.

"They seemed to receive the gospel,—and it would not be strange if they should hereafter worship Jesus Christ in connection with Gaudama and the Nahts; and this is what it is imagined a great many Burmans will do. Indeed, were the gospel to be now suddenly withdrawn from the Province, undoubtedly a few years hence the traveller would find Jesus Christ's image among the idols of Toungoo. On one occasion, as many as thirty promised, and apparently with all sincerity, that they would hereafter worship Jesus Christ. But when they were asked if would cast away their idols,— 'How can we?' they replied, ' the religion of our fathers? We'll worship both, Jesus Christ and Gaudama.' 'True,' they were answered, ' it has been the religion of your fathers for some time past; so has this country been the country of your fathers, but '—here the word was suddenly taken up by a Burman officer standing by, who has enrolled his name as a decided believer,—' but God has pitied us,' he continued, anticipating the thought, ' He saw our distress, under Moung Byu, Moung Kyouk Long, and others, and sent the English to deliver us. Now He sends the Gospel of His Son to liberate us from the Nahts, and all their evils. Good! good! good!'

"Many have been evidently touched with this thought; and tearful eyes have been seen in Toungoo, in four or five instances, when the infinite love of the Redeemer has been portrayed.

" This may appear a slight thing, and unworthy of notice, that a heart should feel when a bleeding Saviour is suspended before them—but it is not so in heathen lands. The mind is so withered and crusted with the mire of demonolatry, there is no room for the Holy Spirit to enter. And yet such hearts as these do soften—repent—believe. We can, as yet, count but two believers who appear to be heartily decided to give up idolatry among the Burman females of this city, but they cry out by scores; ' Don't go away; your words comfort us.'

" One woman came some miles one morning from a distant hamlet to hear of our religion; and after listening with patient attention for more than an hour, she said, ' I think I shall believe. Your words sound good—they seem to make my heart light. But you are going away,—how can we believe? We hear a little—it seems true—but we don't well understand—we can't go alone. Do leave some Christian Burman to teach us. The sun has risen a little way up; but when you leave it will sink back—*and all is gone.*'

"Many a time have I gone to my room with a heavy heart after such interviews, knowing the words were too true. But we try to inspire hope; and sometimes draw the attention to the power of the Christian religion, illustrating it by the new moon increasing to the full, and asking if anything can stay its course? Or when a vessel of palm wine is set in the house, if it will not surely all ferment?

"'Ah, yes, yes!'—they exclaim, their faces brightening, 'you mean the Bible; true, true, that is good; you will leave that with us.'"

The time for departure was drawing near, health was failing, and Dr. Mason was anxious to find a man who would go out to the Bghais, a tribe which had never yet been visited. One of the boatmen, who had navigated their canoe up the turbid waters of the Salween, was a Karen Christian named Shapau. As a boatman he earned much, but he was not happy. He had neglected to speak of Christ and His salvation to his friends and countrymen. One day he was asked, if he would not like to go and work for God? His eye brightened as he replied in the affirmative. As he could speak Pwo Karen and Burmese he was employed as interpreter among the Burmese, and became deeply interested in the work, so that when Mrs. Mason commenced her school in Toungoo she made him her assistant, and he proved to be a very useful and efficient teacher. He was a humble man, and had a very poor opinion of his own abilities, and when first asked to undertake it, said, "I cannot teach, I know nothing myself." Mrs. Mason made him sit down by her side, and began to catechise him and to draw him out, until at last he exclaimed with the greatest simplicity and astonishment, "Why I did not think I knew half so much." When Dr. Mason was inquiring for a man for the Bghai tribe, it was noticed that Shapau looked very thoughtful, and one day he ventured to express the wish that he knew enough to teach the Bghais. "Perhaps you do," was the reply, "but would you be willing to leave your child, your friends, and go among these uncivilized tribes, and work for only four rupees a month; which, you know, is all that we can give you?" He left for a time, looking very thoughtful, doubtless to pray. After awhile he came again, and when the inquiry was put to him, "Well! Shapau, can you go?" he said, "I cannot go for four rupees, but I can go for the love of Christ!" This is an illustration of the spirit of devotedness which actuated these disciples, and led them to surrender up everything to the service of their Lord.

But here our narrative must pause. It was originally with difficulty, and at great hazard that Dr. Mason, in his feeble health, had commenced this mission at Toungoo; but now, completely overcome and exhausted, he was compelled at the very moment when all seemed fairest and most hopeful, to abandon this field of labor. Our narrative has now to record how the Lord of the harvest, in answer to the prayers of his people, raised up from this Karen nation a man gifted with all the needful graces for proclaiming and establishing the gospel. It is to this man's singularly interesting and remarkable history that we have now to direct our attention.

## CHAPTER XII.

### SAU QUALA.

"An example of the believers in word, in conversation, in charity, in spirit, in faith, in purity."—1 TIMOTHY iv. 12.

THE history of SAU QUALA, the first Karen missionary at Toungoo, is an interesting illustration of what, by the grace of God, an earnest, zealous, devoted heart can do, which, consecrating all its powers to the Redeemer's service, seeks to win souls to him. It is a proof also that God does choose the weak things, and the base things of the world, and things which are despised, to work out his own gracious purposes, 'that no flesh should glory in his presence.' Sau Quala was the child of Karen parents, born and nurtured in one of the wildest of their mountain glens. A cascade came leaping from rock to rock, through a deep gorge, just below his mother's dwelling; its bright, clear, dancing waters, a fit emblem of his own future healthful active course. His father's proud nature had long chafed under the bitterness of Burman wrongs, and longed and sighed for deliverance. Often would his full heart give utterance to such expressions as these: " The bamboo leaf falls on thorns, the thorns pierce it. Thorns fall on it, the thorns spear it. Our habitation is a thorn bush. We come upon the Siamese, the Siamese make us slaves. We fall upon the Burmese, the Burmese make us slaves." He hated his Buddhist oppressors. He hated their religion, their pagodas, their priests, everything that was theirs. He hated the taskmaster who ordered him to-day to drag boats, or pull logs, and the officer who commanded him to-morrow to cut bamboos, or ratans, to gather spices, or collect damper or bees-wax. "The iron had entered into his soul," and even his gentle uncomplaining wife could scarcely win a smile from his darkened spirit, as she labored patiently, planted the cotton, weeded it, gathered it, spun it, dyed it, and then wove it into cloth for garments for himself and their children.

Reports, however, had reached them that the white men had come by sea to the Burmese ports, and believing that these white men were destined to be their deliverers, they began to look forward with hope to the day when their galling yoke would be broken, and the oppressed go free. It was about this time that their second child was born, and to him they gave the significant name of Quala—'Hope ;' because, they said : "We hope happiness will come to us in his days."

It was no wonder that the boy should grow up with a thirst for liberty, or that he should treasure in his memory every tradition which prophesied of the emancipation of his nation from the Burman rule. As he kept watch over his father's rice-field, and drove away the peacocks and the monkeys, his boyish fancy was occupied with the time when the promised deliverers would come, and he would sing in wild cadences—

> "The children of God are those who took
> From the hand of God, the Holy Book ;
> The white foreigners are the sons of the Lord,
> They obtained of old his Holy word."

The hour of deliverance did come, and the English took possession of Tavoy, when he was about fourteen or fifteen years old. They had not been in the place many days, when Quala accompanied by his father and mother, went into the city. To their great surprise and alarm, they were no sooner within the walls than they were taken before the Governor and several military officers; but they were soon re-assured by the kind treatment they met with. The Governor would not allow them to prostrate themselves before him, according to oriental custom, but bade them stand erect, and, after talking kindly to them, dismissed them with presents of money, and a turban for each

It was about two or three years after this period, that Ko-thah-byu, the first Karen convert, was baptized, and went forth immediately to preach the gospel to his countrymen. It seems that a "converted Karen no more thinks of asking for a licence to preach, than he would for a licence to pray." The first impulse of his spiritual life is to declare what God has done for his soul, and to invite all whom he can reach to believe and live. Ko-thah-byu was an eminent example of this, and the first house in which he proclaimed the message of mercy, was that of Quala's father.

There the neighbors assembled in the evening, under the impression that Ko-thah-byu would, according to their custom, trace his genealogy, to show that he was not an enemy, but a relative; but he had better things to tell them, and one at least, the youthful Quala, believed to the saving of his soul, and said within himself, "Is not this the very thing we have been waiting for ?"

Quala's father was strongly opposed to the new religion, and the boy had to learn that it was not an easy thing to follow his divine Master, but that it involved taking up the cross, if he would go after Him.

Mr. Boardman, not long after, went to the village to preach, but so strong was his father's opposition, that Quala did not venture to go and hear him. Yet the seed of eternal life had taken root in his heart, and love to the Saviour was burning there too fervently to be quenched. His mother too had embraced the truth and sought every opportunity of hearing the word of life. In Mary's spirit she sat at the feet of the teacher, drinking in, from early dawn till late at night, the word which was able to save her soul. She was a lovely picture, with her large beaming eyes, full of intelligence, fixed upon the speaker, or occasionally, when there was a pause, turning to those near, that she might recommend in tones of persuasive tenderness, those truths which had wrought so great a change in her, and filled her with such bright hopes of future blessedness. She only lived a few years after her baptism, but they were years of spiritual growth: first the blade, then the ear, and then the full corn in the ear, and then the gathering into the heavenly garner.

Quala resembled his mother in many points of her character, especially in her stedfastness and hope. The fierceness of his father's opposition was, at last, so great, that he sought permission to visit an elder half brother, who was living on the eastern side of the mountains; and thither he started one foggy morning with his wallet thrown across his shoulder containing all he possessed on earth, his pruning knife and betel box, and a few treasured Burmese tracts. The path was soon lost in the streamlet, until pressing on, he came to a point where another torrent came flowing in from the north, and upon the spur which rose precipitously between them, his sure foot soon found a pathway, which conducted him to the summit of the mountain. In pursuing the same route fifteen years after, his elder brother was attacked and devoured by a tiger; but the angel of the Lord had encamped round about His young servant, and conducted him in safety to the sanctuary he had prepared. Quala's brother lived in a sequestered dell at the foot of the mountains, and here, in habits of prayer Quala fulfilled his daily duties, assisting his brother in the cultivation of the land. As his mental faculties expanded and developed under the vivifying and strengthening influence of the grace of God, his thirst for knowledge grew also; but there were no books in his own tongue, and he could not read in Burmese, indeed he scarcely understood the language colloquially. His earnest spirit was not however to be daunted by difficulties, which to many would have appeared insuperable, but unaided and alone, he set himself to learn to read Burmese, before he knew how to speak it. His elder brother, who knew a little Burmese, commenced the study with him, and long after the evening shadows had fallen might they be seen by the light of their little lamp, poring over the page, forgetting their weariness in the interest of the work before them.

Dr. Mason says, " In my acquaintance with Karen converts, I have often observed, with admiration, the manner in which the mind when brought into a right moral state, not only craves for knowledge but knowledge of truth, for which it seems to possess an intuitive attraction." Quala had seen Burman books from his early childhood, but Buddhist errors had no attraction for him. It was not until he heard of Christian books, especially the Bible, that the desire for the ability to read was kindled within him.

After spending some months in this peaceful manner, he felt that it was his duty to return to his father, and to tell him of Christ's love to his soul, and of his desire to confess and to follow Him; trusting that his father, seeing his stedfastness, might be induced to let him be baptized. But he met with nothing but reproach and anger; and spiritless and disheartened, his faith failed, and he began to distrust God, and to murmur against his providences. " I will never go to the teacher as long as I live," he said, " and I will pray no more. When the righteous One appears, my father will suffer himself, and I will say, I did not dare to become a Christian on account of my father." He adds, " I felt very unhappy. I wept all day, and thought I would starve myself to death."

But the next day he repented of these feelings, and after a time returned to his brother's peaceful dwelling. Ere long, a company of inquirers went down to the city of Tavoy; amongst them was Sau Quala, and in December, 1830, he made a public profession of his faith, and was admitted into the church of Christ by baptism. Since then, for more than a quarter of a century, he has held on in a stedfast course ; and by his unblemished Christian character has won the respect, confidence, and affection of all connected with him.

As soon as Quala was baptized, he began to tell of Christ, and to read and expound the Christian books that he possessed to those about him. If his father listened and opposed, he would meet him with irresistible arguments in the words of Scripture,—those words, "majestic in their own simplicity,"—until his violent and unbelieving parent was silenced before the mighty truth of God. With the Karen converts, this desire to impart the knowledge of salvation seems a first principle of their new nature. Dr. Mason says, " When I first went to Tavoy, I found amongst the few Christian Karens, one man who could read Burmese very well, but had no power to communicate his ideas with facility to others. Another was unable to read, but was apt to teach and able to speak with fluency and power. Without consulting the missionary, or expecting remuneration for their labors, these men, whenever circumstances allowed, went out itinerating throughout the country. Wherever they got an assembly together, the reader read a portion of the Burmese Scriptures or a tract, while the speaker expounded and exhorted in Karen. Very few men have been more successful preachers than these."

When Boardman, the Karen missionary, was sinking into the grave, as we have before mentioned, he determined to spend his little remaining strength in visiting the jungle homes of the Karens near Tavoy. A party of them came in to assist in carrying the litter and in administering to his wants, and amongst that number was Quala. While encamped in the forest, the dying missionary assisted by Dr. Mason, who had just then arrived in the country, held daily meetings for teaching and prayer with the people. The early morn, the sultry noon, the quiet evening hour were witnesses to those solemn teachings, when one so soon to enter into the holy of holies spoke of life and death, of judgment and eternity. Quala, his mother and sister, were the first to come, the last to go away. They sought too to render every assistance they could to Mrs. Boardman; and when at last his failing strength warned them that their beloved teacher was to be taken from them, Quala was amongst the number who carried that fading form to the little sequestered cove where, beneath the shadow of the broad-leaved trees, he witnessed the baptism of thirty-four Karens for whose salvation he had prayed and labored.

It was the same hand that gently carried him to the boat which was to convey him home, but on the way thither his spirit fled, and " he was not, for God took him." It was the same hand that bore the body to its last quiet resting place, there to slumber in dust, till it shall be reunited to the glorified spirit in the realms of everlasting day. What solemn thoughts must these scenes have kindled in the heart of Sau Quala! They must have given a reality to the great truths he had heard and learned. He had seen that to the Christian death was disarmed of its sting and of its terror, and that to depart and be with Christ, was esteemed by him to be " far better."

From the opportunity which Dr. Mason had of observing the character of Quala at this time, he was convinced that he had no ordinary mind or heart, and he therefore determined to keep him in town, that he might study Karen with him, and that Quala might have the advantage of attending Mrs. Boardman's school. At this time Dr. Mason writes ; "During the first year of my residence in Tavoy, in 1831, I devoted a considerable portion of my time to visiting in every house in the city and suburbs, leaving at each a tract, and a portion of Scripture, thus bringing into actual use the knowledge of Burmese that I was acquiring from day to day. Sau Quala often accompanied me in these excursions, and my knowledge of the language being quite imperfect, he would frequently repeat and enforce the sentiments I had uttered in more 'acceptable words' though he often met with the savage rebuke, 'Who are you? You are just like that dog. He knows nothing but what he is taught, he goes or comes just as his master orders him.' He was unmoved, however, by their cutting sarcasm, and more open abuse. He took the Bible as it said, and Christ at his word, when he read, 'Blessed are ye when men shall revile you, and persecute you, and shall say all manner of evil against you, falsely for my sake : —rejoice and be exceedingly glad ; for great is your reward in heaven ;' then he rejoiced at finding himself in circumstances which entitled him to rejoice, and he looked heavenward for the reward of his labors.

In 1833, Mr. Wade being obliged by sickness to return for a season to America and to abandon the work he had commenced of preparing a translation of the Bible into Karen, Dr. Mason determined, although he had only been a short time in the country, to do what he could in preparatory work, and after consulting Dr. Judson, he determined to send up to Maulmain his two most promising young men, Sau Quala and Kolapau, (who was afterwards ordained pastor of Matah) to study with Paulah, one of the Christian assistants, who had helped Mr. Wade in forming the alphabet, and in adapting the Burman letters to Karen sounds. Dr. Judson in writing home in April, 1833, of a visit to Chummerah, the principal Karen settlement north of Maulmain, says with reference to the school: "The two most imporant students have been a couple of young men from Tavoy, whom brother Mason sent up to learn to read and become qualified to teach their countrymen in that province. They have come down with me and will return to Tavoy by the first opportunity.' These two were Quala and Kolapau.

This journey to Maulmain was a great event in their lives; for not a single Karen in the Tenasserim Provinces had ever been known to cross the river to the north since they first emigrated to the south, untold centuries ago. The traditions of this emigration are treasured up by the Karens, and the names of the Attaran and the Salween rivers, and Balu Island are familiar words. When, therefore, Quala reached Maulmain, it seemed to him like classic ground; and when he gazed upon the ridge of hills crowned with pagodas, or strolled at sunset upon their side, and watched the rolling waters of the Salween as it flows forth into the sea, he thought of the time when perhaps the homes of his ancestors had been there, and when their eyes had looked upon the same beauteous scene. But where were they now? Surely, that affecting thought would animate and rouse the energies of his spirit, as he thirsted to proclaim Christ and his salvation to the perishing souls around! Eighty-three Karens had been baptized at this time in the neighborhood of Maulmain alone, and about one hundred and seventy at Tavoy, but what were they among the many that still remained? After three months' sojourn at Maulmain, Quala returned to Tavoy and continued with Dr. Mason; not only assisting him in the translation of the New Testament, but, as we have seen, accompanying him in his jungle and preaching tours. Dr. Mason says: " It was clear to me at the outset, that to be master of the Karen language, so as to be perfectly familiar with all the words and constructions I heard, would only be a small advance towards the knowledge of the language necessary to an adequate translation of the Bible. To supply this deficiency I employed Sau Quala to write down all the traditions in prose with which he was acquainted, and when he had exhausted his own memory. I sent him to different individuals reputed to be particularly versed in these traditions, to collect whatever they remembered with which he was unacquainted. I found also, that without a written literature they had a mass of fictitious stories in their memories, which in the long rainy nights or in their leisure hours, they were in the habit of repeating to each other. Sau Quala, therefore, was employed in committing to paper every poem or story that any one knew. In this way, Quala created for me and others after me, a Karen literature in prose and verse, of several manuscript volumes. Among the fragments are several singular pieces in relation to the Karen Bible or book, which have manifestly been composed since Europeans went into India; and notwithstanding their fabulous character, they show the high estimate the Karens have ever placed on Karen books, and how well they were prepared to appreciate the Bible, when presented to them in their own tongue."

"Again," Dr. Mason adds, " there are many ambiguous passages in the Bible, especially in the Old Testament: and it is the duty of a translator to present such passages in his version, precisely in the same dubious light in which they appear in the original, whenever it is possible to do so. It requires far more skill and knowledge of the language to render such passages correctly than the definite ones; and Quala, after the various aspects of a passage had been shown him, would often exercise his philological skill to discover a word or form of expression sufficiently generic to embrace all the specific significations which might be extracted from the language."

There can be no doubt, that a course of study like this must have been one main source of the power with which he preached. For while his mind was supplied with such variety of illustration, it must have given his language much fulness and precision of expression. Earnestly did he thirst also for a more full and perfect understanding of the Scriptures. As soon as the New Testament was translated, he was anxious for a work in Karen, and Kitto's Cyclopædia is perhaps an embodiment in English of his idea. In the *Morning Star*, a Karen periodical which Dr. Mason commenced in 1842, and for which Quala often wrote, he says:

"Consider the generation of the fathers, they had no books; they had none to teach them of the things in heaven and the things on earth—they knew nothing; but now, through the grace of our Lord Jesus Christ, the American teachers from the West have come and taught us, and we have obtained books in our own language. Then when they instruct us, and explain to us the Holy Scriptures, we ought, every one of us, to seize on their instructions and to retain them; for if it had not been for the teachers, we should have remained without books, in ignorance and darkness, to this day. Let us, then, in the strength of God, put forth strenuous efforts to acquire a knowledge of books, for should the teachers leave, we should be left as orphans. While they are with us, let us make every possible effort to study, so that we may understand for ourselves independently; and, should the teachers be no longer with us, that we may be able to instruct each other.

"Teachers, there is one thing I want you to do for us above all things. I wish you to publish notices of the ancestors, and biographies of the persons mentioned in Scripture. Were you to explain completely the things in the Bible, there would be afterwards no room for doubt or difference of opinion. Then if the teachers should die or leave us, our means of knowledge would still be full and accurate. We love our children, yet we can only benefit them while we are with them; but the teachers are able to benefit future generations. When our parents died, their possessions were gone; but the possession of the teachers will remain. Our parents could benefit us in this life only, but the teachers benefit us both for this life and the life to come. Brethren, had not the teachers come to us with the word of God, we should have known nothing, but have been still in darkness."

At this time his father was very earnest in trying to induce him to return to the jungles. He was promised an equivalent for his son's services, and from that time never troubled him again. Quala wrote at this period: "I was very zealous in studying the word of God, and prayed with brokenness of heart. I thought of nothing else but to be skilled in the books. This occupied my whole mind continually." Thus this young disciple grew in grace, drinking in the word of life, which was able to save his soul.

In his early childhood he had, according to the custom of the East, been betrothed to a little girl in another village, but they had seen nothing of each other, and grew up strangers in sympathy and affection. After Quala's baptism, the subject of his marriage at times induced serious thoughts, and led him to commit his way to the Lord more earnestly. One of the elders of his village, according to the Karen custom, was deputed to visit his betrothed, to ascertain the nature of her feelings towards him. The only remark she made was, " Oh, yes ; I love Sau Quala amazingly, now he is baptized. Had he not been baptized I should not have loved him at all." This signified, according to their mode of expression, a decided rejection, and here their engagement ended, and they never met again.

About this time in the little class of Karen girls under Mrs. Mason's care, was one named Muphau, "Celestial flower ;" she was indeed a flower of heavenly birth and growth, and between her and Quala an attachment sprung up, ending in a union which has been eminently blessed to both. She has greatly strengthened her husband's hands, encouraged his heart under all his labors, and has set a bright example to her Christian sisters of what a Christian wife, and especially a pastor's wife, should be. When her husband had an offer of lucrative employment under Government, she never for one moment yielded to the temptation of a position of greater ease and emoluments ; but when an opportunity of a larger field and increased labors in the service of their heavenly Master was presented to them, she was ready for the call, and said, " This makes me happy," literally, "*hits my heart*." A Christian officer, who once accompanied Dr. Mason in a preaching tour in the jungle, was much struck by her appearance, as they came suddenly upon her, standing on a projecting cliff before them, her long tasseled shawl thrown round her graceful figure, and the embroidered scarf wound round her head like a coronet, setting off her fine expressive features to perfection. " Surely Quala has got the flower of the jungle," he exclaimed, " she reminds one of Scott's description of Helen Mac-

Gregor." She was indeed one of its flowers, and long may she be spared to grace the home of her husband, and to adorn her Christian profession in all things.

From the time of his marriage, Quala used often to accompany the missionary in preaching tours into the jungle. Many were the happy hours thus employed, when laden with the message of salvation, they would start forth in the balmy freshness of a tropic morning. As the air perfumed with fragrance, and the light mists rising upward with the sun revealed more and more of the bright landscape before them, how often would the heart exclaim :—

> "If God has made this world so fair
> Where sin and death abound,
> How beautiful beyond compare
> Will paradise be found!"

Very interesting were some of the discussions with the simple sons of the forest. The following is a specimen of the way in which Quala would address them. To an idolater he would say, "Can the image save those who worship it? Think! How can it posibly save them? How many trees have sprung up which the image has created? How many clumps of bamboo are there, that the image has made? How many men has it formed? Where are the animals, or even the insects, that it has brought into existence? It has done nothing. Nor is the image self-existent: it was made by man. Rather than worship the image, ought we not to worship the man who made it, for his superior power? But the maker was a thief.

"Do you doubt it? Consider! earth, wood, stone, gold, silver, lead, and copper are, because God created them. He who makes an image, takes God's earth, God's wood, God's rocks, God's gold, God's silver, God's lead, God's copper. Does he ask for it? No! he takes it without leave, says he will form an image and worship it; thus making himself a son of folly. Were we to disobey our parents and treat their commands with contempt, following our own will in everything, would they not be angry? Now, He who is greater than father, greater than mother, the only true God, who cannot die, or cease to exist, commands; 'Make no image, worship no image, worship me.' Against this God have we sinned, in all our thoughts, in all our deeds. There is no part of us free from transgression. The hand has transgressed, the foot has transgressed, the eye has transgressed, the ear has transgressed, the mouth has transgressed, the mind has transgressed, the heart has transgressed. Our transgressions are greater than the hills, loftier than the mountains. It is not fitting we ascend to the presence of God. It is fitting that we descend to the lowest depths of hell, and the great grace of God alone still keeps us here. These heavens so wide, this earth so great, everything in the many waters and numerous lands, God created. He formed man holy, exempt from old age, sickness, and death; but he disobeyed God, obeying Satan; and thus brought misery on himself and all creation. Still God did not give us up. He had compassion upon us, and sent His only Son to save the slaves of Satan, and who had no rest in his service. To deliver us from the hands of Satan, and to give us rest, He bought us with His own blood, He had no compassion on His own great life, but He had compassion on men who were going down to hell. He died on the cross for us, on account of our sins, and thus threw open the gate at the foot of the road, so that man is made again acquainted with God. Surely, the children of earth ought to worship God, ought to perform His work, ought to observe His word, ought to follow His path, ought to obey His will; but man makes himself obstinate and his ears crooked. He worships not, he serves not, he obeys not His word, follows not His path, submits not to His will. But he thus fulfils the language of the elders, who said, 'Children and grandchildren, words good and white are scarcely received. Rottenness has many associates, sweetness few.'"

When addressing Karens who expressed their determination to follow in the path of their ancestors, he remarked; "Some of you object;—'The tortoise dying dies in its shell. Our mother dying, let us occupy our mother's chamber; our father dying, let us take our father's hall. The tigress striped, the cubs striped. Let not the tree depart from its shadow. If mother has gone to hell, we will go after her; if father has gone to hell, we will go after him.' Let those who speak thus think of suffering on earth, not to speak of hell. If a tiger devoured our mother, dare we go out and give ourselves to be devoured by tigers. If a crocodile killed her, or fire devoured her, or she was drowned, dare we go out and give ourselves to die by the crocodile, fire, or water? We can be very bold while the tiger is out of sight; but when we meet it face to face we are panic-stricken, and scatter, one one way and two two ways. Our father and mother did not hear what we hear, did not know what we know. It is of God's special grace that these things have come to us. The elders of antiquity yearned to hear the word of God, but heard it not. That blessing was reserved for us. Still it is according to the saying, 'If the lake is pleasant the fish remain.' In a large lake where there is nothing to devour, the fish and its waters never fail, the lake is pleasant. Yet if there be no fish in it, it does not call the fish to come unwillingly. If the fish wish to dwell in it, they remain; if not, they depart. God is the lake, we are the fish. Unless we are in God, ere long something will come and devour us. The fire of hell will devour us. Then dwell in God."

A caviller once remarked: " God is possessed of infinite power, and has a perfect knowledge of all things. Why did He create Satan? Did He not know that he would come and deceive man? If He knew that he would come and destroy why did He create him? If God compassionates man, if He loves him, why did He create the tree of temptation? Did He not know that if a man ate of it he would die? And if He knew, why did He create it? Why has He made men so that some come forth from the womb blind, some hump-backed, some with dead limbs, some with twisted limbs, some with crooked limbs, some white, some black? And why are some born dead? Why do some die in infancy, some in childhood, some in youth, some in manhood, some in old age? Why are some insane, some idiots, some fools, some wise? Why are some masters and others slaves; some rich and others poor? Could not God make them all alike? Or is it because He loved some and did not love others?"

Quala replied: " God is above man, above kings, above all. Kings are obeyed without asking reasons. We ought not to reply against God. He is our Father. The child understands not what the father does. The axe and the knife kill, yet without them the father could not obtain food for the child. He does not allow the child to handle them, but one with crooked ears, when unobserved by its father, takes hold of them and cuts himself. Parents give children many playthings; but because they love them they do not allow them to play with the axe and the knife. God acts according to His own will. The house-owner builds a house, and decides in relation to its parts. He disposes of the timbers or bamboos according to their proper positions. That which is too short he lengthens; that which is too long he shortens;

that which will not answer his purpose he throws away. That which is shortened does not say to the builder, 'Why hast thou shortened me?' nor that which is lengthened, 'Why hast thou lengthened me?' The timbers or bamboos do not say, 'Make us this way or that way; make us not that way or this way.' The materials know nothing, but the owner of the house knows, and directs everything according to his own will. God is the Owner of the house, and we ought to submit to His dispensations in silence. Then He will use us as parts of His building; that is, we shall become His children and servants. But if we murmur and complain against God, we become like the bamboos and timber, which being unsuitable for the building, were rejected by the builder, and thrown away. Some of God's judicial arrangements are in order that we may praise Him, some that we may repent of our sins, some that we may discern between good and evil, some that we may not hope in transitory things on earth, some that we may avoid hell, and go to heaven. None are made for our disadvantage, but all for the advantage of man. To those who murmur, the Holy book says, 'Who art thou, O man! that repliest against God? Shall the thing formed say to him that formed it, Why hast thou made me thus? Hath not the potter power over the clay, of the same lump to make one vessel to honor, and another to dishonor?'"

To nominal believers in the Christian settlements, his language was: "Not having become true Christians your profession of faith and your avoidance of external vices are of no avail. When you are with Christians you do as Christians do; when you are with the world you do as the world does. You regard yourselves as worshippers of God, and still in heart you follow the will of Satan. You do not love God, you do not fear sin. You say, 'Ah, we have not been baptized. If we do sin it is of no consequence. The sin will be done away when we become disciples.' Think, and repent of your sins quickly. The Scriptures say, we cannot add a cubit to our lives; so, that death may not find you in your sins, avoid iniquity; and first of all things put your trust in the Lord, accepting cordially His commands. The Bible says: 'Blessed are the dead that die in the Lord.' Wherefore, to obtain this blessedness, let it be the first thing with you to rouse yourselves with energy from your lethargy. Remain not between Christ and the world, ever vibrating from one side to the other. The Holy Scriptures say, we cannot serve two masters; so choose the Master who is able to save, and confide earnestly in Him."

It was in this way that Quala was trained for the ministry. For fifteen successive years he accompanied the missionary in his jungle tours, sometimes extending to three or four hundred miles, till every hamlet was visited in the provinces of Tavoy and Mergui, in which Karens were likely to be found. Frequently they left the usual passes, and branching off across the chain of mountains in four or five different directions, would visit every secluded nook, and coming down the Tenasserim upon a frail native raft, would sometimes scarcely escape being overset in the rapids. Often has Quala shared with the teacher these hallowed labors, sleeping under the shadow of the same forest tree, where, perhaps, the tiger's footprints might be traced in the morning, not many yards from the place where they had slept. Together they laid the foundation of many little churches in these regions, and travelled and preached from hamlet to hamlet, from glen to glen, watching for the first dawnings of grace, for the first fruits of the Spirit; until this young servant of the Lord was himself well furnished in every good word and work, for the service of the ministry and the responsibilities of the pastorate.

But we must hasten on. The Karen New Testament was completed; and Dr. Mason, no longer requiring the services of Sau Quala for this work, determined to place him in charge of the church at Pyeekhya. It was the most central and the most important of the little churches gathered on the mountains, and gave him a position in which his influence might be felt and exerted in the country round. Excepting in the administration of the ordinances, he was the pastor of the church from the beginning, but he was not ordained till five years afterwards. Sau Quala had been early impressed with the duty and desirableness of the native churches taking measures to support their ministers and schoolmasters. He endeavored, therefore, to inculcate the importance of this duty upon his people. Without its having been suggested, he and his wife kept an accurate account of all that had been given by the disciples for this purpose during the first year, and no less than three hundred and eighty-seven presents were brought in.

It was not long after Quala's settlement that Dr. Mason visited him. After slowly ascending the mountain by a steep and narrow path, they seated themselves to rest upon a little level spot upon the hill side. Ten or twelve years had passed since they had first sat together there. Quala had cut down some bamboos which impeded their view to the west. The spotless blue heavens were over their heads, while the clouds, like snow-drifts, were moving lazily far beneath their feet. The Pyeekhya, Putsauoo, and Palouk rivers were discovered here and there peeping from beneath the bright green verdure, as they meandered through glen and gorge, dale and valley. In the direction of Mergui on the south-west, huge rocks towered in grotesque peaks over the ocean's waves, and near at hand every dell and dingle was adorned with the loveliest flowers. They could say with truth,—

> "Our rocks are rough; but smiling there,
> The acacia waves her golden hair,
> Lovely and sweet, nor lov'd the less,
> For flowering in the wilderness."

Karen hamlets lay hidden at intervals throughout the wide extended forest below; ten years before not a single Christian heart beat in one of them.

"When," said the teacher at that time, "shall these vales resound with the songs of the redeemed? When shall we look on Christian churches in these green fields?" Ten years before Quala had answered: "Hereafter, teacher, hereafter." And now as they gazed again upon that lovely scene of hill and dale, and rock and ocean, although the face of nature was unchanged, the Spirit of the living God had been at work among the simple-hearted inhabitants of the hamlets, and in Pyeekhya alone Quala could rejoice over a hundred souls who owned Jesus as their Lord. From Putsauoo, Palouk, and Toungbyouk on the north where little churches had grown up in the interval, they could almost catch the echoes of their hymns of praise; and when they looked to the south upon those hills where their feet had first carried the message of salvation, and could count, in hamlet after hamlet, some precious souls born of God, the depth of their emotion was too great to find expression in words. At last Quala observed, "God will do greater things than these;" and God has done greater things, and will, we trust, continue to do so, "until all Burmah worships the eternal God."

About this time Dr. Mason, in writing to the Executive Committee at home, said: "Sau Quala is the assistant that has been writing by my side every rains for eight or ten years; and he has been the almost constant companion of my travels ever since I entered the mission. With him I first began the study of the Karen language; and with him I commenced the translation of the New Testament, and he has continued with me throughout the work. Besides copying for me, I have constantly consulted him as I went along for words, their signification, and their construction, precisely as in cultivated languages a student consults his dictionaries and grammars; while I have thus been gathering knowledge from him, I have not been unmindful of imparting knowledge to him.

"I have often thought that could I leave him, when my labors close on earth, an able minister of the New Testament, I should not have labored in vain; and, latterly, I have indulged the pleasing hope that God would more than fulfil my desire, and make him a useful minister even while I live. Formerly his mind was exceedingly obtuse, as are the minds of uncultivated people generally, and utterly unable to make any rational distinction between words and things that differed; but he now possesses, comparatively, quite a discriminating mind; and I am sometimes surprised at the nice distinctions that he occasionally points out as existing between the signification of words. I do not suppose there is any one of his nation that can make any approach to him in the matter of judicious criticism on Karen composition. This is saying nothing to the disparagement of any one else, for no other has had the same years of discipline that he has had. He has, however, obtained something more valuable than a power of criticism; he has obtained a very tolerable knowledge of the principal parts of the New Testament and of the sentiments of Scripture in general. Furthermore, he is 'apt to teach,' and a very good preacher. When in the jungle he is continually engaged in informal preaching, from house to house, and by the way side; I often set him to preach at evening meetings, when I have an opportunity of hearing his more regular productions; and he frequently gives an exposition of Scripture, of which an educated man at home would not be ashamed. In addition to his other acquirements, Quala has grown in grace so much latterly, that, were there any particular necessity for it, he might be ordained."

In 1844, Dr. Mason, accompanied by Mr. Vinton, visited Pyeekhya, and remained with Quala and his people for about three weeks. During that time they were visited by one of those remarkable outpourings of the Holy Spirit's influence which are not uncommon in America, and with which we have occasionally been blessed in our own country. Here Quala witnessed some of those extraordinary means which the Spirit of all grace is sometimes pleased to use in bringing sinners to Christ; quickening dead souls to life, and reviving the slumbering graces of the children of God. Here, too, his faith in the power of believing prayer was strengthened, and he learnt something of the deep import of those gracious words—"Ask, and ye shall have." In describing the scene he said; "When the teachers and disciples prayed in earnest, the Holy Spirit came down upon the unconverted, and they came forward, requesting to be baptized. Many of these were people with whom I had labored and exhorted before the meeting, and some said to me, 'We will wait a year;' others, 'We will wait two years;' others, 'We will look on a little longer;' but when the Holy Spirit touched them, they repented and became Christians. Many of those who had been among the unconverted came forward and confessed their sins and transgressions publicly. They took up the habit immediately of private prayer in the jungle, and became very anxious for their unconverted relatives, going and inviting many to the meeting. Some confessed sins that had been committed in secret, and prayed with sobs and tears.

Many others resolved to become Christians, and many Christians grew in grace. Brethren, these things are the work of the Holy Spirit, but they are spiritually discerned. Those whose minds are enlightened see the power of God in them, and wonder and praise the Lord. The advantages of these meetings for prayer for the outpouring of the Holy Spirit are great. The graces of Christians are increased, the unconverted obtain new hearts, and those who listen understand the easier."

There was one case of conversion in connection with this revival which we cannot forbear mentioning. Mr. Vinton had desired the assistant to write down the names of the principal unconverted people in the neighborhood, and one evening they were read out, as subjects or prayer. Among the names was that of a Bong-ko, or religious teacher, a man of some note among the people, who, hearing that his name had been so used, was very angry. He wanted no prayer to be made for him. One evening, some time after, to the surprise of all, he and his wife walked into the meeting. He said he had not come to be a Christian, but to hear. It was felt that God had led him there and had purposes of mercy towards him, and before another week had passed away, he had openly declared himself to be the Lord's. He was determined to be a Christian, and that *now*. As soon as their son-in-law heard of their determination, for his wife also was converted with him, he became greatly enraged, and declared he would leave them, which he ultimately did. It was a great grief to the old people, for, according to the Karen custom, the sons-in-law usually cultivate the field and provide for the parents of their wives. But under this trial they remained calm and unmoved, trusting in the Lord, and have gone on stedfastly in His ways.

At the close of these heart-stirring scenes in Pyeekhya,

Quala accompanied Dr. Mason and Mr. Vinton to Newville, the Karen station north of Maulmain. Nearly ten years had passed since Quala's first visit in 1833, and great changes had taken place in that interval. Then the eighty-three Karens who had been baptized were just entering on the Christian race : now they had completed their course, or were tried Christians among two or three hundred more recent converts. At Newville they held similar meetings to those at Pyeekhya and with similar results ; and Quala must have returned to his mountain home with quickened faith and hope in the glorious promises of God.

It was on the 28th April, 1844, that Sau Quala was ordained to the office of the ministry, and in writing at that time he says : " This is of the grace of God. Great is God's goodness. O Lord, when we were in darkness thou placedst us in the light ; when we were in distress and difficulty thou placedst us in prosperity and ease. We will praise thy goodness to us as long as we live, throughout our whole existence. Make our light, our wisdom, our understanding of the Holy Scriptures, of Thee, and of thy love, to increase. Give us, O God, to understand the deep things of Thee. Thy mercy and thy watchful care over us we can never sufficiently praise. Have mercy upon us and watch over us to the end."

We are now brought to the time in Quala's history when his mind frequently dwelt upon the desire, early formed, to be the Lord's messenger of salvation to the province of Toungoo. In the wise and inscrutable providence of God, the door which had been so long closed to the entrance of the gospel was about to be opened, and already he was working in the heart of this man. We have the following interesting account from the pen of Mr. Cross of Tavoy.

" Some three years before the last Burmese war, a Karen

by the name of Dumoo, a native of the region of Toungoo, fell in with a company of Burmese in his own country who were going to the south. He accompanied them in hopes of finding his daughter, who had married and gone with her husband in that direction. This company, according to Dumoo's story, were seized by the British Government on suspicion that they were dacoits. One of them was a Tavoyer: and when they were liberated, Dumoo chose to accompany the Tavoyer without any assignable reason, apparently without any end or aim. He thus wandered nearly two hundred miles still further from his friends and among strangers, as if led by a hand as unfelt as it was unseen.

"These two men arrived in Tavoy at a time when the small-pox was raging with great violence and destructiveness through the whole city and province of Tavoy. Dumoo came within a few yards of the mission premises. But he had no wish to see the missionaries; he knew there were white men in Maulmain and Tavoy, but he had no special interest in them, but to avoid them. Wandering about in the city as he was, without any settled purpose, he was soon smitten by the fearful plague which was destroying so many victims around him. While enduring this disease he was sheltered in a Burmese kyoung or monastery. In this condition, hanging for a long time between life and death, his thoughts were turned within to the nature of the soul, and its prospects of misery or happiness after death, and this subject began to assume an overwhelming importance when he recovered. He did not, however, seek the missionaries, but soon left the city for the jungles, wandering here and there among the heathen Karens in the province. Hence, though he had been a number of months among the Karens, he got no idea of the Christians or their books; yet the desire for a book seemed to occupy and haunt his mind. He learnt that a Karen who had set up claims to divine inspiration, had invented a method of writing the Karen language. He almost immediately made his way to that person, and soon found that his ability to write was all a mere deception to gain credit and increase the number of his followers. Dumoo turned away from him with disappointment and disgust. He had gone quite across the province of Tavoy to the borders of Siam to see this wonderful pretender, but though he was disappointed in his object, his journey was not in vain. He fell in with two young men from the Karen theological school in Tavoy, who were spending their vacation in the jungle as Scripture readers, and endeavoring to exhort the people to repentance. As soon as Dumoo met these men with the New Testament which could be read, a book uttering by means of letters declarations concerning his soul and the God who made it, so exactly answering to the deep longings of his spirit, his inmost soul cried out, 'I have found what I want.' Nor did he separate himself from these young men, or give them rest till he learned from them the wonderful magic of the alphabet.

"When these young men returned to their school, Dumoo repaired to a Christian village and attached himself to the native pastor, and showed a docility and earnestness which were regarded with astonishment by all who saw him. But his earnestness and fire were not only an earnestness and an inward burning to be able to read books in his own tongue, but the love of the Saviour and the power of the Holy Ghost seemed to have taken possession of him. He remained in the village trying to learn to read, and publishing to all around what a Saviour he had found. When the missionary made his pastoral visit to the village, he met Dumoo foremost of the multitude and the heartiest to greet him, not with the cringing common to natives who have never seen a

European and expect attention from him, but with the upright frankness of a Christian, in which distinctions of flesh and blood are lost in the stronger promptings of the soul. This man was baptized, and from that time he never ceased his efforts and entreaties. By his exhortations and representations he stirred up a missionary spirit in the mind of Quala and others in the province, and induced them to pledge themselves to return with him to his native country. He was sure the great multitude of the people would believe without hesitation and become Christians. And already, as if the result had become a reality in his own mind, he could not refrain from exhorting the people in these provinces to emulate the example of the Christians that would be in Toungoo. They would support their teachers, they would greedily and earnestly seize upon the book here so little prized by the disciples, etc.

"Dumoo entered the theological school in Tavoy and spent the term of two years. He learned to write his own language, and acquired considerable knowledge of the Bible. But all his efforts and his enthusiasm had a single aim; one burning desire seemed to possess him continually and everywhere. It was to go back and preach the gospel to his countrymen, and to induce others to go with him from this place. It was with him that Quala determined to go, for his spirit moved him more than the opposition and entreaties of all the disciples here. The churches could not spare him, and the oldest and most experienced missionaries then here thought the project chimerical and preposterous.

"But, just at the right time, Quala and Dumoo with two others from this province started for Toungoo. Dr. Mason had preceded them a few weeks, an invalid destined soon to return to America. He was able to remain just long enough to receive Quala at Toungoo, and see him baptize two persons who had already been converted, and then leave the work in his hands. Quala and Dumoo, after meeting with many hindrances in Maulmain, finally succeeded in ascending the river, but they separated before they reached Toungoo. Quala proceeded to join Dr. Mason, and Dumoo turned to the south and east, and entering the Shwaygyeen district, began the work there.

"This seems to be the history of the beginning of this great work. God chose his own instruments and his own way of leading them into the field which he had prepared for them. How wonderful, when the hand of God is revealed, are the seemingly insignificant events chosen in the distance, exactly timed in their occurrence, and unerringly connected and accumulated until a miracle of grace and of mercy is the result!"

As soon as the war broke out in 1852, Quala would have proceeded to Toungoo immediately, but he was advised to wait until things assumed a more settled aspect. When, however, Dr. and Mrs. Mason were settled in Toungoo, Quala followed them. The churches in the southern provinces were very unwilling to let him go; but it was in vain that they endeavored to detain him. A memorial signed by every assistant south of Tavoy, and by their churches, remonstrating in affecting terms against the departure of one whose instructions were so much valued by them was presented to the association. "What was to be done?" writes the missionary, Mr. Thomas. "Here was a man who, under various circumstances, had been under the eye of the missionaries from boyhood. He had been for a long time pastor of the most important church in his vicinity, and had frequently visited other churches in the missionaries' stead, to settle difficulties and administer the ordinances of the Lord's house; and had never been guilty of anything requiring discipline. This man for more than a year had desired to visit a distant region, a region never yet visited by a minister of the gospel, there to plant the standard of the cross. We looked at the subject carefully; we spoke, we wept, we prayed; and all the adverse memorialists rose with tears, and voted to approve his going." Dr. Mason also, in writing of what the Karen churches have done for the extension of Christ's kingdom, adds, "They have done more than give money. They have given men for mission work;—not their youth to study and qualify themselves for becoming missionaries, but their tried ministers; not the mediocrity, but the most talented, best educated, most efficient, and most highly esteemed. When the churches of America send the most useful, most learned, and most valued in New England or New York, to Burmah, then they will have made a sacrifice equal to that which the churches of Tavoy and Mergui made when they gave Quala for Toungoo."

Accompanied by two assistants qualified to be common school teachers, Quala reached Toungoo in December, 1853. The first baptism took place in the following January. The ordinance was administered by Sau Quala, in the presence of more than fifty Burmans, whom he addressed in a most judicious and eloquent manner. The Colonel and one or two other pious officers of the 5th Regt. of N. I. were present, and were much gratified with the fearlessness, dignity, and propriety of demeanor exhibited by the administrator. Before the close of the year the number of converts was seven hundred and forty-one, who were associated in nine churches. In May, 1856, they had increased to thirty churches, with an aggregate of two thousand one hundred and twenty-four members, all of whom had been baptized within two years, and more than two thousand of them by one man.

Truly God had fulfilled Dr. Mason's desire to see Quala a

"*useful* minister while he lived." Mrs. Wade writing home in April, 1855, says of him; " If our dear brother Mason had done nothing else in Burmah besides training this Karen missionary, he would have done a good work. But he could not thus have trained his pupil had he not travelled and preached year after year, building up churches, and disciplining them according to the rules of the Bible. And besides this, Quala having assisted brother Mason so much in the translations, the word of God dwells richly in his mind, so that after being an excellent pastor and leading minister among these lovely southern churches, he has gone forth with our full confidence as a missionary; has baptized—formed churches, superintending them with excessive labor and fatigue like an apostle. Having no salary, one and another of the disciples gives him a garment when he needs; and having no home, he gets his food where he labors."

How striking is this testimony to the simplicity of faith with which these noble men go forth to the help of the Lord against the mighty! They remind us of the little fountains bubbling up in their own distant hills shining like silver threads in the thick jungle, and sparkling like diamonds in their healthful activity, impatient to bear their tribute of fresh waters, to swell the river which rolls beneath, and not only so, but rejoicing and blessing all whom they reach within their course. How unlike the pestilential inactivity of the stagnant pool, which settling itself down in its listless selfishness, neither rejoices man or beast, but spreads malaria all around! Not so with the Karens; they have no sooner tasted that the Lord is gracious, and learned that their highest happiness is " to glorify Him and enjoy Him for ever," than they start forth into a new life of holy devotedness. Men and women, young and old, unite in the happy service of seeking to win souls to the knowledge of that Saviour whom to know is life eternal. Faith in Christ is their commencement, progress, and end.

The following letter from Sau Quala will exhibit something of the spirit which animated him in his labors amongst this people.

"Because God has showed me my work I rest not. I go up the mountains and down the valleys, hither and thither. One day in a place, one night in a place, continually. Still I know that I do the work of God imperfectly, and my heart is exceeding sad. Some come to me from a distance, and reprove me, saying, 'Teacher, thou sayest thou hast come to exhort men, and thou hast not been to our stream, to our land. Dost thou not love us?' Then I feel unable to open my mouth, for I know when the judgment-day arrives, that many who know not God will charge sin upon me, and I can only *stammer*.

"Therefore, though my flesh be tolerably comfortable, I count that nothing. I desire that the Kingdom of God be established all over the land of Toungoo more than I can express, and among the man-killers, far beyond words. Because God has given evidence that He purposes to save them, my heart is strong, though my flesh is weak. Brethren—teachers—teacheresses, pray for me!"

An instance of his disinterested spirit must be mentioned. The 'Taubeahs,' or 'wild Karens,' hearing of the teacher in Toungoo, were anxious to be allowed to come nearer, that they too might hear of the Eternal God; and sent a petition to this effect, which was forwarded to Major Phayre, Commissioner of Pegu. Major Phayre subsequently went up to Toungoo, and wished to induce Quala to be a medium of communication between these oppressed tribes and the Government, for which he would pay him twenty-five to thirty rupees a month. Sau Quala gave an account of his interview with Major Phayre, when this office was offered to him. "The Commissioner arrived at Toungoo on the 9th March, and I went immediately to visit him. He shook hands with me, and asked me concerning the Bghais, Manniepghas and Pakus; and in respect to their listening and becoming Christians, and concerning all the unordained assistants; finally he said, 'Teacher, I have spoken to the Government concerning you, and that you should become a head and overseer among the Bghais, Pakus and Wild Karens, for which you shall receive thirty rupees a month.' I replied, 'Sir, I cannot do it. I will not have the money. I will not mix up God's work with Government work. There are others to do this thing. Employ them: as for me I will continue in the work in which I have been engaged.' The Commissioner asked: 'Where do you obtain money to live on? Why do you not like money? We will give money, and you may continue your work as teacher, as heretofore. Will it not make it easier for you?' I answered: 'No, Sir. When I eat with the children of poverty I am content (literally, 'my heart sleeps'). I did not leave my dear wife and come up hither in search of silver or agreeable food. I came to this land, that its poor benighted inhabitants might be saved. Be patient with me, Sir. Were I to take your money the wild Karens would turn against me.' He said to me again; 'Well, teacher! think of the matter a day or two.' So I left him, but I went to the Christian chief Kwailai and the Shan who had been baptized, and I persuaded them to take the office. The next day I visited the Commissioner again, and presented these two men, as willing to receive the appointment. He agreed to give them the office; so I am free with clean hands. Teacheress and teacher, do not be anxious about me. I have no desire for this work, neither is my wife pleased with it. When I was in Tavoy and Mergui, and was urged to accept the office of Magistrate, she threw all the difficulties in the way she could ; but when I became a teacher, that pleased her (literally, 'hit her heart'). The Holy Scripture says : ' If a man desire the office of a bishop he desireth a good work ;' why should I go back to things that are worthless ? May the Lord help me, draw me by the hand, and guide me to the things which are pleasing in his sight."

## CHAPTER XIII.

### RECENT LABORS IN TOUNGOO.

"He called the name of it Rehoboth ; and he said, For now the Lord hath made room for us, and we shall be fruitful in the land."—GEN. xxvi. 22.

FOR two years Quala continued to labor, not even allowing himself the leisure to visit his wife and family, whom he had been obliged to leave at Tavoy. For a long time he had only three native assistants, Sau Papau whom he placed among the Sgaus, Sau Shapau among the Bghais, Sau Pwaipau among the Pakus; these were true "fellow-laborers," of whom he had no need to be ashamed. Amongst the Bghai tribe they soon had upwards of thirty stations, attended by seventeen native assistants, who were again superintended by Sau Quala. We have a very interesting notice of the appointment of six native preachers as missionaries, one especially dedicated to assist Quala at Toungoo, at the quarterly meeting of the Bassein Mission which took place in May, 1855, at Kau Nee, a Karen village on the bank of the river, about five miles above Bassein. Although the chapel had been greatly enlarged, it was impossible to accommodate all who came, and many of the number, who were estimated at upwards of twelve hundred, had to seat themselves on the ground outside ; these were principally the people of the village who with true Christian courtesy gave up the whole of the interior of the chapel to their guests. Thirty-nine native preachers were present on that occasion, besides many of the younger men who had been engaged as missionaries and teachers. It was a beautiful sight to see so many gathered together in one bond of holy brotherhood, commemorating the dying hour of Christ their Saviour.

Six missionaries from amongst the number were appointed at that time: Sau Plomai for Toungoo. His wife seems to have been a person of uncommon energy and zeal, and soon after his settlement at Baumu he sent for her. The following letter was written after she had joined him : " Originally I lived in the land of Bassein, and while there, I saw on the 5th of last April, a company of Rangooners approaching me. They brought me a letter from my husband in Toungoo, who wrote that I must 'go up and join him,' for he said, 'Here is a place to work.' So I started with my mother, we two alone, till reaching Rangoon, when we were joined by ten others, men and women, and we all travelled together. At Shwaygyeen a part of our company left us taking boat to Toungoo ; but I kept on by land, and on the latter part of the journey we were left quite alone again. As soon as we arrived at my husband's village, the children all came around me, and I commenced at once to teach them to read. The children, however, learn with difficulty, and the women whom I try to instruct to the best of my ability do not understand much. Indeed I do not understand much myself, having studied but little. I am often very sorrowful when I think of my deficiencies both in explaining things to them, and in setting them an example. But I trust in God ; my confidence in Him never fails. To the extent of my ability I endure patiently, and labor in earnest with unceasing effort. Therefore, dear brethren and sisters, to whatever church you may belong, I entreat you to remember me in your prayers. But more than this, I desire that men and women everywhere, may offer united prayer, that the Kingdom of

God may spread abroad and come before all other things quickly, throughout the whole earth." Such was the spirit manifested by the workers at Toungoo, and so greatly did the Lord bless their labors, that it was thought desirable that Mr. and Mrs. Whitaker should go up to aid and counsel them, at least till the return of Dr. and Mrs. Mason from America. Accordingly in May, 1855, they started. On reaching Shwaygyeen Mr. Whitaker found it impossible to take his family on at once to Toungoo; he determined therefore on leaving them with the mission family at Shwaygyeen, and proceeded by himself to Toungoo. There he was continually surrounded with inquiring Karens, all eagerly anxious to see the teacher, and to facilitate his remaining among them. So effectually was their aid given, that in six days a house was made tenantable for the family. Quala, who had been out on a lengthened tour, arrived to see Mr. Whitaker, and gave a most encouraging account of the continued progress of the work among the different tribes. Early therefore, in September, Mr. Whitaker returned to Shwaygyeen for his family; when he found both Mr. and Mrs. Harris prostrate with fever, and the mission plunged into the deepest sorrow under the chastening hand of God.

In a former chapter we have mentioned the first Mrs. Harris. After her death, Mr. Harris went to Rangoon to consult with the brethren there as to his future course. It was then arranged that Miss Vinton, who for fifteen years had been laboring amongst the Karens, and who needed rest, should go to America with his children, leaving Mr. Harris free to return to Shwaygyeen. In April 1855, Miss Vinton returned from America, and was married to Mr. Harris, and together they entered on their work with renewed earnestness and zeal.

In vigorous health, with a perfect knowledge of the language, loving the people, and with the most earnest desire for their salvation, she went out with her husband into the jungles, her favorite hymn expressing the desire of her heart.

> "In these deserts let me labor,
> On these mountains let me tell
> How he died, the blessed Saviour,
> To redeem a world from hell."

So devoted were her labors, that her praise spread far and wide, and when at last she was taken from them, the Karens in the distant hills who had not yet seen her, said, "We cannot eat, we have no appetite for food, our friend is gone."

When Mr. Whitaker reached Shwaygyeen the fever was not severe, and from its intermittent character both she and Mr. Harris were at times able to move about. On the ninth day, she seemed no worse, and in the afternoon begged that the Karen children might sing their hymns to her. She herself then sang a sweet hymn on *rest*, and after sleeping till about twelve at night, asked to be raised, and her head falling on her husband's shoulder, she was gone without a struggle to be for ever with the Lord.

It was an affecting sight to see those for whom she had so zealously labored, and in whose ears her words of gentle teaching had scarcely ceased to echo, called in to take their last long look of those beloved features, before they carried her forth to her last resting-place. Surely we may inscribe upon this mission, "in deaths oft;" but it has been life also, life to the dead in trespasses and sins; life, eternal life, to the many who have believed.

Mr. Harris bravely struggled on for two long months, but disease was too strong for him, and at the close of 1856, he was compelled to seek a renewal of lost health and strength in America. We had the privilege of seeing him at that time, weak in body, but strong in faith, counting all his sorrows light, if he might but win his beloved Karens to the excellency of the knowledge of Christ Jesus his Lord. In speaking of those whom God had given him among from the heathen he said, "God is *always* faithful to his promise, *always*. 'There is no man that hath left parents, or brethren, or wife, or children, for the Kingdom of God's sake, who shall not receive manifold more in this present time, and in the world to come life everlasting.'" Before Mr. Harris left Shwaygyeen eight hundred had been admitted into the Christian church by baptism.

When Mr. and Mrs. Whitaker arrived at Toungoo, they were thronged with visitors; at one time about two hundred were present for several successive days, all anxious to hear of Christ, and to receive instruction. The total number of baptisms in the province of Toungoo amounted at this time to two thousand six hundred. Among the numerous tribes east of the town, there appeared no opposition to the gospel, but on the contrary in all the villages there were those who listened, while the whole population was more or less brought under its life-giving influence. The number of people thus reached, could not be less than twenty thousand. We have many interesting notices, in one of Mr. Whitaker's tours in the jungle, of their earnestness in prayer, and thirst for the knowledge of God's word, their love of holiness, and zeal for the ordinances of God's house. How great the change effected in a few short months! Then nothing but the sound of savage strife was heard in these villages and on those hills, but now peace reigns wherever the blessed gospel has found its way. In some of the villages the people possessed rare gems, which had come down to them from their ancestors, and which they regarded with superstitious reverence. But on bringing them to Mr. Whitaker for inspection they asked;

"shall we throw them away;" evidently willing to do so, had it been considered right. Some of the chapels they had built were so large and commodious that they would hold from four to six hundred people, and these were filled to overflowing. At the association meeting which Mr. Whitaker held with them in the 1st January, 1857, upwards of sixteen hundred were present, many earnest applications were made for school teachers, and there was a universal readiness on the part of the preachers to rely on God and their people for support.

Mr. Whitaker gives an interesting account of a Sabbath spent at Wathaukho, where Pwaipau began his labors among the Klenla people. When Pwaipau first went amongst them, he found only one man willing to hear him. After faithfully preaching to him he was about to turn away, but the man earnestly entreated, saying that if no one else would listen he would, and that he would learn to read *the book*. Pwaipau sat down to teach him, and in a fortnight he had a school of forty boys. All went on well until the father of two of the lads sent to call them home to the celebration of a feast to an evil spirit. The boys stoutly refused to go, and the next day the school house was surrounded with thirty or forty men armed with spears. One of the boys leaped out at the back of the house and concealed himself in the jungle, the other was secured, and ordered off to the ceremony on pain of death. He of course obeyed, but light had entered, and soon that first learner was the assistant in charge of a church of two hundred members four or five miles in extent. Pwaipau watched over another flock still more numerous; the two number nearly five hundred. Peaceful and happy they dwell under the shadow of the Almighty. May his banner over them be love.

Well might Mr. Whitaker "thank God that he had been permitted to spend four years on heathen ground, and for the miracles of grace and power he had been permitted to witness." His hands were full of labor, and his heart buoyant with hope that the fulfilment of God's richest promises was at hand, but in the midst of labor and of hope the hand of death was upon him, and after a brief illness he entered into rest in August, 1857.

It was at the close of 1856 that Dr. and Mrs. Mason returned from America. On reaching Calcutta there was some difficulty in obtaining a passage on to Burmah for the whole party, and Dr. Mason determined therefore to proceed alone, leaving Mrs. Mason and the children to follow him as speedily as possible. After an absence of three years Dr. Mason reached Toungoo in January, 1857, and was welcomed by the Karens with the most fervent joy. Finding the elephant upon which he travelled moved but slowly, they made a palankeen of bamboos, and placing him upon their shoulders they bore him on from village to village, through the Manniepgha hamlets to the Paku settlements and on to the Bghai mountains. His course was like the triumphant procession of one whom the Lord had blessed. He says:—

"I left Shwaygyeen for Toungoo by land with two elephants, and reached the borders of the province on the 2nd of January. When the Christians heard of my arrival, twenty men started to meet me and cut a road for my elephants, the bamboo scuff being quite impassable. In the interior I had taken the road to another village, the inhabitants of the village connected with Shwaygyeen having volunteered their services to prepare the way before me; while the chief and his followers of a third village were busied at the same time in clearing a path for me to their hamlet. Missing both these parties I proceeded onward to the village of Khupghai. The road being exceedingly difficult and the mountains so steep that places for the feet of the elephants to step in had sometimes to be dug in their sides, and gorges so narrow that the animals could scarcely turn aside and pick a practicable track among the rocks with which they were filled, it was not until the morning of the third day we reached our destination. The first night I slept on the top of a paddy crib in an old field, a thousand feet above the plains seen in the distance ; and darkness overtook us on the evening of the second day, when the natives proposed to encamp out again, but having no tent, and the north wind at this season blowing very keenly over the hills, I refused—determined to go to the village if we travelled till midnight ; so on we went, up and down, with a beautiful moon peeping now and then through trees. We were in a deep dell, when the path required us to ascend a precipitous mountain side but on turning the heads of our elephants through weariness they positively refused to go, and when goaded by their drivers they made the forest resound with their bellowing, but not a foot onward would they stir. For once I had to acknowledge myself fairly beaten, and the next best thing to be done was to find the nearest dry spot on which we could spread ourselves down ; for in these glens the ground is frequently very wet. After retracing our steps a few hundred yards I called to a man on foot, to feel if the ground was dry in the green palm grove through which we were passing ; when my attention was arrested by the figure of a stranger in the shade. He announced himself a Christian, and urged us to come and spend the night at his house which was about a quarter of a mile from the road, on a little hill with a gentle ascent, the only difficulty in the way, a deep stream, he said he could overcome by leading us to a practicable ford. It appeared that he heard the tinkling of the bells that hung to the necks of the elephants, and the report having reached him that I was somewhere in the jungles, he came down with his son after us to see if it were not the teacher. His hospitable mansion was reached about ten o'clock, where the most comfortable place in it was spread with mats for my reception. When we had dined (for we had not stopped before from early dawn) I announced prayers, and the only daughter of my host, a pretty girl of sixteen, brought forward a New Testament and hymn book, joining with her sweet voice in the praises of God. Fancy my emotions! Three years ago not a soul in these jungles had heard of the Saviour, when it was my privilege to be first to proclaim His precious name. Now, the first house I am led to enter, in the field of my charge, is furnished with a family Bible and hymn book, whose owners prize them as precious treasure. Surely 'it is the Lord's doing, and is wonderful in our eyes.'

"Before we could reach Khupghai next morning, the news had reached the village that the teacher had come; and the hill sides were covered with men, women and children who had come out to meet him, each anxious to seize his hand before he could descend from the elephant. In one corner of their very neat meeting house was a place matted off for my sleeping room, and curtained all around with new Burmese silk, such as the wealthier Karens wear for their best dresses. My Karen guide wore a lower garment for which he paid twenty-five rupees, and above it a Shan jacket of considerable value. The native preacher here I found well provided for by the church, without requiring aid from any other sources.

"The next evening found me at Kholu, in the midst of some of the grandest alpine scenery I ever gazed on. It stands on the mountain side, one or two thousand feet above Yan Creek at the base; and looking across the valley, mountains are seen piled on mountains as far as the eye can reach, with forms as varied as the pictures of the kaleidoscope. On the mountain range where I stood, which bounds the valley on the south, are six Christian villages, and on the northern range are no less than fifteen. When I look around me I find myself in a Christian country, raised up as if by magic from the darkness of heathenism in three brief years.

"The next day, after travelling a few miles, a difficulty arose as to which village I should go to, the road dividing into two, and the path had been cleared for my elephants to both. I found no way to decide the matter, but to declare that Quala's wife was my daughter, and that I must go and see my daughter. Twenty-five years ago she was Mrs. Mason's favorite pupil,—so on we went to the village of Lenkla, where Quala makes his home. At present he is away preaching the gospel to the Red Karens, seven days' journey north-east of Toungoo.

"When the Sabbath was over, the chief of this village came to me and asked how many nights I had slept at Lenkla, I told him two; 'Then,' he said, 'you must come and sleep at least two in my village. I spent a Sunday in your house in Toungoo, and there first heard the gospel from your lips. I want too, so much to see the teacheress. Will she not come on to the mountains to see us? My wife and I will go to the city to visit her, so soon as we hear of her arrival.' In reply to his invitation to come to his village, I told him I had dismissed my elephants, the time for which I engaged them having expired, and that I was unable to walk so far. 'We do not want you to walk,' he continued, 'we will carry you and all your things, if you will say, Go.' I gave the word, and he turned to a man at his elbow saying, 'Make a dooly for the teacher and bring twenty men to carry his things.' In a few hours a very comfortable affair was constructed of bamboo, on which my bed and myself were put, and borne by four men, relieved at short intervals by four more, a dozen being in attendance, away I went at a trot over several hills and valleys to this village, which stands on the very top of a mountain spur, with the whole plain of Toungoo to the Prome mountains spread out on the west, and the magnificent scenery of the Bghai mountains on the north, with the tortuous course of the stream on which our most interesting Bghai villages are located, distinctly visible by the deep chasms through which it runs.

'I am now among the Manniepghas, and at every village I find more or less applicants for baptism, but I reserve statistics for another letter This illustrates the gratitude of the Karens to their teachers for bringing them the gospel.

"I have got the Sermon on the Mount into Bghai, a third of Matthew, and Genesis begun. I have now to request the patronage of the Society for an edition of three thousand copies of Genesis, and as many of the Sermon on the Mount.* * *

" The evening your letter arrived I found a little Bghai boy, not a dozen years of age, reading by the way, an old smoked catechism in Sgau, which, to preserve, he had sewed between two bits of old Burmese pasteboard on a kind of spring back of a bamboo splint. I send it to ask if such a people who will take such care of books, not a tithe of which they can understand, shall be denied the Scriptures.

"Would that you could stand with me on these mountain tops, and see now two, now three, and then five other clusters of Christian habitations. You would then feel that ' the half was not told.' The duty of giving a full support to their teachers the churches fully recognise, and, though it often requires much self-denial on the part of the assistant in places where the people are few and poor, yet they are ready to admit that they ought to look for their means to live to their congregations. Still, in the present incipient state of things, we ought to assist those who need help, as many do. One young man, who has a wife to support, told me that the 'Wild Bghais,' among whom he is located, could give him nothing but rice, for it is all they have for themselves. Many wear scarcely any clothing, and are at constant warfare among themselves and have to be ever prepared for attacks from their neighbors. Yet in the hearts of these people the Spirit of God is manifestly at work, though none have been baptized, and they come to meeting on Sundays in great numbers, armed—like the old covenanters—with swords, spears and cross-bows; muskets they have none. To supply his necessities, the young man above-mentioned has repeatedly come down into the plains, and labored as a cooly. In such instances, and there are others, the missionary should be able to step in with the necessary funds and keep the man at work."

The following account of a meeting on the Bghai mountains is very striking: he says;

"Like the prophet in his vision, I feel overwhelmed with the scenes that are passing before my eyes. Three days ago, the first meeting of the Bghai association was held in this place. I was called to the chair, and as I looked from the crest of the hill on which it assembled, on two thousand of the wildest Karens the jungles can boast, I seemed to be seated in an assembly of all nations. There were men robed in silks in the Burmese costume; others with the blue pants and padded jackets which distinguish Shans; and a few were buttoned up in the cast off red coats of English soldiers. Among the ladies, there was a sufficient variety of silk handkerchiefs, white cottons, and diversified calicoes to supply a small linendraper's shop; but the larger number were in their native dresses. The Pakus were known by the horizontal stripes on their tunics. One Bghai tribe was easily recognised by the tunic being striped perpendicularly with red lines, and the other by their short pants reaching half way down the thigh. Many of those from the distant mountains had their swords by their sides, and not a few might be seen on the distant margin of the congregation listening as they leaned on their spears.

"Forty-five stations were represented, each of which has its teacher, and all, with a very few exceptions, are natives of Toungoo, raised up from among themselves. At twenty-four of the stations, the foundations of churches have been laid, and there are many candidates for baptism at most of the stations. Three hundred and sixteen persons were baptized during the year, making the present number of church members in good standing among the Bghais alone, (there is a still larger number of Pakus and Manniepghas)—one thousand two hundred and sixteen. The aggregate of the pupils reported in school is six hundred and eighty-eight. In the Paku and Manniepgha districts there is a still larger number, there being exactly fifty stations. Thus there are ninety-five schools, and as many school teachers and preachers to the extent of their knowledge in eastern Toungoo, all, with the exception of about ten, natives of the province and converted within the last three years. This is the most remarkable feature of this most remarkable work. These young preachers exhibited in the discussion of questions brought before the association, forensic talents which I have never seen equalled in the best educated of our native assistants, and which it would be difficult to surpass in our schools at home. When I told Quala at parting, to thrust into the work every promising young man instructed by himself or his three associates, without waiting for them to take a regular course of education, I little thought to witness such glorious results. When the work became too great for one man, Shapau took the lead among the Bghais, providing teachers from among his pupils for that tribe, and Pwaipau among the Pakus. Both, as well as Quala, are in fact bishops, and no bishops ever acted more judiciously, more uprightly, or more successfully than they have done during the last three years.

"Were the plan of bringing forward the natives to places of responsibility followed out, we should soon have a band of missionaries raised up on the ground, to go to the regions beyond, with tenfold better qualifications for their mission than all the universities can give their students, and at little or no expense. Is it to be done? Or are native preachers, whose labors God blessed beyond example in the history of missions, to be kept in everlasting pupilage, and made nonentities in the eyes of their fellow countrymen?

"The raising up of such a body of assistants is, I think, unequalled in the history of missions, and scarcely less remarkable is the fact that all the congregations come forward and engage to support their teachers; and at every station which I have visited, I find the assistant better clothed and in a better house than any of his congregation. Several of the churches gave their teachers twenty rupees in money last year, and one gave thirty. Added to this, they have paid into the mission about a thousand rupees for books; a larger sum than has ever been contributed for books, I imagine, from all the rest of the missions during the quarter of a century they have been in existence. Medicines which were always given away, I believe, at the expense of the mission till I commenced selling them to the Karens of Tavoy, meet with a ready market here, affording the dealer a clear profit of twenty-five per cent. Finally, they have contributed for the Home Mission Society a fraction over two hundred and eighty-one rupees, which with two hundred and eighty-three rupees contributed by the Paku and Manniepgha churches, and more than two hundred of balance on hand, will, after paying for the printing of the minutes, be devoted to Mr. Whitaker's school during the rains in town; and the amount is larger than will be necessary to expend.

"I had written thus far when I arose for an evening walk. On the edge of the village I came upon four little girls with sparkling eyes looking from dirty faces, like morning stars peeping through clouds. The eldest was not seven years of age, the youngest about five. One of them had two torn leaves of an old hymn book in her hand. After winning them out of their bashfulness, I found all could read; and they finally sung one of the hymns through to a good English tune, as accurately and as harmoniously as I ever heard little girls of their age sing anywhere. Truly God's ways are wonderful, and He puts to shame the wisdom and works of man. Here is a professedly Christian population of more than ten thousand souls, upwards of two thousand of whom are members of Christian churches; schools in ninety-five villages, with praise proceeding from the lips of babes, in tunes with which our mothers sung to us cradle hymns; indigenous teachers in almost every village, using books that they have purchased; and to enable a few to obtain a better education than the jungles can afford, ample funds are provided to support a school in the city: all this, and more, in three years through native agents, who from the foundation of the mission to the present time have not received in the aggregate two hundred rupees. Where shall we look for a parallel in the history of missions? But the work has only just begun. These young Bghai preachers are going to form a phalanx of missionaries to evangelise the other wild tribes in the 'regions beyond,' as far as the Hohangho and Bramahpootra. These men will be better qualified, with a little instruction, for their work than it is possible to qualify white men in all the colleges throughout Christendom.

"You recollect St. Anthony's chapel, of course. Well, my Bghai hermitage occupies a very similar position. I am on the top of a hill, with a precipitous mountain behind me, like Arthur's seat, but much higher. On one side of this mountain is a deep gorge with a steep ascent, precisely like Victoria Road. In the other direction, looking down as it were to Edinburgh, is a rapid stream running through a deep glen, bordered by precipices higher than that on which Edinburgh castle stands ; and in the far distance are lofty mountains as seen beyond the Forth.

"The country is not more Scotch than are its inhabitants. The Bghais are as like the Highlanders of olden time as can well be imagined. They are divided into small clans that have been so separated by old feuds, that a mountain ridge between them could not be crossed by either party. If a man was found on the grounds of his neighbors his life was the price of his temerity. The people were ever in a state of apprehension, for one clan or another was constantly making forays into the weaker or less prepared villages.

"The young man who is writing by my side lost a sister several years ago by a party of Pant Bghais who attacked the village, killed and wounded several persons, and carried away some half a dozen captives, who were probably sold into slavery to the Shans, or some other tribe to the eastward. Quala tells me that he saw a number of slaves among the Red Karens who had been captured in this region, but they were well treated, had become domesticated with their masters, and manifested no wish to return to their native land. Christianity will put a termination to this state of things, but Government cannot. This young-man's family cherished the purpose to attack the Pant Bghais whenever a favorable opportunity occurred, and obtain a substitute for his sister but when they embraced Christianity the avenging design was, they say, abandoned for ever. Beyond the Christian settlements, notwithstanding the English power, kidnapping, killing, and plundering, are going on while I am writing. There seems from the physiognomy of the people to be a great difference in the character of the Bghais. A party of thirty from a distant village stopped here a few days lately, and some of them had certainly as brutal countenances as my eyes ever rested on. Others again appear to have mild dispositions. The young man who is school teacher appears to me, after a two months' intimate acquaintance, to be a very amiable youth. Some are very stupid, and some appear remarkably intelligent. A few Sundays ago I had the teacher of a neighboring village to preach for me in the evening. I sat and listened to him with admiration and astonishment. I recollected him as one of the young men who came to Mrs. Mason's school in the city. He was then anxious to learn, but the Burmese, who did all in their power to keep the Karens from our house, spared no efforts when they did come to frighten them away again, and succeeded by their tales of terror in driving him away after he had been about a week with us; but when Shapau came out here he went to his school, and stayed with him a month. Here then is the amount of his education, six days in the city and thirty in the jungles; yet he certainly preached as good a sermon in every respect as you will hear from one half of our ministers who have been three years to college and three to the theological seminary. His text was, 'As Moses lifted up the serpent in the wilderness, &c.' In the introduction he gave as accurate an account of the circumstances under which the serpent was made, as it would be possible for the most experienced theologian to furnish, with the necessity of looking on it to live; and applied it to Christ with an earnestness and animation that would have secured the attention of any audience. He is very anxious to have me supply his place and allow him to go to school. He is just the kind we wish to have instructed, but we cannot spare him from the field. Shapau placed him at one village where he taught for a couple of years nearly, when more than forty of his congregation were baptized. Shapau then removed him to a frontier settlement where thirty-five are now requesting admittance into the church. But such men are few everywhere. We need to pray for more laborers, and for the right kind of laborers."

Again on the 8th April, 1857, Dr. Mason writes from ' Independent Bghai-dom :'—" The people here are the Pant-wearing Bghais, who boast that they never paid taxes to any Government, but have maintained their independence from time immemorial. The Burmese denominate them Loo-Yaing or ' wild men,' and not without reason. Though only one short march from the villages of the Frock-wearing Bghais, from whom a large revenue was collected, this people never allowed a Burman to return if he once appeared amongst them. Though many thousands of them are nominally under the English Government, no taxes have yet been asked of them; and they now show themselves boldly in the city to purchase salt and a few other articles. As they become Christianised we may expect they will be taxed, which will not make Christianity popular. As I am the first white man that has ever been to their village, I may not improbably, when they come to be taxed, have my name handed down to posterity as a spy of the English Government. However, I came here by their own invitation, and they carried me on their shoulders all the way.

" This is the most north-easternmost point to which the

conquests of Christianity have reached. Here light and darkness meet. None of the villagers have been baptized, but a list of thirty-two applicants for the ordinance has been brought in, and I have an assembly of two or three hundred every evening at worship who are all professed believers in Christ. But it is astonishing to find how stupid the old people are on all subjects, while the young appear as bright and intelligent as European children. Would we rouse the people we must educate the young; there is no other way. The old may obtain grace to save their souls, but never knowledge and intelligence to give them a place among civilized nations.

" This is only one of three villages in which there are professors of Christianity, in the same little valley, and all are visible from the top of the hill that overshadows us. My present locality is the very antipodes to the one I last wrote from. The village is down in a little basin on the banks of a stream, completely encircled by high hills which shut out everything but the sun. The thermometer rises seven degrees higher here than where I last sojourned.

" The work accomplished in Toungoo appears great on paper, but when I take my stand on one of those hills, and the eye sweeps round from the northwest to the southeast on an unbroken mass of heathenism lying at my feet, and on, on, on, till the imagination is lost in the darkness, I sink paralysed at the view of the ' much land which yet remains to be possessed.' Still these uttermost parts of the earth have been promised by One who never fails to fulfil His promises. Promised, however, on the condition that they shall be asked for; and we have reason to inquire, Has the condition been fulfilled ?

"The season for itinerating is close upon us, and throughout the rains the natives will be confined to their stations and their schools, with the exception of short excursions into the neighboring villages. Quala has made one valuable trip this year among the Red Karens, but valuable mainly for the knowledge he brings us of the people, for he failed to find a single individual who gave any attention to the gospel. But one great obstacle was, he could not speak their language, and had to converse with them through a Shan who was inimical to Christianity. Shapau, our next best assistant, has made a more successful tour on and over the eastern mountains in the southern part of the province, and before his return he saw *six* zayats built in as many different villages, settled six teachers in them and thus laid the foundation of as many Christian communities, where the worship of God was not before known. One of the villages that received a teacher promising him his support and engaging to obey the precepts of the gospel, is on the eastern side of the dividing chain of mountains, and is the first village that has received Christianity beyond the English territories. * *

"Shapau has made one trip among the Pant-wearing Bghais in the northern portion of the province. While absent he wrote me : 'I have reached the land of Kannee, and several of the villages are about to build zayats. I intend to go as far as the village of Koo-oo; I hear many of the villages in that region are about to erect chapels. Should I remain here till the zayats are completed I shall be delayed a considerable time. I have a number of people with me, and shall leave a teacher in each village that prepares for his accommodation. Teacher, pray for us.' Since he wrote the above, a body of wild Bghais from the north attacked the village of Koo-oo, to which Shapau was bound, killing three men, and carrying off seven persons into slavery."

In June, 1857, Mrs. Mason reached Toungoo, and again

commenced her work amongst these people. In writing of her first impressions on her return, she says : " Three years and a half ago I gazed over these mountains and plains where the fallen angels have held supreme power ever since the days of Noah, wondering if there were any of the chosen among them. Now our missionary boat-man Shapau stands beside me, pointing to the north, south, east and west, and says, ' Teacher, among these hills and valleys are ninety-six churches, chapels, and schools.' Three years ago I looked upon troop after troop of wild mountaineers with their short-striped growns and unwashed faces, wondering if they could be civilized. Now I look upon a hundred young men and lads, all neatly dressed in clean new gowns and blue pantaloons, with their hair nicely braided under tasteful turbans.

" Three years ago I sent to them the first book they ever saw in their own tongue ; yesterday I sat in the midst of twenty young preachers, fine intelligent youth, all following the speaker, with open Bibles, turning from page to page, from paragraph to paragraph, with perfect ease and the deepest interest. I could not but exclaim, ' What hath God wrought !' Several of the preachers say their hearts are to go beyond the frontier to carry the gospel. May God strengthen their holy purpose."

Mrs. Mason went up to Toungoo with the hope and determination of being able to establish a self supporting female normal school, for the training of young teachers for the village school. She felt there would be many difficulties and obstacles in the way, but she went forward strong in faith, believing that God would prosper and bless the work. Some of the chiefs having heard of her design, three girls were sent in, but nothing was said as to their support. The crisis had come, but how to meet it was the difficulty. If the girls were sent home, Mrs. Mason felt sure no more would come; to support them herself was neither possible nor desirable. Her heart was lifted up for guidance to Him who giveth wisdom liberally and upbraideth not. That evening a man came in who was not at first recognised, but who proved to be the very man who had formerly come back with the little book, "The sayings of the elders." He was now a Christian, and was private agent to the Commissioner, and one of the most influential men of the jungles. After cordial greetings M. s. Mason, amongst other things, mentioned her plan for the school, her hope of obtaining a grant of land from Government, of erecting a school-house, chapel and teachers' dwellings, all of which was to be made over in trust for the Karens. He seemed to see at once the advantage of such an establishment; the desirableness of instructing the women, of making them the *teachers*, and of sending off the young men as *preachers* among the heathen. He urged Mrs Mason to secure a tract of land on the eastern side of the river, so that when the Karens came down from the mountains they might there find a resting-place. The Commissioner had entered most kindly into Mrs. Mason's wishes, and had been over every part of the city and its environs, which is on the western side of the river, looking for an eligible site, but in vain; and when Mrs. Mason found that the Nah-Khan's advice was to settle on the eastern side, although removed from all civilization and surrounded by jungle, she determined, if possible, to do so, in the hope that some of the Karens might be induced to come and settle round her. Before leaving, the Nah-Khan inquired how the institution, &c., was to be supported. When Mrs. Mason replied that she trusted in God, whose ravens were still upon the earth, he understood her, and with a sympathising glance said in an under tone to those who stood by, " I must send the mamma my great pig!" And in a few days after down came the great pig, and eleven rupees for the girls' support.

Thus a beginning was made, and that by a chief of considerable influence, who assured Mrs. Mason that the people would send their daughters and provide for them. Shapau also entered warmly into the scheme; and although at a most unhealthy season, went out to make it known in the jungles: in a short time Mrs. Mason had twenty Karens and two Burmese girls, from thirteen to sixteen years of age, gathered into the school. Letters, too, came pouring in from the different villages, expressive of their hearts' good will and desire to support the institution. Some of these letters are very characteristic; we give the following as specimens.

"Letter of the Ta-wa-la-khe-ites.—Teacheress; Formerly we knew not God's word. Not one of us knew what was right: we saw nothing but transgression. Hence God had mercy on us and sent us books; but although he had sent us books we knew not of them,—not a single man of us. While we were in this state of ignorance, according to the command of God, teacher and teacheress Mason came to us children of sin. We heard as the teacher preached to us. We believed, and rejoiced exceedingly. Now, as we are unable to devise for ourselves, the teacheress has devised for us to erect a large school-building, which we approve, all and each of us. Teacheress, as you have ordered for us we will do and study."

There is another from the Mopghas.

"Letter of the Pelekhe-ites—Teacheress; Your erection of a large zayat for the Karens *hits* our hearts *exceedingly, exceeding greatly.* We will send our children and grandchildren to study, and we will most assuredly furnish their food. The teacheress building a large school-house harmonizes perfectly with our own minds, and we will moreover assist the teacheress. It is our heart's desire to become skilled in the books, and we will study till we are skilled in them, both male and female, and become teachers of God's word.

"We give our word of honor for that to which we here agree. We are also pleased with the Committee of seven.

"May great grace and peace rest upon the teachers.

"Mercy, love, and peace abide with the teacheress for ever!"

Another wrote:

"DEAR TEACHERESS; Formerly all of us in Toungoo were under the dominion of Satan; we drank arrack, cursed, reviled, told lies, fought and devoured one another, until no one dared to go to a neighbor's house. We hated and dreaded each other. Now behold the change: we love one another!

"Two years ago I heard of the Eternal God's commands, and of Jesus Christ our Redeemer. I believed and worshipped with my whole heart, and according to the command, I have ever since preached Christ to my countrymen according to my ability. I try much, but very imperfectly.

"When I heard of your work for the Karens I rejoiced with great joy. If God and the white foreigners had not pitied us, we must have remained in darkness and sin, for we were full of all unrighteousness.

"Now we have heard, and we have learned a little with delight.

"Now the teacheress is building a great house and a holy city, that the young women may increase in understanding, and God's kingdom be extended. For this I rejoice much, *much, much!*

"Formerly we looked for a deliverer but none came. Now God has sent to us, therefore our hearts are very hot, and we are determined to study with all our might.

"Because formerly we worked hard in wickedness, now we ought to work the harder to do good.

"We send five men to help build the girls' rooms, and when they leave, others will take their place. They will buy their own food.

"Dear teacheress, I never saw you, but I beg you will pray for me, and remember the little church which sends this letter.

"Janquate."

This is a literal translation, word for word. The young teacher who wrote this letter had no instruction but such as he had obtained in the jungles.

Nothing could have been more favorable than this commencement; and probably since the sending forth of the little tract, no work had awakened such a glow of enthusiasm in these Toungoo jungles. Thirty-two acres and a half of land were made over by the Commissioner to the institution. And the next work was to clear, and drain, and build. Fifty Karens came in at once to offer a willing service, and the work was at once commenced. In addition to land, Major Phayre gave orders for a supply of teak, free of charge. The rains had now set in, and it was impossible to do anything in the jungle. Dr. Mason was at work with a translation of the Scriptures into Bghai, and in June, 1857, wrote:—

"The rains are pouring down upon us, and all travelling is nearly closed till the fair weather comes again. I regret that we have so few men at our outpost, for it is hard work. One wrote me that the village where he was teaching was enfiladed by an uninterrupted series of traps, so that no one could enter after dark without being speared. The village, like most of the Bghai villages, consists of one house with a hall in the centre, and the only way of access at any time is by a ladder let down from the centre of the hall, which is taken up at night and the trap-door let down. Thus the people live in constant fear of attack from their enemies. Some of the inhabitants of another village had killed two Burmans. Two of the murderers were brought to town through the efforts of some of the Christians, where they died in jail before trial, if I recollect right, since my arrival. Recently a part of this village went out to revenge the death of the men that died in prison, and the first object of their vengeance was the daughter of a Christian chief, whom they speared to death on the banks of the brook where she had gone to draw water. One young teacher had to run away from the village where he was located with half the inhabitants intoxicated after him, because they said they would kill every man that forbade them drink.

"After allowing for much chaff, God has still done a wonderful work here in taming so many of the wild men around us; but unless He continue to work, 'the watchman waketh in vain.' All our efforts, all our machinery, is naught."

In this letter was enclosed the following translation of a letter from Sau Quala.

"I have received the affectionate letter which you wrote me, and I rejoice exceedingly with much thankfulness. We Karens, wild and ignorant sons of the forest, are not worthy of anything from your hands, for we have been a rejected people from days of old. When we fell among Talaings, the Talaings persecuted us; when we fell among Shans, the Shans persecuted us; when we fell among Burmans, the Burmans persecuted us; father and mother, grandfather and grandmother, generation on generation. Thus we became children of destruction, unworthy to receive anything from the hands of respectable people, and undeserving the privilege of addressing you, Madam.

"When I was fifteen years of age, English white rulers, the sons of the west, reached this country of Burmah, and my father and mother said: 'Now happiness has reached the land! They have come by water. Children, you have fallen on the time when they arrived.' After a short interval, the American teacher Boardman came; when many believed, and I was baptized. A brief period elapsed when teacher Mason arrived and teacher Boardman died. I was many years with teacher Mason, and then became a preacher and was located at Pyeekhya in the southern part of Tavoy; being subsequently ordained.

"In the lapse of years I came to Toungoo, where after being a short time with teacher and teacheress Mason, they left the country; and I then went to the Commissioner O'Riley. He said to me; 'Teacher, do not be anxious: if anything happens, come and tell me.' Many persons, Bghais, Mopghas, Pakus, and Manniepghas, believed. Some of the Burmese headmen began then to obstruct the work; so I wrote to the Commissioner O'Riley, and he ordered the Burmese headmen, saying; 'A great teacher has gone out to the Karens on their mountains, and if they learn to read, or build zayats, throw no obstruction in their way.' Some of the Burmans then said: 'The Karens are in league with the white foreigners, but when the Burmans obtain the city again, they will kill the whole of them.' Others said, 'When the time arrives, the white foreigners will take all that learn to read, in their ships, and give them for food to a man-eating monster.' Some of the Karens were much frightened, for the Burmans bore them malice because they were on amicable terms with the English.

"Subsequently the Commissioner O'Riley came into the jungle, and many of the wild Karens visited him; to whom he gave turbans and money, while I preached to them the word of God and exhorted them to learn to read. After this teacher Whitaker came. The Commissioner made another visit to the jungle when he called me to accompany him to the Red Karens; and he purchased food for me, for I am not one of those who eat wages. This Commissioner is a most excellent man, and all his decisions please the poor people exceedingly; but he has now left Toungoo, and the whole of the inhabitants of Toungoo mourn. But now, Madam, teacher and teacheress Mason have returned to Toungoo.

"As to the Red Karens, they are Bghais; but speak a different dialect from the Toungoo Bghais; and the Pakus differ again from them. The Pakus and Manniepghas are of the same race as the Sgaus. The Mapghas are a small tribe whose language differs from all the others, and I therefore think they had the same origin as the Pghas. I send you a few specimens of the Bghai, Mopgha, Paku, and Manniepgha dresses.

"All the inhabitants of Toungoo, both Bghai, Mopgha, Paku and Manniepgha, are apprehensive lest the English should leave the country, for the Burmans will then persecute them. The Burmans often threaten, saying: 'When your white foreigners go away, you will know it!'

"Teacher Quala's letter of Christian affection, May 26th, 1857."

In October 1857, Quala started on a tour through the province, and such were the applications for baptism that he wrote to Dr. Mason recommending the ordination of four of the principal assistants, but Dr. Mason considered that two only were in a state to justify their admittance to the office of pastor. At this time we have a letter from Quala addressed to the American churches.

"Brethren, children of God in America, rulers, nobles,

chiefs, elders, great and small, male and female, rich and wealthy, poor and indigent, young men and maidens, children and aged, the grey-haired and the toothless, all, every one of you, may the only one God our Father, the Lord of heaven and earth and all things, Jesus Christ, and the Holy Spirit, bless you greatly with happiness, abundance, success, skill, and permanency; giving peace to your towns and cities, your lands and your waters, your kingdom and your realm, your houses and your villages, both to yourselves, and to your children, and grandchildren, generation on generation, continually without ceasing.

"Dear friends, I am Quala, a wild man, a son of the forest, an uncultivated one who neither knows nor understands any thing. I, a dark-minded unworthy one, send you salutation. I am not your equal, yet through the grace of God I call you brethren.

"Dear friends, you truly abound in ability, in patient endurance, in love, in mercy, and goodness. Behold, my dear friends, had you not sent the teachers and teacheresses to us, wild men, the sons of the east, living in darkness, we should have gone on to destruction both in this world and the world to come for ever.

"Dear friends, the grace that the white foreigners the sons of America have displayed is so much, so great, that it cannot be expressed by words. It is exceedingly great, for you have saved us from death. Formerly we knew not God; we had no books, and being destitute of instruction we knew nothing.

"When you sent the teachers and teacheresses among us, and they told us that God loved the world so much that he gave us His Son Jesus Christ, who came and purchased us by his blood we became Christians, and became able to discern between right and wrong; and when the teachers made us books, our knowledge increased greatly. Still, the signification, the reason of things, we understood very imperfectly, and we should have never known, had not the teachers and teacheresses taught us and explained them to us; because my dear friends, we are habituated to darkness, and things of light we understand with great difficulty. Still some make their ears crooked, will not give attention, and do not believe; but on the contrary revile. Pray to God for them that they may repent, believe, obtain new hearts, and all become disciples like ourselves.

"God has now displayed his power in Toungoo; and many sons of the forest, living in darkness, have believed, and your kindness is great in sending two teachers to help them. As to myself, being of a race of uncultivated men, I am of no value; but through the grace of God I became a disciple of Christ in the days of your teacher Boardman; then I studied a very long time in the hands of teacher Mason, and I came to know and understand the truth as one in a dream. Still I became a teacher to go about preaching and administering baptism. This was through your kindness, for when I was studying with teacher Mason, you sent the money which you gave to teacher Mason. My relatives were unable to support me, and had it not been for your money I could not have studied nor by any means have acquired the knowledge I have. When I think of your kindness, I feel as if I could not extol it sufficiently. Though I die, I will praise your goodness to my children and grandchildren, and the generation following. I am now growing old, my hair is grey, my sight dim, and through sickness my strength has failed, so that I have not the vigor I had when I studied with teacher Mason; but my strength in God has not decreased in the least: pray for me

"The favor you have shown me, my dear friends, is exceedingly great. When teacher Mason and the teacheress returned to America, I told them the things I would like to have, and they procured the whole of them. They obtained for me black alpacca two suits, a white blanket, with many other articles of clothing, and a spy glass of the very best kind, besides a large quantity of medicine. I also received, through your kindness, a cloak from teacher Cross. But, brethren, we have received not worldly things of you merely, we have received spiritual things also, and forget you, can never. Though I cannot speak with you personally, yet my love and remembrance of you is uninterrupted, and I hope to be able to converse with you in the Kingdom of God, and associate with you eternally. My dear friends, the greatest favors you have shown us are sending us teachers and teacheresses who came and taught us the word of God, made books for us, taught us figures, and instructed us in the things of light.

"Through the power of God, may your towns and cities, your lands and waters, your kingdom and domain, your houses and dwellings, your plans and devices, your works and deeds be established, increased and perfected in goodness, happiness, and light, generation on generation for ever.

"Teacher QUALA,
"*July* 26*th*, 1857. A Son of the Forest."

In November Mrs. Mason writes, "We hear of new stations rising up in the Bghai and Paku regions, and the prospect in Toungoo is still very bright. Shwaygyeen is waking up, and we have had four embassies from that province bringing 'letters of introduction,' and desiring to join us in the national institute. We propose establishing a Young Men's Normal School to be conducted on the same principles as the female one, to be under my superintendence with the aid of native assistants, Dr. Mason giving lectures and taking the higher branches. We have now nearly one hundred letters or pledges to the support of the institution from the native churches.

"A few days ago, a young preacher came in on his way to the western Sgau region towards Prome. He had two other preachers with him and a train of five or six pupils, all going out to do battle with the powers of darkness. I asked him for his history, and he gave me the accompanying letter. Although there is nothing striking in it, it shows the *onward* and *upward* spirit of these young preachers. They were going out of their own free will without scrip or purse, and when I suggested they might be in want,—they answered: 'We go to work for God. When did He ever let his teachers die of hunger ?'

"'*Toungoo, November 6th*, 1857.

"My Dear Teacheress,

"'Blessings be with thee for ever!

"'You ask about myself. I will tell you. At first I lived in Bassein, I sought only worldly pleasures, and served the devil with a full heart. The Holy Spirit sent from heaven, stirred up my mind to study the sacred Scriptures, so that I could not rest. Then I went to Maulmain and studied a year; after which I heard of teacher Quala in Toungoo, and longed to come and help him. God enabled me to come to the Paku region to the people of Jauthadeu, where I remained and instructed them until one hundred believed and embraced the gospel. Then I thought to return and study more, but sickness prevented whenever I made the attempt, so I turned my thoughts to the unbelieving Sgaus in the west and went out to visit them. On returning from this tour, I concluded to return no more to Maulmain or Bassein, and wrote for permission to marry in Jauthadeu. Then I took a wife of the Paku tribe, and went out on another tour to the Sgaus. At this time one house believed and desired to learn so I left one of my pupils to instruct them, and returned to my people. Now, about twenty in that country believe, and they seem to me like my children, so I am now going again to visit, and encourage them. Pray for them, teacheress.—SAUKA.'"

At the annual association in January, 1858, Dr. Mason in writing from the Bghai mountains mentioned many interesting facts descriptive of the habits of the people, and their uncivilized state before the gospel subdues and corrects them.

"An incident occurred during the Paku association which illustrates the state of society among the Toungoo Karens better than could be done by a formal description. I was on the ground several days before the time of the meeting, and one afternoon I went up the mountain with my prismatic compass to take bearings. A village was pointed out to me in a recess of the mountains which had never been visited by a teacher. The people had declared they would spear the first teacher that appeared on their domains. The name of the village is Htie-thie-pu or 'the dried fountain.' While the meeting was in progress, a Bghai rushed hastily into my presence from a Christian village, saying that on Saturday, the day I was looking at the place, the people of Htie-thie-pu attacked their village, killed two, wounded four, and carried off ten into captivity. Our Deputy Commissioner, Captain D'Oyly, was with us the next day, and declared at once that he would punish them severely for the depredations. He had a dozen Europeans with him at a neighboring village, and after collecting a few Karens, he went and attacked the village, killed two men, burning and destroying every thing in the place.

"How interesting is it to see some of these notorious robbers and murderers brought under the sound of the gospel. A day's journey beyond the English boundary is a village, which, when Quala was there last January, was notorious for its depredations. In fact it was a band of robbers, and the chief was their captain. Many are the men they have killed, and the women and children they have carried into captivity. These people have within the year solicited and obtained a teacher, and there sat the brigand and forty of his followers at our meetings for several days, until their rice was exhausted. The chief is a fine looking man, and one of the last among the twelve hundred present that I should have judged capable of the deeds which are attributed to him. Of a widely different physiognomy was the chief of a village on the ledge of a precipice, seen from the place of assembly on the opposite side of the gorge. The village, as seen at some six miles distance, looks like an eagle's nest, with an immense precipice rising to it, and ascending above it. Tradition says, that some two hundred and fifty years ago, at the destruction of Pegu, a party of Talaing men fled from their own country, and took refuge on this rocky mountain side. Here they made friends with the Karens, took Karen wives, and their descendants have nothing to distinguish themselves from their Karen neighbors, but the ability to make an old fashioned species of earthenware. Their habits of committing robbery and murder are as thoroughly Karen as their language, which does not retain a trace of the Talaing. Some two years ago, two unfortunate trading Burmans ventured too far with their wares into the Karen community, and being met by a party from this village, they were considered a lawful prize, killed and despoiled of their wares. Mr. O'Riley, being informed of the outrage, undertook to bring the guilty party to justice, but that could not be done by direct means; so the chief of the next village was engaged to ferret out the offenders. He succeeded in ascertaining who the actual murderers were, and by coaxing and promising to make himself responsible for the lives of the men, he succeeded in persuading the murderers and a large party of others to start on a visit to Mr. O'Riley, but on the way they began to suspect treachery, and all ran away except two, who were secured; one was guilty but the other was innocent. These two men were put in jail in Toungoo, and I think, but am not certain, that they were both tried and found guilty. Be that as it may, the Government in Calcutta were asked if these men should suffer death according to the English law; the response was; No, that they were ignorant men not knowing the guilt of their crimes, and that they should therefore be dismissed with a rebuke. But in this the Government showed ignorance, for a Karen says that blood should be shed for blood, and he never allows a homicide to pass unrevenged, if possible, though the person may have been slain by accident. Just as the order for the release of the prisoners arrived, they were both taken with cholera and died in jail the same night. The village to which they belonged had now their death to avenge as much as if they had been hanged; and when Mr. O'Riley passed near their village, they determined that his life should pay the forfeit; and they would have speared him while sleeping in his tent, had not the elephants created a disturbance which awoke him and his people. Being defeated here, they turned on the neighboring chief that had assisted in bringing the criminals to justice, first robbing him and finally spearing to death his daughter, as she went down to the brook to draw water; but of the murder there is no direct evidence, though no one doubts who the authors were. The chief is a very bad looking old man, but for more than a week, during which we usually had four meetings a day, that man was never missing from the assembly. In our early prayer-meetings when we often came together before there was light enough to see to read, he was always there before I was. I watched him closely, knowing his history, and though I cannot believe him a converted man, I must regard him as one with whom the Spirit of God is striving. When I conversed with him personally, he replied to my remark, ' If you are a follower of Christ, you must love your enemies.' ' Yes, I love my enemies as myself.' Time will test his character."

We add an account of the first ordination in this remarkable province. It was in February, 1858.

"The first ordination in Toungoo occurred this morning where the Karens have lived independent of all Governments, Burmese, Talaing, or Shan, from time immemorial.

"A Council was convened of which Quala was appointed Moderator, and Shapau Scribe ; when after prayer, the Council examined the candidate Pwaipau, on his religious experience, call to the ministry, and views of doctrine ; which, proving satisfactory, it was unanimously voted to proceed to his ordination. The order of exercises was as follows : reading of the Scriptures by Ahtso ; prayer by Waleuhtie ; sermon by Shapau; ordaining prayer by Quala ; hand of fellowship by Dr. Mason of Toungoo; charge by Diepo ; benediction by the candidate. Pwaipau belongs to Tavoy and was a member of my theological class, when I made over the school to Mr. Cross, under whom he finished his education. When I put forth the Macedonian cry for Toungoo, he volunteered for the work and accompanied Quala when he came up and joined me. He assisted Mrs. Mason in her Normal school till we left, when he removed to Klenla in the centre of the Pakus country where he soon had a self-supporting school of one hundred pupils. Klenla has been his home ever since; but he has constantly itinerated, from the Manniepgha country on the west to the eastern boundary of the province, and beyond, into the independent Karen districts bordering on the Red Karens, and supplying the new stations that he founded with teachers from his own school. His field of labor embraces about one hundred villages, and his ordination effects no change in his circumstances beyond that of authorizing him to administer the ordinances. God has made him a bishop, and we in ordaining him have only said, AMEN."

Dr. Mason further wrote:

"No feature of the work among the Karens seems to me so full of promise as the eagerness with which the young preachers seek for information on biblical subjects. During the three or four weeks spent with our associations, whenever I sat down to eat, there were always, more or less, around me some who were seeking information on difficult passages, and when I strolled into the forest at evening, a long peripatetic train questioned me at every step. Sometimes I would seat myself to rest on a granite rock overtopping the plains thousands of feet below, when all around would quickly seat themselves, a crowd of young men with their open Testaments, each eager to ask me concerning some passage or another that he found difficult to comprehend. One desires me to explain Paul's remark, 'For me to live is Christ, but to die is gain:' another, the expression, 'I am crucified unto the world, and the world is crucified unto me.' A third finds it difficult to understand, 'I could wish myself accursed from Christ;' and a fourth cannot comprehend our Lord's language in relation to John the Baptist; while still another is perplexed with Peter's statement that 'David has not ascended into heaven,' 'David who wrote the Psalms, he observed, 'has surely gone to heaven! Were there two

Davids?' Some have chronological difficulties to settle; others ask for historical information, and others still have numerous inquiries to make on the natural productions of the Bible; while not a few have questions to ask that Gabriel could not answer. Thus a single lecture is diversified, like mosaic work, with theology and botany, exegesis and zoology, metaphysics and lightning wires, history, sacred and profane, geography, ancient and modern, with a sprinkling of almost every other subject of the past, the present, and the future. Often after lying down to sleep, I hear the young teachers inquiring of their seniors, the signification of various passages, and asking information on numerous topics on which they have been instructed. In this way the knowledge communicated to one is passed on to tens, twenties, and thirties; and my school of theology is as wide as the province, and its pupils as numerous as the students within its borders. Many in this anomalous way, without pausing in their labors, learn more than those immured for years within brick walls, who complete a curriculum under half a dozen professors; and it is an undeniable fact that when we need a man to go to a station where there is real self-denial to be endured, it is not the man who has had a regular course of instruction who goes, but one of this irregular corps. These are the men that occupy all our new stations, the very out-posts of Christ's kingdom, and these are the men whose labors God pre-eminently blesses. They are the cream of the churches, rising by the law of moral power, a law as immutable as the law of gravitation."

Shapau was also ordained and afterwards we had the following account of his first baptisms.

"Shapau accompanied by Quala has just made the circuit of the principal Bghai and Mopgha villages. He has baptized one hundred and nine persons, laid the foundations of four new churches, and established one new station. In one Bghai church seven were suspended; one Mopgha church was found still in the use of charms; and two or three Bghai churches had difficulties with each other, concerning the boundaries of their lands. With these exceptions, and we have not yet reached the period in the history of the church when such exceptions are not to be anticipated, the work progresses both in depth and surface. One church among the Mopghas lately purchased between twenty and thirty New Testaments in addition to their former stock, after contributing seventy rupees in cash for educational purposes; while they were sending their men by twenties and thirties to work on the school buildings and grounds. The Bghais are by far the poorest of our people, living as they do without any permanent cultivation, in a much wilder state than the other tribes; yet when they get money to purchase a copy of Matthew in their own language, they almost universally prefer to pay half a rupee for a bound copy, to a quarter of a rupee for one in paper covers : 'Because,' they say, 'it will last longer.'

"Still the prospect of 'the regions beyond' saddens the heart. Quala writing from one of our most northern stations says; 'The people have here recently professed faith in Christ. How numerous the impenitent are around them, it is impossible to say. I went up to the top of mount Leu Kentha and looked to the south, the north, and the west; and there were visible fields and villages as far as the eye could reach, and none of them have ever heard the word of God. They are men of contention, spearing those who offend them, regardless of law, yet were they to hear the word of God, they would be subdued without difficulty. Children of God, what shall we do? They are all wild Bghais, and when I look around upon them, the language of our Lord

Jesus Christ is suggested : ' The harvest is plenteous, but the laborers are few.'

" ' he gad flies here bite dreadfully, and the mountains are piled up ridge upon ridge, one above another, exceedingly high. Pray for us that we may have strength given us to do the work of God fully and thoroughly.'

" A few days afterwards he writes from another village : ' These also are wild Bghais. They pay no taxes, permit no Government to rule over them, and know very little of God. Still they have a zayat with a teacher, and we have hope for their conversion hereafter ; for God is able, and, having commenced the work, he will carry it on till completed. Let us then rejoice and pray fervently with glad hearts.' "

During the time Dr. Mason was attending the association, Mrs. Mason finding that the Karens experienced great difficulty in getting down the timber from the jungle, determined to visit them, and to assist them with superintendence and advice, as well as with sympathy and encouragement. Her presence seems to have produced the happiest results ; frequent hindrances had arisen, from one chief refusing to obey another chief, one clan or tribe another tribe ; but these difficulties appear to have vanished under her influence. Every evening they met for united prayer and reading of the word of God, and made the silent forest resound with songs of praise.

The following is a sketch of one of the Sabbaths spent amongst one of the tribes, and re-introduces to us the Taubeah chief who visited Mrs. Mason in Toungoo in 1853. She writes :

" Last Sunday I assembled with the Wethaduies on the Mopgha mountains, and had a very pleasant interview. I was in a bamboo tent only a few miles from the village, and could not refuse their earnest solicitations, so climbed up the mountains. We started with an elephant, but found the path so very steep and rough, I sent it back. The path led over three sharp alpine-like peaks and through as many deep glens, then out gushed broad sunlight over an immense open paddy-field, with here and there a wee bit of a shanty, and I began to congratulate myself on finding a resting spot again, when I chanced to look forward, and, lo, there were the boys who carried my little bundle away on the tip top of another cliff almost as far as the eye could reach. I had been quite ill the night before with fever, and was far too weak for such a jaunt, but it was useless to look back when once started; and besides we could not look downward without clinging to the bamboos, or we should have gone to the very deeps. So we went plodding on, and even after reaching the narrow opening up in the sky, by clinging to the roots, rocks, and whatever could help us, still no house appeared, nor the slightest vestige of any village, but following our guide we wound along over the sides of the hill down, down, down, and were about to step off into a ravine as black as night, when a dozen hands were raised and a whole flood of mountain music burst up the ravine, and held us spell-bound! It was a little congregation, yet far distant, at prayer, and singing

> 'Rock of ages, cleft for me.'

"We stayed our steps and listened with emotions indescribable, glancing over the whole history of the past four years in almost as many minutes, until lost in bewildering joy; for well do I recollect the first visit of these Taubeahs to our house, and the man who came 'to see if Jesus Christ was in Toungoo, or Maulmain, or Bengal,' and who, when I told him he had gone to heaven, would not stop a moment, but grasped his bamboo spear and stalked away. Now he came smiling down the glen to meet me, his babe in a blanket upon his back, for me to *bless!* And on reaching the house, every mother to the number of a hundred, I should think, brought forth their infants for me to lay my hand upon their heads. I did not know what to do, whether to gratify them, or refuse, for it seemed fearful to think of standing in the place of our blessed Redeemer. However I patted their little heads and shook hands with some four hundred, then went into the chapel, and explained to them who alone could bless them and their little ones. The whole village consists of one house only, besides the chapel and teacher's residence. Imagine a house some four hundred feet long, and thirty wide, divided into some thirty rooms; then another house parallel, just separated by a verandah three feet broad; then still another parallel, separated by a verandah just the same, and all three alike, except the central row which is some ten feet shorter at each end, leaving an open court in the front and a space for work behind. This central row belongs to the chief and his relations, and he holds his court in the first hall. Each room has its little bed-rooms just large enough to stretch oneself in, with cooking box and all manner of jungle apparatus, while beneath each room is a pig-sty, walled up with bamboos to the floor, which is about six or eight feet from the ground. There are three separate roofs to the building, and under the eaves extend long bamboo spouts. This constitutes the village of Wethadue, the largest village of the Mopgha tribe of Karens.

"I found forty boys and girls in this village who could read very well and repeat the catechism by heart. Several of them have been baptized."

On her return from the jungle, Mrs. Mason wrote: "I felt very sad about spending time in the jungle traversing pathless mountains and glens in search of timber, but now I see the hand of God leading me onward, for in no other way could I have come so near to the hearts of the people, or been made acquainted with their individual characters. Now I know whom to trust, and how each can be made most useful.

"It was one of the most interesting nights I ever spent, when we encamped at the mouth of the river, after three months of hard toil, six weeks of which I had spent with them, teaching them to make roads and drag logs up the mountains. Now there lie the logs strung to bamboos filling the river.

"A hundred Karens were stretched round six or eight camp fires, covering the long sand bank just below my tent, which was pitched on the overhanging cliff. The full moon was rising behind the trees, its soft light shining upon the waters, and lighting up the dark faces of the Karens. We all knelt down and poured out our hearts in grateful praise, and after singing a hymn, I got into my little boat and came down to the city, reaching home at midnight.

"I am thankful that I was able to be with them for it cheered them not a little, taught them to think and reason more correctly, and through God's mercy prevented much sickness. During the last week many have come in to see the logs and look upon them with great delight and satisfaction. No doubt it will be far better for the people that they have had to work hard for the timber, for had I purchased it, they would never have valued it half so much. Now they are pouring down to settle round the Institute, and thirty houses are already erected, and four streets are regularly laid out."

Finding that the Burmese and Karen girls would not amalgamate, a house was secured for a Burmese school on the city side of the river. Every night Bible classes were held with the workers on the land. One evening the subject had been the two great commandments, and as Mrs. Mason was returning home afterwards, a wild looking Karen met her on the steps and said, " I wonder, teacheress, if I love God with all my strength. The chiefs say if we do, we shall *work for Him* with all our strength : I am thinking if I can do this." He wished Mrs. Mason to supply his men with rice or even paddy, and ten men would remain and work a week at the buildings, buying their own curry. Mrs. Mason was obliged to tell him she could not do this, but after discussing the matter with his men he finally came back and said they would go home, and make some baskets, and bring them down, and buy for themselves. This they did, and soon returned with their heads loaded with baskets, to sell for their support while building a school house for their nation. These men were from the Bghai mountains, wild and uncivilized, but who will say they cannot be taught patriotism? Mrs. Mason says, " One of our Karen board of managers thought the other day we ought to have more hands at work, so calling for a writer he sent off letters in all directions, and in three days we had fifty more men here putting up the dormitories, all feeding themselves and working like men. All brought letters from their teachers saying how many had come, from which I learned that those who remained at home contributed areca nuts, rice, fish, and all sorts of things for those who came.

"It is most pleasing to see the interest felt in making our new town a holy place. Every one brings a letter of introduction, and has to pass through the ordeal of criticism; as the chiefs are called on to state what they know of every one, so that it is not easy for a bad or lazy person to get into our little community. Every one gives a pledge that he will not be idle, and we have put up a large board at the entrance of our highway, on which is written in large letters :—

'*No idlers here.*'

"Each one who lives or stops to rest here, is compelled to attend worship every night.

"One of the Board examines all on the place on Saturdays, and brings me a report which is read on the Sabbath. But what encourages me not a little is to see the pig-pens vanish. Last year the two men who first settled here put up pig-pens right under their doors, according to their custom. I mentioned to the Nah Khan, the Commissioner's agent, how offensive it was, and that hereafter we would not have them. 'O Mamma,' he exclaimed, 'if you do so, not a single one will live here.' So I let it pass, and the pens have remained just six months. A few weeks ago when they were building new houses I spoke of it in the chapel, and that it would grieve me to see them. The next morning, away went the pig-pens, and every yard was swept neatly. It has become a custom for every follower of Christ's law to come forward and give his hand, which is saying, 'I am with you;' but they have, for all this four years, been in the habit of giving their hands, just as they chance to be, covered with earth or lime, or anything else. Last year I did not dare to speak of it, but now they know me all over the jungles as a friend, and so I am trying gently to change that, by telling all to lay off their loads, go to the river, and wash and put up their hair, then I shall know who they are. A few have walked off, Bghais, who are the filthiest people I am sure in the world, but generally now they rush for the river before coming to give the hand. All this I trust will have more or less effect upon their hearts, and lead them to more watchfulness.

"Then again our village school will I expect become a model for all the Paku, Mopgha, Bghai, Sgau, and Red Karen villages. It numbers forty pupils, some young women, and it is such a pleasure to look in and see them every morning with clean hands and faces and neatly dressed hair. Many have got new dresses, and the little looms are cropping out in every direction, and yarn, and dyeing even, among those who are encamped on the ground, their houses being yet unbuilt. This shows that they are getting some idea of whole and clean clothes, and of providing them for themselves, instead of looking to the missionary to give them. Besides, I am going to discourage foreign dress, and allow my girls to wear only their own manufacture. Their own cloth is very durable, and their own costume neat and pretty, except the men's gown, and even that looks well with the thin loose Shan pantaloons which many wear."

In the beginning of 1858, Dr. Mason in writing of the trials, hopes and present aspect of the Mission in Toungoo, gave the following condensed report.

"Though funds in America fail, God is with us, and if He has prepared a field for the seed and sent the sower into it, as he has done here, he will most assuredly send him tools to work with.

"I append the statistics of the Toungoo Mission, premising that the name of Christ was first proclaimed in the province in October, 1853, from which date the mission commences.

    Associations . . . . . . . 2

*a.* The Paku Association, embracing Pakus and Manniep ghas.

*b.* The Bghai Association, including Bghais and Manniepghas.

    Stations . . . . . . . 101
    Churches . . . . . . 42
    Village schools . . . . . . 101
    Preachers and teachers (native) . . 103
    Ordained native preachers . . . . 3
    Pupils in village schools . . . . 2,420

| | |
|---|---:|
| Baptized in 1857 | 129 |
| Excluded | 7 |
| Suspended | 29 |
| Restored | 14 |
| Died | 66 |
| Present number | 2,640 |

"We have also a Karen Education Society, which was founded in 1857, and has in its charge two boarding schools, The National Female Institute, and a Young Men's Normal School, open to all the native tribes of Burmah. This society embraces eighty-six chiefs, who have sent in letters pledging themselves and thousands of their people to support permanently the Institute; except the teachers, who for the present are dependent upon friends in India, England and Scotland. The pledges are not yet all received for the Young Men's Normal School, but it is confidently expected that they will assume the responsibility of carrying it on, as they have the girl's school.

"The Female Institute was opened in May 1857, and numbered during the first session twenty-four pupils, besides nine that were sent back to the jungles for the want of room. These include Sgaus, Pakus, Manniepghas, Mopghas, Bghais, and two Burmese. None are received under twelve years of age, none for a less period than one year, and all are taught in their own vernacular tongues. The studies embrace reading, writing, geography, history, mathematics, something of natural philosophy, physiology, and the Holy Scriptures, with plain sewing, cooking, washing, and general cleanliness; together with nursing the sick, and training children. There is also an ornamental department, intended principally for the Burmese and Shans, which no one is allowed to enter till she can read and write well in her own language. This school is entirely in the charge of Mrs. Mason, aided by four native assistants, but a young lady is expected from the United States in the present year to assist in the Burmese and Shan department.

"The Young Men's Normal School commences with the approaching rains, and will be limited, like the female school, to fifty pupils. It will be instructed in Biblical exercises, mathematics, philosophy, and practical land-surveying by myself, but in all minor branches by native teachers. This school is on the grounds of the Institute, and the boarding and all the other financial matters are in the hands of Mrs. Mason. For this department the chiefs have built a large bamboo school-house, and a boarding-house of one hundred and fifty feet by fifteen, also a good house for the teacher, the first with a wooden frame and floor ever built by the Karens of Toungoo.

"For these schools the Karens here contributed—

- 970 Rupees in cash,
- 1 Elephant,
- 3 Goats,
- 4 Pigs,
- 170 Fowls,
- 200 Eggs,
- 65 Mats,
- 15 Baskets,
- 12 Large chopping knives,
- 150 Long ratans
- 10 Large bundles of bark rope,
- 1580 Large bamboos,
- 2000 Small "
- 1 Boat,

"They have also felled and brought to town fifty teak logs, six cubits by thirty, given by Government for the school-building, and eighty iron-wood posts, some of them very valuable, fifty feet in length. This is a very remarkable performance for mountaineers, since, though wholly unacquainted with the water and unable to swim, and knowing nothing of the timber business, they brought them down a large stream and then several miles down the Sitang. They have also built twelve bamboo houses for families to live in as a protection to the Institute, and are now making four streets in a village of thirty houses growing up around the grounds. The Indian Government has liberally granted thirty-two acres of land to the Institute lying upon the Sitang river, and 1400 rupees for the buildings. The Calcutta Tract Society has given books to the value of 100 rupees and a valuable set of illustrative prints. A publishing house in Philadelphia has sent us a set of large outline-maps; and friends in Calcutta an excellent prismatic compass. All the land, buildings, apparatus, furniture, and everything pertaining to these schools is the property of the Karen Education Society, which held a convention in August, 1857, and chose a band of managers, consisting of one Paku, one Manniepgha, one Mopgha, one Tunic Bghai; Capt. Doyly, Deputy Commissioner, Toungoo, agreeing to act as President. The whole is entirely independent of every missionary association."

## CHAPTER XIV.

### THE CONCLUSION.

*" Who knoweth not in all these, that the hand of the Lord hath wrought this ?"—JOB xii. 9.*

A GLANCE at the various other stations must conclude these sketches. Never were the prospects of the mission, generally, brighter than now, and never were the missionaries laboring more earnestly in their calling. Differences of sentiment, however, have divided them, and no longer are they all connected with the same Missionary Union in America.

When Dr. Judson was at Serampore in 1811, he adopted the sentiments of the Baptist churches, and his connexion with the Board of Commissioners for Foreign Missions terminated. He went forward to Burmah, not knowing whether the Baptists in America would form a Missionary Society or not. The Serampore Missionaries, however, supported him, and ere long the American Baptist Missionary Union was established. It was by that Board that the mission in Burmah was maintained till recently. In 1853, a deputation from the Union visited Burmah, and eventually some differences arose respecting the measures then adopted, and the reports subsequently made in America; the result of which is that Mrs. Vinton, Mr. Brayton, Mr. Beecher, and Mr. Harris are now in connexion with the " American Baptist Free Mission Society." Mr. Kincaid occupies an independent position. On the other hand Dr. Wade, Dr. Mason, Mr.

Thomas, and others, continue their former relation to the Missionary Union. It is not needful or desirable to enter further into this subject. St. Bernard's sweet saying, "It will be one of the felicities of heaven that the saints shall no longer misunderstand one another," must be our comfort, when here on earth we see no present prospect of reconciliation. Happily the differences of opinion among real Christians generally do not appear so wide as once they were, and the greater part, with the late beloved Bishop of Calcutta, Daniel Wilson, can rejoice that " we no longer maintain the old and fatal mistake that Christian men are not to co-operate in anything till they are agreed in everything. We now hold the antagonistic and true maxim, that Christians should act together so far as they are agreed." May this ever be the rule in Burmah, in America, and in every land where Jesus reigns in the hearts of men as the Prince of peace! We shall now proceed to a review of the different stations.

### Tavoy.

In the year 1857, we find at Tavoy in the Karen department, Mr. and Mrs. Cross, and in the Burman part of the mission Mr. and Mrs. Allen. Mr. Cross, during the season, made extensive tours among the churches in the jungle. He found them in various conditions; some declining, others flourishing like watered gardens. At Pyeekhya more especially every thing was prospering, and the little flock appeared like a well organized Christian body, full of intelligence, and walking in the fear of God.

The pastors of the churches are mentioned by Mr. Cross as being "men fully consecrated to the Lord, submitting to much self-denial, for the privilege of preaching the gospel. They seldom obtain from their churches more than five or eight rupees a year, such is the great poverty in this province;

but they are content, and the spirit manifested by them when they heard that the American Mission was in difficulty was beyond all praise. Cheerfully they surrendered the small pittance they had been accustomed to receive from its funds and would have willingly given every man his coat also, had we asked it."

The following extract from Mr. Cross's journal is given as a specimen of the character of his labors during the past year.

"I have never been more encouraged than I am now by the stir among the heathen, and the new spirit which seems to be awakened among them. I trust it will not be long before better days will come for us in this region

"The deacon of a little church, with their preacher, accompanied me on this tour, and surprised me by the power of his arguments to convince the ungodly of their sins, and to rout them from their strong-holds of superstition and error. On one occasion a man who seemed to be much interested and who lingered after the sermon in the evening to converse presented one of the constant objections against the goodness and government of God, that He allowed men to sin, and had not so created them that they could not fall into evil. He said; 'Why did God create man with this liberty or possibility within him?' The old man replied, 'Ask me why God created fire, and your difficulty will be settled. Without this substance with all its qualities, who could be happy;— Who could live? Who could eat or breathe? See the coldness and death that would instantly take the place of life and warmth which now cheer the world. But over what are we obliged to maintain a stricter watch? You never leave your house without first ordering your children to be careful about fire; and when it rages, there is nothing so full of the power to inflict injury. What was evidently created for the greatest good becomes instantly the source of the greatest evil when it transcends its limits and is wrongly applied. Your liberty was created for good. Without it death takes the place of life, and coldness the place of warmth. But when your liberty is abused and misapplied, like the breaking out of fire, it riots in evil. But to check this evil all liberty must not be destroyed, any more than to save your house all fire must be extinguished from the earth. It must be put out only in the extreme, where it destroys. It is not to destroy fire, but to save a burning house, that efforts are made. Because of the nature of fire, many houses will needs be burned; yet without it no man would exist. So, because of liberty, many souls will be ruined; but without it, none would exist. Consider this illustration, and you need have no more difficulty about the question,—Why God has made man capable of sin.' Such was the old man's argument. It is worthy to be uttered by a philosopher of other pretensions than a simple Karen, whose only book has been his Bible.

"This man was one of the first of the Karens who heard the gospel in this province from Mr. Boardman. His language often is,—' None ever was or could be more wicked than I have been. There is no oath which I have not uttered, none of the Nats which I have not worshipped. With all this I was a drunkard. But when the teacher asked me, Will you repent and believe? I immediately said, 'Teacher, yes.' I felt that there was no other way to be saved from my sins. And I did not wait to break off from them by my own strength; but I cast myself upon Christ—and He has saved me. I am now happy. I do not fear death. I say, "Let death come when God shall send it."' Such a mind as this, and such faith, exist in a body covered with rags, and of so inferior personal appearance that the man would be taken by a stranger to be even below the majority of his degraded and filthy race. Yet the depth and originality of his ideas in regard to the gospel seem almost to border upon inspiration. His religion is not merely for the Sabbath. He says, 'I can do nothing without prayer. When I go to my field, before I begin my work, I stop and lift up my heart to God, and say, "O God, drive all evil from this place. Let no lurking beast of prey or evil temptation come nigh me while I am at work, and let the work of my hands be blessed. Let the field which I am now to cut for my rice, be fruitful." When I have thus prayed, I feel happy and cheerful to begin my work, and believe that God will defend me and bless me."'

Mr. Allen's labors were confined entirely to the Burmans, and in his tours this year he seems to have found the people very accessible. The influence of the priesthood seems also to be dying out. He writes:

"Formerly there were six, ten, or twenty priests in every village. Now nearly half of the villages have none at all, and but few have more than two or three. It is almost impossible for parents to keep their sons in the kyoungs. To do this at all they have to take them from their own villages, transport them across the river, and place them in a kyoung on the opposite side where they are strangers. Even then, they will run away and leave the kyoungs. This is an encouraging feature in one respect. When the priests all leave the kyoungs, the people will be more free to think and inquire; and I cannot but believe that they will be more anxious for religious schools and school teachers. Yet one thing is certain;—without the Spirit of God shed upon us and them they will never become true Christians."

The following sketch of a visit to a Burman village is interesting: "In the morning, after trying to tell the people of the two houses of Enga-wendwin how they might be saved, I started for a village a mile or two below. I preached to all I met on the way; some three or four houses being scattered along under the mountain, whose very base was washed by the ocean. On arriving at the village called Kyoung-nee-man, I was much struck by its beauty. It is situated on an elevation which overlooks the sea, and where at all seasons of the year, can be inhaled the bracing breezes of the Indian Ocean.

"The people were no less cordial than their village was lovely. I was at once invited to a house, which was soon filled with listening hearers. After discoursing to them for more than an hour without a word of opposition, I stopped and asked them if they had understood what I had been telling them. They said they understood all. They then invited me to come and lodge in the kyoung, saying that their priests had all left. To this I, of course, readily consented.

"After breakfast, and the tide serving, having walked back to the upper village, we put our goods into the boat, and descending to Kyoung-nee-man, moored our bark at the foot of the hill and placed our effects in the kyoung. Here we remained two nights. I never had more attentive listeners than at this village. They all assented to the reasonableness of the gospel, but they were not quite ready to receive it. The kyoung in which we stopped, like all kyoungs, had a great quantity of idols. I proposed to the people to throw these idols into the jungle, saying, if the idols would return of their own accord I would also worship them; but if not, the people should forsake them, and worship the eternal God. To this they would not consent. Still, on leaving the village, I could not but feel that the time is not far distant when these villages will receive the gospel."

## MAULMAIN.

At Maulmain Dr. and Mrs. Wade continue to conduct the Karen Theological Seminary. When the school was re-organized in 1858, Dr. Wade found but fourteen pupils; the number, however, gradually increased to about fifty, while their piety as well as the proficiency in their studies gave him great satisfaction. During the three months' vacation the young men used to go out preaching or teaching in distant Karen villages. Mrs. Wade writes: "The school has continued to increase in interest to the present time; a good number of young men have finished their three years' course of study, and have gone forth to the 'fields white for the harvest,' while new classes have taken their places. The preaching talent of these young Karens, their ardent desire for biblical knowledge, and wish to enter the ministry (though they have no worldly prospects beyond such as the Karen churches can give them,) seem to us quite as remarkable as the conversion to God of so many of their countrymen.

The school was for a time in some difficulty from the want of funds, but we have reason to believe this obstacle was soon, in some measure, removed; and it is interesting to find Dr. and Mrs. Wade still pursuing their patient labors on to the close of their long and useful lives. Mrs. Wade recently wrote:

"If we have been enabled to labor faithfully, and with some degree in success, for more than thirty years, in this good work to which the Lord called us, we attribute much to the encouragement we have ever received from the friends we left behind, and especially to their prayers. And now that our poor labors are nearly finished, we look forward with sure and humble hope to those bright mansions where, through grace alone, we expect soon to rejoice together with these precious children whom the Lord has given us in this dark land.

'Better than daughters, or than sons,
Temples divine, of living stones,
Inscribed with Jesus' name.'

"I feel it a great mercy, a most undeserved blessing, that the physical, and especially the nervous debility, induced by a long residence in this hot climate, is seldom permitted to dim the fair prospect of heavenly glory. As I approach nearer and nearer the 'dark waters,' the mild light from the other side shines more and more upon my pathway. My courage may fail when called to go over; but Christ will not fail the soul which trusts humbly, penitently, and believingly, in his rich, free grace."

A new arrangement has lately been made for the Theological Seminary. Dr. Binney, who formerly for some years conducted it in Maulmain with great ability, is now returning from America to resume his charge. The school will be established at Rangoon, and Dr. Wade in the evening of his days will be relieved of a large part of his arduous duty.

Mr. Hibbard is in charge of the Karen churches round Maulmain. They were in trial from the effort to introduce the self-supporting system, which was considered to be essential to permanency and strength. Notwithstanding their difficulties, every pastor remained at his post, the richer churches contributing to assist their poorer brethren; while several of the pastors worked with their own hands a part of the time to help to support their families, while ministering to the little flock over which the Holy Ghost had made them overseers. Schools also have been established in some of the larger villages, in which their children are taught to read, supported entirely by themselves. "Thus," wrote Mr. Hibbard, "I feel confident that these churches will live; they are trees of our Heavenly Father's planting."

Mr. Bennett superintends the printing department, while Mr. Haswell still labors among the Burmans and Talaings at Maulmain, with occasional visits to Amherst and the out-stations.

## SHWAYGYEEN.

At Shwaygyeen, deprived of the succor of Mr. Harris, Mr. Watrous, since the end of 1856, has been laboring alone, but the blessing of the Lord has been with him, and thus "judgment has dwelt in the wilderness, and righteousness remained in the fruitful field." Ere long Mr. Harris hopes to return to the midst of this interesting people.

## BASSEIN.

We have had occasion before to refer to the Bassein Mission. Mr. Van Meter, after laboring there for some years, has been obliged to return to America for a time, but he has left the impress of his labors behind him. Mr. Beecher, after a visit to his native land, again resumed his work among the Karens of Bassein in the beginning of 1857. In February of that year he wrote the following interesting account of one of their meetings:

"The churches of this mission have just held another annual, or Associational Meeting. The exercises of the meeting commenced on Thursday, A.M. the 26th of January, and closed on the Sabbath evening following.

"Mauyay, one of the ordained pastors, was chosen Moderator, and Thahree, an intelligent young pastor, was appointed secretary.

"Zoepoe and Pokyan, head teachers of two more advanced village schools, were appointed assistant secretaries.

"Mr. and Mrs. Vinton of the Rangoon Karen Mission were present by the special invitation of the Karens, and Mr. Thomas of the Henthadah Mission by the direction of the Executive Committee of the Missionary Union. Their presence added much interest to the exercises of the occasion. After the preliminary services, the first important business was the reading of the letters of the churches. More than fifty churches, comprising a membership of 5345 persons, were represented by letters and delegates.

"It was just ten years since I attended, for the first time, the associational meeting of these churches. How great and how gratifying the progress which has been made in this short period is indicated in the contrast between the character and contents of the letters presented then, and those read on this occasion, or perhaps I should rather say in the contrast between the almost entire lack of anything like regular reports from the churches by letter or delegates then, and the carefully prepared and comprehensive letters read at this meeting!

"Then, too, the preachers came to receive aid from the missionary, and had much to say about their poverty and trials, and were for several years accustomed to receive through the missionaries from three to seven hundred rupees. Now, the letters report that the churches, besides giving their pastors from seventy-five to two hundred baskets of paddy each, contributed various other articles of food and clothing, and have altogether paid their pastors in money during the past year more than 1400 rupees. Besides this, they have unitedly contributed more than nine hundred rupees to the funds of their Home Mission Society; given to the poor, 173 rs.; expended in erecting chapels, over 800 rs.; paid their school teachers 901 rs.; and contributed about 100 rs. to aid me in erecting mission buildings. The whole amount of what they have expended in the past year for religious and educational purposes exceeds six thousand rupees.

"In the course of the meeting it was proposed that the churches should pay for, and hold as their property, the mission buildings which I am now erecting. Much zeal and determination was manifested by several of the leading pastors, to have more done for the education of their children in this province than is now being done for that purpose. Some were quite anxious that I should devote myself chiefly to this work; but when they saw that I could not do this without neglecting the churches, they conceived the project of calling another missionary from America who should devote himself wholly to this work, and whom they should support. All the pastors present were ready to vote in favor of the resolution, but thought it would involve such new and heavy responsibilities, that it would not be prudent to undertake it without consulting with their churches, from whom the means of supporting such a missionary must come. They concluded to consult with their churches, and separately inform me of their decisions at an early date. I have since heard from several of the feebler churches, that they have many misgivings about their ability to support such a school, and it is my impression that if they pay for the mission building this year it will be as much as they will be able to accomplish, if they carry forward all their other benevolent enterprises.

"The fact, however, that they have, entirely of their own accord, seriously proposed to call and support such a missionary or educator, is a most gratifying indication of the progress which they are making in Christian benevolence and enterprise, and is full of promise for their future stability and instrumentality in evangelizing their own and surrounding races.

"The Home Missionary Society appointed five young men to accompany Mr. Kincaid to Ava, and to proceed from thence as Providence shall seem to open their way to preach the gospel to the heathen Karens in the 'regions beyond.'"

In April 1857 a most terrific cyclone swept over the entire province of Bassein, leaving whole villages and cities in ruins. The Christian Karens, besides having their houses and chapels injured, and much of their paddy destroyed, had many of their books completely spoiled. This loss was the more serious, as some of the books, the Karen Bible especially, were out of print. Mrs. Beecher refers to this want in the following letter. She writes:—

"I have been both gratified and surprised at the intelligence and desire for knowledge shown by two young women, who have come in from a village a very short time ago sunk in heathen degradation. They said they had studied the books of Moses, and I have been examining them in Genesis, and find that they not only remember very correctly and fully everything, but that they have a good general understanding of the facts; and not only so, but that they have some idea of types and of an inner significance, which is a very rare thing indeed. They understand my imperfect Karen very readily, and take notes of the references and explanations I give them. I never saw brighter, or more hopeful scholars, especially considering that they have never been with a missionary, but have only studied with their native pastor, whose own advantages have been very limited.

"But I should greatly mislead you, if I gave you an idea that these are at all fair representatives of the Karen women of Bassein. I have been greatly grieved and sometimes quite discouraged by their stupidity, ignorance, and absence of desire for knowledge. Multitudes of them cannot read at all, and *very few* read the Bible. Indeed, the most discouraging feature of the Karen mission here is the scarcity of Bibles, and the general absence of Bible reading among the people. Sometimes my heart sinks. How can they be holy, how can they grow in grace and avoid the institutions of the heathen, if they do not get the pure milk of the word?

I have been in villages, Christian villages, where there was not an entire Bible! They come to us to buy; but we have them not, and are obliged to send them empty and grieved away. But you know the course of human nature. The more the Bible is read, the more it is desired; and the less we read it, the less we care for it,—and so it is with these people just emerging from the lowest depths of degradation, —the deprivation of God's holy book to so great an extent, and the absence of an opportunity to become better acquainted with its truths through the missionary for several years, are already showing their sad fruits in many ways, and one of the most discouraging is an increasing indifference to the study of the Scriptures. There is great need of earnest prayer and effort lest this great and glorious work should decline. Many of the native pastors feel and lament this state of things, but the more ignorant and those who need instruction very much, seem quite indifferent about it.

"Will you not pray for us that God may revive his work here? And I do trust that Christians both in India and America will aid in providing God's holy word for these poor ignorant people, that they may be sanctified through the truth, and not relapse into the heathenism from which they have so lately escaped."

While Mr. and Mrs. Beecher were thus giving their attention to the Karens, Mr. Douglas was no less earnestly laboring for the good of the Burmans of Bassein. During the years 1857–58, he had been able uninterruptedly to pursue his work, especially in the jungles, visiting from village to village, preaching the gospel, and distributing tracts. In some of these villages his heart was cheered by many a listener, sometimes by a few inquirers, some of whom gave evidence of their faith in Christ, and love to his name. But the work amongst the Burmans here as elsewhere, is attended with difficulty, and as compared with that amongst the Karens the missionary meets with little encouragement. At the same time labor amongst them has been owned and blessed. God has shown mercy to some, and who shall despise the day of small things?

It has long been the opinion of some of the missionaries, that a large number of Karens, if not the body of the Karen nation, lived north of Ava. This impression had produced a strong desire on the part of some of the churches to send missionaries into that region. No steps, however, had been taken to this end until October, 1858, when at the meeting of the Karen ministerial conference, and Home Mission Society at Bassein, the subject was brought to the consideration of the native preachers. The meeting had been marked by a spirit of fervent prayer, unity, and love, and when the call for volunteers to go to the Karens north of Ava was made, many expressed a desire to go, but none were appointed until the following Sabbath evening. Mr. Douglas then asked if the Rev. Poe Quay was not the man. He appeared at first surprised, but after a little hesitation confessed that his mind had been filled with a strong desire for this work, and that he only wanted the concurrence of his brethren to believe it to be his duty to leave his church, his wife and his children, and to go forth as a herald of salvation to that vast region between Ava and Assam.

The concurrence of his brethren was cheerfully and promptly given, and Poe Quay and two other young men were at once appointed to the work. Mr. Beecher then addressed the Society on the important and serious responsibilities they had assumed, and reminded them that they must continue in persevering prayer, while they consecrated all they possessed to the service of God. More than one hundred rupees were then contributed by the Karens for the mission.

Poe Quay and his young associates will go two, three, or four hundred miles north of Ava, and after spending some months in exploring the field, and preaching, he will locate the young men in suitable places, and return to report not only upon their reception, but as to the number of the Karen population, and the dialects spoken. Poe Quay is a man, from his fine intellectual powers, education, eloquence, and devoted piety, well fitted for the work, and, with the blessing of God, it may not be less glorious in its results than Quala's at Toungoo. Mr. Douglas proposes accompanying the little embassy as far as Ava, and hopes not only to aid them in their mission, but to accomplish something amongst the Burmans also.

## HENTHADA.

At Henthada Mr. Thomas superintends the Karen mission. When he first went there in 1855, being able to speak the language of the people, he entered at once on a wide field, where the light of the gospel had not permanently shone. He took with him three native assistants, and was soon joined by as many more.

The first work was necessarily to preach the gospel to the heathen; for the Karens until they have made up their minds to become Christians, will not learn to read, nor will they permit a book to remain in their houses. During the first traveling season the missionary's work therefore was to proclaim the gospel, and that, " in season and out of season," whether they would hear, or whether they would forbear. In this tour Mr. Thomas went through many populous regions of Karens in the Henthada province, and penetrated at several points into the Tharrawaddy district, and not only preached Christ "where he had not been named," but stationed assistants in every place where the people were willing to receive them. Thus before the rains set in, in which season it is impossible to travel, many native helpers were at work among the people.

The work of assistants was two-fold. They preached from house to house and taught to read all who were desirous of learning. The first educational operations were thus commenced in the houses of these new converts. There the people learned to read and write in their own tongue. At the close of a few months a few were regarded worthy of receiving baptism. Then commenced the normal boarding school in the city. The first term of the school was composed of young men from those young converts, who could read and write, and some older Christian men from the borders of Bassein, whom Mr. Thomas hoped to make useful as preachers and teachers.

The next six months were passed by the missionary in town, almost daily preaching to the heathen visitors, but laboring more especially to train up a native ministry.

The second dry season passed as the first, except that there was here and there a little flock, which after its gathering, had to be tended, while the village schools became more systematic, and were removed from dwelling-houses into chapels. Before the second rains closed in, there were nearly three hundred baptized disciples in this and the Tharrawaddy districts, for God had poured out His Holy Spirit, and had made this wilderness to blossom as the rose.

From these disciples, a second normal school of about twenty was formed in the city. These were not mere boys, they were men, many of them married men, who a year and a half before, were in the depths of heathen darkness. The pupils were intent upon the object for which they came to the city, and the school was one in which Mr. Thomas felt a deep interest. Another dry season passed away, during which time, aided by twenty imperfect assistants, nearly the whole of the two provinces were visited, and many new stations formed or supplied with teachers. Thus the work progressed, and in July 1857, nearly six hundred disciples were formed into sixteen little flocks, widely scattered over these two districts. Principally from these churches have been chosen the present normal school of upwards of sixty pupils. This school embraces a large proportion of younger lads, who, it is hoped, will remain in the school many terms, and acquire a comparatively thorough education; but the elder pupils can remain in school but a short time, some of them having left their families and churches behind, while they study with the missionary one term. For the secular instruction of these youths two good assistants were employed, while the missionary devoted his time almost exclusively to teaching the Holy Scriptures to the whole school; upon him also devolved the "care of all the churches."

Thus notwithstanding the dark clouds of trial and pecuniary difficulty which have rolled over the mission, God has not left it without witness of his blessing, in souls redeemed, sanctified, and saved. At the meeting of the churches in 1858, in the Henthada and Tharrawaddy districts, it appeared that one hundred and fifty adult believers had been baptized; that eight new churches had been formed; that another man had been ordained to the work of the ministry; and that schools were in operation in connection with nearly all the churches. Thus in this new mission of about four years standing, there are thirty little churches with an aggregate of more than seven hundred believers. There are also a large number of those who worship with the Christians, but who have not yet been baptized; and there are not only native pastors and assistants in connection with all the flocks, but many who are endeavoring to raise up churches "in the regions beyond." On the very spot where, four years ago, the Burmans were cultivating their paddy fields at Henthada, there now stands the new modest dwelling of the missionary and his family. Associated with Mr. Thomas at Henthada is Mr. Crawley, who labors for the Burmans. Although, as we have before remarked, the success amongst them is not so great as with the Karens, yet the Lord has not withheld His blessing, but to the faithful labors of His servants does from time to time give them souls for their hire.

## Prome.

In the early part of 1858, Mr. Kincaid returned from America and proceeded to Prome, where he and Mr. Simons have been laboring with much success. In February 1858, Mr. Kincaid wrote : " Since reaching Burmah, I have been almost constantly in the country among the villages to the east and south-east of Prome. In thirteen villages we have baptized disciples, but I have visited and preached in over forty villages, seven of which were entirely Karen, the others Burman. I found many earnest inquirers, and some nine or ten who give evidence of saving faith in Christ, and will before long be baptized. A few days since I baptized a young Burman of great promise. For ten years he studied in one of the most celebrated schools in Ava, and then became the head of a monastery, built and sustained by the population of four villages. It was one of the largest establishments in this province. More than a year ago, he first heard the gospel from one of our native Christians: he ordered the man to be driven from the monastery, but not long after heard again, and then was more mild, and was smitten by the perseverance and kindliness of this Christian man. He took some small parts of the New Testament, and read and continued to read, and soon the light began to dawn upon his mind; he proclaimed to the priests under him, the wonderful truths revealed. Some months passed, and he began to see the inconsistency of his position, and boldly threw aside his priestly robes, and proclaimed himself a disciple of Christ. The people of those villages were amazed as they listened to the doctrines preached by this young man, before whom, for five years, they had bowed, and whom they had called their Lord and Master. He is profoundly taught in the principles of Buddhism; has a clear understanding, and speaks with great fluency and power; he is now living with one of our most distinguished native preachers, and is giving himself to the study of the New Testament. We trust he is raised up for some great and good work. In one of our Prome villages, nine have been baptized within a few days; in two Burman villages there are eleven candidates for baptism; seven Karens have been baptized, and six or seven more give evidence of faith in Christ. This people are found in great numbers in this province and further north along the eastern side of the Yoma mountains. In their traditions, manners, and customs, they are much like the Karens. I have not yet visited one half of our stations where the work has begun, but expect to do so before the rains begin. We have twelve native assistants, including one man at Ava, who are evangelists, and proclaim the gospel publicly, and from house to house. Some of them in the truest sense of the word are preachers, and all are fellow-laborers in the gospel. Besides these, we have two other men of great promise, who are now in their own localities spending all the time they can spare in going from house to house reading and teaching. It is only four years since the first blow was struck in this province; all was then unbroken heathenism. We have now seven Christian congregations widely separated, four Burman and three Karen, in many other cases we have one, two, and three converts in a place, indications of much fruit. After much thought and prayerful deliberation, Mr. Simons and I have resolved to dismiss none of our native laborers, even if obliged to effect a loan to meet the expense. The state of feeling in many parts of this district, both among Burmans and Karens, and I may add among the Khyens also, is very encouraging; there is a spirit of inquiry unusual, *especially* among the Burmans.

Mr. Simons, writing in August, 1858, gives the following interesting particulars. "Besides the three assistants at Thayet, six others are employed, three of whom give their services gratuitously in preaching occasionally, as lay-members do in Christian lands. There are also a few promising young men coming forward who are employed as school-teachers and colporteurs. We try to enlist into the service of doing good as many as we can. There was a female prayer-meeting at our house yesterday, and one of the females, of more than common intelligence, came to me for some tracts for a relative living some distance off; she did not want large books, but small tracts which they could easily read and understand, such as 'The Glad Tidings,' 'Investigation,' and 'Father's Advice,' also the 'Mother's Book.' We give tracts to all who wish them, and portions of Scripture, such as 'The Life of Christ,' 'Digest,' and Psalms, to the more intelligent of the applicants. The New Testament is given to individuals on their becoming members of the church, and the whole Bible in quarto form to the assistants who preach.

"A lay member, a farmer at Enmah, some distance from Prome, came to me some time ago, and said he wished to possess the whole Bible. I told him that as it was an expensive book, we gave it only to the preachers. He replied that he did not consider himself a preacher; but he could say that he could not live if he did not make known to his relatives what he knew of the religion of Jesus Christ : of course I gave him one. Two female relatives of his were baptized lately, and others are favorably disposed."

## Rangoon.

The work at Rangoon seems to have been uninterruptedly prospered since the time of the Annexation. Mr. Stevens, who has for long labored with such stedfastness in the Burman department of the mission both at Maulmain and subsequently at Rangoon, sent us the following interesting account of Moung-Thet-nau, one of the Burman preachers. He writes:

" Moung-Thet-nau I regard as an assistant of more than ordinary value, alike for the correctness of his Scriptural knowledge, his experimental acquaintance with divine truth, the practical turn of his mind, his commanding influence, and the apparent sincerity and fulness of his devotion to the work of the Lord—all which point him out to my mind as peculiarly fitted to sustain the pastoral relation. I was unusually interested in the account he gave me of his conversion, and as I have no doubt you will also be, I will give you the principal facts.

" He had heard of one of his friends intending to become a Christian. He visited him for the purpose of dissuading him from a step which, he represented, would bring disgrace on himself and his friends. That friend, as they commenced conversation, handing him a little tin box containing prepared lime used in chewing betel-nut, asked the question, whether that little box could have made itself? 'By no means,' was the reply. ' How then could this great world have come of itself?' The truth thus simply suggested, became like a barbed arrow in him. Night and day thinking of it he found no rest, because he could not tell whence came this world. At length, returning to his friend, he asked for a tract, yet dared not allow any of his acquaintances to see him with it, but sought a private room where he could read it unobserved. On opening the tract, the first words which met his eye were the first of Genesis, 'In the beginning God created the heavens and the earth.' They came as a flash of light upon his soul, and he was instantly absorbed in the thought. Then, said he, *God is first* and all things *from Him! That is the truth.* From that moment he was fully satisfied that the book of the missionaries was the true one. He immediately sought out the preacher, from whom he obtained a full account of Christ, which revealed to him the wonders of God's love. He received the gospel with all gladness, and without the least hesitation his resolution was at once taken to be baptized. For this purpose it was necessary for him to go to Akyab, as there was no missionary or native pastor in Ramree where he then resided. He told his wife of his intention; but as he knew it would be a terrible blow to her, added, that he would not subject her to the shame of being the wife of a Christian if she were determined not to be so; and gave her her choice, wishing her to decide within four days, when an opportunity offered for him to go to Akyab, whether she would remain with him or not. If she would consent to remain, he promised to be to her a faithful husband. If she chose to leave him he would put no obstacle in her way, allowing her to take all the property, he leaving with only the clothes he had on his back. She heard his proposition in silence and in tears. The fourth day at length arived, and not a word had she spoken in answer to his proposition, only showing by her tears the depth of her feelings; when he told her the time had come for him to leave, and he must know her decision. She answered she would not forsake him. With a light heart he left for Akyab, sought the house of the missionary, the late Mr. Ingalls, and immediately asked for baptism. Mr. Ingalls of course hesitated, and the suit was so earnestly pressed from day to day, that he thought the man must be actuated by some worldly motive, and it was not until a month had elapsed that, being satisfied of the sincerity of the candidate, and the reality of his conversion, he administered to him the ordinance. Moung-Thet-nau's subsequent course has corresponded, as far as I can learn, with the hopes excited by such an experience, and, as it seems to me, we may reasonably hope from him the usefulness which belongs to a consistent minister of the gospel. Such evident marks of the Spirit's work are peculiarly encouraging to our hearts, amid the general indifference and opposition of the Burmans to our message of love."

On the 31st March, 1858, the Karen mission at Rangoon sustained a severe loss in the death of Mr. Vinton, who for more than twenty-five years had devoted all the remarkable powers of his mind and body to the evangelization of this people. The first portion of his missionary life was spent at Maulmain and in the country round, and there he was greatly blessed in gathering many souls to Christ. He also made extensive evangelistic tours, and finally, after the war in 1852, proceeded to Rangoon, where in the first year he baptized no less than five hundred Karen believers. At Kemmendine, a suburb of Rangoon, Mr. Vinton formed a most interesting central Karen station; Mr. Brayton laboring with him for the Pwo Karens. Mrs. Vinton and Mrs. Brayton, assisted by native teachers, had a large school of nearly one thousand pupils, and during the rainy season, when prevented from itinerating, Mr. Vinton would instruct in his verandah a class of more than fifty young men in the Holy Scriptures, who at the close of the rains would go forth as teachers and evangelists in the villages around. In 1856, Mr. Vinton had, connected with this station, forty-two Karen churches, and Mr. Brayton four Pwo Karen churches; numbering about two thousand four hundred members; supporting thirty-nine native preachers, and thirty-six village schools; building their own school-houses and chapels; and contributing six hundred rupees a year to the Normal or High School at Kemmendine. And when the Missionary Board were in pecuniary difficulties, and means were wanting at home, the Karens came forward and voluntarily assumed the responsibilities which had been necessarily incurred for the erection of the dwelling-houses for the missionaries and school-houses for the children.

Mr. Vinton in writing home in March 1857, of the great Association meeting north of Shwaygyeen said: "The churches in this Association are included within very narrow limits, and embrace but a very small part of this great field. So, in the outset, it was in Rangoon and Bassein; and, I may add, so it is now.

" When the work first commenced, everything for a time, within a given limit, went with a rush. (It was different in Maulmain and Tavoy.) Beyond this limit, little was attempted for the conversion of the heathen for the next twenty years. On coming to Rangoon, I was surprised to find that the Christians occupied a district only some fifteen to twenty miles from north to south, and from thirty to forty miles from east to west.

" All beyond these limits was given up to the dominion of heathenism, and nothing was being attempted for the great masses that were pursuing their downward way to death. In 1850, it was the universal opinion that the Karen Mission had reached its culminating point. From 1852 to 1855, God was pleased to grant us great enlargement; three new districts were taken possession of in the name of the Lord; a large number of new churches constituted; and more than twelve hundred baptized. During the past year I am pained to say the native preachers have again shown a disposition to make themselves comfortable, and little has been done to advance the interests of the cause and save souls. This is the greatest trial of missionary life. The anguish of my spirit is so great, that if God does not send deliverance, I feel I cannot long survive, nor do I wish it, for if to live be not Christ, life itself becomes a burden. Since returning from Shwaygyeen we have attended the meetings of our two associations. Both meetings were blessed to some of our native preachers, I trust, and there appears to be a waking up; but whether the movement will prove permanent, remains to be seen. Of one thing I am confident, and that is that spasmodic religion will never convert the world. It is so unlike God, so unlike the primitive type of Christianity, and so ill-adapted to the present condition of the world. To-day heaven and hell are great realities, to-morrow mere fictions of imagination. To-day, knowing the terrors of the Lord, we persuade men; to-morrow say, 'Am I my brother's keeper?' and no man cares for his neighbor's soul. Nothing but the *continuous* out pouring of the Holy Spirit, and adding ' to the churches *daily* such as shall be saved,' will hasten the coming of the Redeemer's Kingdom.

"After the meeting of the Maubee Association, I prepared to cross the Yomah mountains, at a point a little north of Pegu; but my guide took me a long way to the north, and we crossed at a point midway between Shwaygyeen and Toungoo. The way for elephants was so difficult, that at one time we thought we should have to retrace our steps. I found, however, a large number of Karen villages that had never heard the first word on the subject of the Christian religion, and had never seen the face of a white man The Karens received us with the greatest cordiality; listened to everything we had to say with the greatest interest; and promised to receive teachers, build chapels, &c. . Here then is a new field of equal promise to those of Shwaygyeen and Toungoo, at the outset. Shall it be overlooked? I know of three other fields of equal promise, which I visited between 1836 and 1842, that are not yet occupied, because the means at our command have been unequal to the undertaking The prospect now is that we shall die before the work is half completed, and before this great field shall have even been half surveyed. ... At times I have seen the cloud as big as a man's hand, and have not doubted that the rain of grace would begin and that the latter would be more glorious than the former rain.

"I had written thus far when a letter from one of our young men, who is in the employ of the Superintendent of teak forests, and now on the mountains at the back of Prome, comes in saying; that the Karens upon those mountains are very numerous, have never heard anything on the subject of the Christian religion, listen with the greatest interest and are anxious to have teachers sent among them, &c. Here then is another field to be supplied. What is to be done? Are these Macedonian cries from so many parts of the Karen jungle never to be heard? Now that there is no part of the Karen world to which the gospel message has been sent, but thousands and tens of thousands have turned to the Lord; now that the occupancy of Shwaygyeen has resulted in the conversion of from one to two thousand, of Rangoon from two to three thousand, of Bassein from five to ten thousand, and an equal number at Toungoo; shall it be known in the Judgment, that not only the three fields brought to the notice of the Christian world in 1836, and following years, were long left uncultivated, but that these new openings were left disregarded? But language fails me. My hand is tremulous with emotion. My eyes run down with tears. My heart is full, and in the anguish of my soul I say; O God, how will Thy professing people answer to Thee for the loss of these tens of thousands of priceless souls, to whom thou hast sent messages of eternal love? What will they say when in the light of the Judgment, it is seen and known that each messenger of mercy sent, gathered from one thousand to five thousand precious souls into the garner of our dear Lord, and yet they refused to multiply the number of those heavenly messengers, and even refused to sustain those who are pouring out their life-blood in this more than angelic service?"

Such were the fervent aspirations of this man of God! Well might one of his brethren say of him, "We look around in vain for one to fill his place! He was a man of ardent piety, untiring zeal, great practical wisdom, and great physical energies, and as a successful preacher in the Karen language, he stood unrivalled." While another adds, "Who can take his place and do his work? No one man could do it, and there is not even one to spare from other fields."

We have the following letter from Mr. Kincaid, which gives an interesting description of his character and labors. 28th April, 1858; "On the 8th of this month I reached Thayet from Ava, and the first word uttered by the native Christians was, 'Teacher Vinton is dead!' The shock was so great I could hardly speak for more than an hour. As soon as I had rallied a little, I went off to the military cantonments and called on a pious officer to learn if indeed this was true. 'It is too true,' he replied, 'Major Wheeler has just come up from Rangoon and confirmed all.' That night I left for Prome, and the next day about noon arrived. Brother Simons and the disciples were deeply afflicted in view of this sad bereavement, but few particulars had yet reached Prome. Soon after a steamer came up having on board the Commissioner, Major Phayre, and several other officers. From them I learned many facts; all were at the funeral, some of them were present when he died. His death they said, was beautiful, so calm, so peaceful, so much like going home. Without a struggle or a sigh, he fell asleep. Such was the language of those who stood by and saw this man of God as the curtains of death were gathered slowly round him. A person in British Burmah has never died more deeply or universally lamented. As Major Phayre said, 'His death is a calamity to the country : who can supply his place in these provinces ?'

"His influence among the Karens was remarkable. In preaching he labored in season and out of season. He was exceeding zealous of the honor and glory of God, and hence his mind dwelt intensely on the ministry which God had given him to fulfil, to win souls to Christ; and not only to win them to a saving knowledge of Jesus Christ, but to lead them on to higher attainments in the divine life ; to make them feel and comprehend, that they were redeemed unto God for great and noble purposes to be fellow laborers with God. Beyond all other men I have ever known, he had the talent of winning the confidence and love of the natives. They saw that he had no interest separate from theirs. He prayed for them as few men can pray. He preached as few men can preach. His heart was in all he did. The sick, the afflicted, the oppressed, soon learned to seek his aid and counsel, and in him all found a friend, and if not relieved, went back comforted. His influence among the Karen Christians was wonderful. They saw that he willingly sacrificed all his great powers of body and mind to their temporal and spiritual interests, and they were ready to make any sacrifice for him. He was careful to deal justly and kindly with the natives, and hence among the heathen he was honored and revered. I have known him for twenty-three years, and every succeeding year has only increased my respect for the purity of his life and my admiration of his untiring devotion to the great work for which he came to this heathen land.

"All the gifts which God gave him were employed in evangelizing the heathen, and in planting and training Christian churches. Besides those he raised up in the Maulmain province, here in the Rangoon province are about forty churches planted through his labors. They are also raised to a state of efficiency, such as has rarely been equalled in modern times. The amount of labor which our departed brother has performed during the past six years, since he came to Rangoon in 1852, is amazing; and most of the time, under difficulties that few men could have endured. For six months he has travelled over a district as large as one of the New England States, without roads, amidst a people poor and ignorant. Now forty-two chapels and thirty school-houses have been opened; and between eight and nine thousand worshippers meet in these chapels every Lord's day. About one hundred pastors, evangelists, and school teachers, have been educated and trained for the work.

"The very means for travelling and for teaching have been raised in a large degree by his individual efforts. Imagine if you can, the amount of labor and privation to accomplish such a work, in such a climate, and under such circumstances. He has fallen as a noble general amidst the trophies of victory, and thousands of Karens weep around his grave. A large number are now beside me talking of their beloved teacher, some of them weeping because they will see his face no more.

"Just before sunset, I preached from Acts, 'In the last days, saith God, I will pour out of my Spirit upon all flesh.' We have had meetings every morning and evening for four days in this chapel. Four villages are in sight. Mrs. Vinton has had a female prayer-meeting in the middle of the day, above a hundred females and children present. O for a time of refreshment from the presence of the Lord! Mrs. Vinton will not leave the field of her husband's labors, and this in no small degree soothes the heart of this afflicted people. That this bereavement may be sanctified to us all, should be our earnest prayer. During brother Vinton's last tour he visited some new fields, and among others was on the mountains between the Line river and the Sitang Valley. The heat was fearfully oppressive, and for four or five nights he had to sleep in a dense bamboo jungle, and one day rode not less than forty miles on an elephant across burning paddy fields. Still when he came home he was apparently well and in a delightful frame of mind. He went about giving directions, and superintending a large amount of work which was necessary to be done before the rains set in, and he was intending to leave in four or five days on another tour, on which his heart was much set, but in two days he was taken ill with fever. Still he was able to walk about the house and to go from one room to another, and was full of hope that he should soon be able to go into the mountains again to accomplish the work on which his heart was bent. On the fifth day, he was worse, and on the seventh he breathed his last without a struggle, and with the same expression of calm and holy joy upon his countenance.

During his last tour he had written Mrs. Vinton several brief letters, all breathing in a remarkable degree an intense desire for the salvation of souls, and a readiness to depart and be with Christ. The five young men who went with him have all been ill; and one of them has since followed him to that rest which belongs to the people of God The elephant which he rode was also taken ill, and is now blind. The young men he left in the mountains to teach the people to read, and to instruct them in the gospel, fled down to the plains when they heard of their beloved teacher's death. The Karens are overwhelmed with sorrow. One of the pastors after the sermon last evening, addressed the congregation in a deeply interesting narrative of their teacher's labors, and closed by urging them to earnest prayer for a large measure of the Holy Spirit. He said, ' Our teacher *pleased* God, and so God took him. Now what we want is a man like our teacher Vinton, and God alone can send such a man. We must all pray that God may pour out His Holy Spirit upon us, and then we shall please God, and He will send us the teacher we need.'

"Had you known our brother and labored with him as I have done, you would have said, ' Why was he taken ?' The Karens seem to understand this ; they say, ' He was taken because he *pleased* God.' "

Mr. Stevens gives the following interesting and affecting account of the last hours :

"You are prepared to sympathise, I know, in the heavy bereavement which has befallen us in the sudden decease of Mr. Vinton, of which you no doubt heard by the last mail. On the evening of the 23rd March, he reached home after a tour among the mountain Karens, the last two days of which he was exposed incessantly to the burning sun, with but a slight protection, which together with the fatigue of riding on an elephant induced a fever. But the remedies which were resorted to seemed to act so favorably, that his physician thought him in no danger, nor was he undeceived until the very night preceding the morning of his decease. During his illness he spoke but little of himself, seeming to have no apprehension of his approaching end. On the contrary, in reply to a remark of Mrs. Vinton, inquiring if he did not think his work was done, 'No,' he said, 'I feel that I may yet live these twenty years.' And such was the impression which his ordinary appearance in health would be likely to produce on any one. Disease, however, had taken a relentless hold on him, and its work was rapid. As his end approached, and it became manifest to all that the hand of death was on him, we were glad to observe that consciousness was still perfect, and although unable clearly to articulate, in reply to the question, 'Is the name of Jesus precious to you?' he distinctly answered, 'Yes, O yes,' and soon after, turning himself over, as if to adjust himself for death, he rapidly sank away, leaving attendant friends, who had been hastily summoned to his bed side, in all but mute amazement, as though they had heard a voice speaking to them, 'Be still, and know that I am God.'

"This sad event was scarcely less a shock to us, than it undoubtedly has been and yet will be to friends at a distance. For he had been so hale and strong, with such evident signs of fitness for yet many years of labor, that certainly any one of our circle would have been selected by us as the next victim for the Destroyer before him. But he is gone! and his death has left a wide chasm in our ranks. Mrs. Vinton bears up remarkably under the stroke, for which indeed she seems to have been specially prepared by a kind providence, in a presentiment which she had had, even before Mr. Vinton came down from the jungle, that he was not long to continue with her. The Lord, we trust, will now be her stay, an ever-present help in trouble.

"It was affecting to observe how the Karens were exercised under this heavy affliction. All seemed astounded as though they could not believe their own eyes, when they saw the robust form of their revered teacher lying lifeless before them. Many wept, of whom some, his more immediate co-workers in the kingdom of Christ, remembering the hand of God, seemed lost in the inquiry, 'Why has he done it?' while yet they would acknowledge with Abraham, 'The Judge of all the earth must do right.' Perhaps by taking from them one on whom, in an eminent degree, they were accustomed to lean, God intends to draw them more fully to stay themselves on His everlasting strength. Mr. Brayton too, the more immediate associate of our deceased brother, especially needs our sympathy and prayers. For under the crushing weight of the accumulated affairs that will now devolve on him, I am sure he feels that none but an Almighty arm can keep him from sinking.

"How comforting it is to reflect, in view of this and similar dispensations of Providence, so seriously, as we should say, affecting the prosperity of the missionary cause, which depends for success so much on continuous effort, that the enterprise originated with Him, the instruments He provides; so that how frail soever they are, and however rapidly they fail in the using, He remains the same, and His resources are infinite; and He will continue to provide and adapt the instruments to the successive stages of the work, until the grand result He aims at is attained."

We have thus endeavored to survey this field which the Lord has blessed. Our readers will judge if, viewed as a whole, the work in Burmah has not (as we stated at the commencement) realized the New Testament idea of a Christian mission. The broad outlines of such a mission are seen on the very surface of the Acts and the Epistles of the Apostles.

The first opening of the gospel message after the ascension was Peter's sermon, ending with, "Therefore let all the house of Israel know assuredly, that God hath made that same Jesus whom ye have crucified both Lord and Christ." (Acts ii. 36.) Thus he again addressed the people, when they marvelled at the miracle wrought on the lame man (iii. 12—16); thus he addressed the council (iv. 12, v. 31); and these were the words spoken to Cornelius (x. 36—43, and xi. 14), whereby he and all his house should be saved; thus Philip preached at Samaria (viii. 5); and to the Eunuch (viii. 35); and thus the scattered disciples as they traveled abroad "preached the Lord Jesus" (xi. 20). Beaten by order of the Jewish council, and commanded not to speak in the name of Jesus, the Apostles daily in the temple and in every house "ceased not to teach and to preach Jesus Christ" (v. 40, 42); and when secular work pressed upon them in ministering to the poor, they sought to be relieved, that they might give themselves continually "to prayer and to the ministry of the word" (vi. 4).

Immediately on his conversion Paul "preached Christ" at Damascus, (ix. 20;) and afterwards from Antioch to Philippi; from Corinth to Athens; from Ephesus to Rome; to the Jews and the Gentiles; to the populace and to individual inquirers; to the Roman Governor and to King Agrippa: this was his message. "From Jerusalem round about unto Illyricum he fully preached the gospel of Christ." (Rom. xv. 19.) It was evidently his *habit* thus to preach: "I determined," he said, "not to know anything among you save Jesus Christ and Him crucified." (1 Cor. ii. 2.) At Thessalonica, "Paul, *as his manner was*, went in unto them, and three Sabbath days reasoned with them out of the Scriptures, opening and alleging that Christ must needs have suffered and risen again from the dead: and that this same Jesus whom I preach unto you is Christ." (Acts xvii. 2, 3.) And in the full anticipation of his coming trials, he said to the elders at Ephesus, 'None of these things move me, neither count I my life dear unto me, so that I might finish my course with joy, and the ministry which I have received of the Lord Jesus to testify the gospel of the grace of God." (xx. 24.) On this gospel his confidence reposed: "We preach Christ crucified, to the Jews a stumbling block, to the Greeks foolishness; but to us who are called, both Jews and Greeks, Christ the power of God, and the wisdom of God." (1 Cor. i. 22.) "I am not ashamed of the gospel of Christ: for it is the power of God unto salvation to every one that believeth." (Rom. i. 16.)

The work of the preachers was the Ministry of Reconciliation: as it is written: "Now then we are ambassadors for Christ, as though God did beseech you by us, we pray you in Christ's stead, be ye reconciled to God." (2 Cor. v. 20.) The first proclamation of the gospel was at Jerusalem, according to the commandment, (Luke xxiv. 47;) but the disciples were appointed to be witnesses unto the Lord, both in Jerusalem and in all Judea, and in Samaria, and to the uttermost parts of the earth. (Acts i. 8.) From Jerusalem therefore the word went forth to all the greatest cities of the age. But it was not confined to them. As Jesus Himself went about all the cities and villages teaching and preaching, (Matt. ix. 35,) so his faithful followers in the same manner, as debtors both to the wise and to the unwise, preached his gospel to the neglected poor of all the countries they visited. "Philip passing through Azotus preached in all the cities till he came to Cæsarea." (Acts viii. 40.) Peter passed throughout all quarters till he came down also to the saints which dwelt at Lydda. (ix. 32.) They that were scattered abroad upon the persecution at Jerusalem, "went everywhere preaching the word." (viii. 4.) When Paul and Barnabas departed from Antioch to the work unto which the Holy Ghost had called them, (xii. 2.) they travelled to Seleucia and thence to Cyprus, and "went through the island to Paphos," (xii. 4—6;) preached in Antioch in Pisidia; and "published the word of the Lord throughout all the region," (49,) thence travelling and preaching from city to city, they preached the gospel not only in Lystra and Derbe, but also in "the region that lieth round about," (xiv. 6, 7;) and subsequently "they passed through Pisidia," (xiv. 24:) afterward Paul went "throughout Phrygia and the region of Galatia," (xvi. 6;) and again a second time went "over all the country of Galatia and Phrygia." (xviii. 23.) In the same manner "he passed through the upper coasts" ere he "came to Ephesus," (xix. 1;) and "not alone at Ephesus, but almost throughout all Asia, persuaded and turned away much people," (xix. 26;) and so when about to depart on his second journey to Macedonia, "he went over those parts and gave them much exhortation" before he sailed for Greece. (xx. 2.)

These are sufficient indications of the plans of the Apostles: how God "made manifest the savor of his knowledge by them in every place." (2 Cor. ii. 14.) It was a vast circuit traversed by Paul, and others doubtless labored with unwearying zeal. His journey by Illyricum was immense. He traversed great regions, inhabited and uninhabited, full of "perils in the city, in the wilderness, and in the deep." (2 Cor. xi. 26.) The fruits in all places were alike, a great variety of men heard the truth. Jews, Samaritans, Ephesians, Corinthians, Athenians, Romans, the islanders of Cyprus and of Crete. There were votaries of an idolatrous superstition at Corinth; Roman colonists at Philippi; Jewish priests full of envy, (Acts v. 17,) of whom nevertheless "a great company were obedient to the faith;" (vi. 7,) and barbarians at Melita.

But the same simple gospel was addressed to all. The Apostle testified that "the grace of God that bringeth salvation hath appeared unto all men, teaching us that, denying ungodliness and worldly lusts, we should live soberly, righteously, and godly in this present world; looking for that blessed hope and the glorious appearing of the great God and our Saviour Jesus Christ, who gave himself for us that he might redeem us from all iniquity, and purify unto himself a peculiar people zealous of good works." (Titus ii. 11, 14.) And this purpose was largely accomplished. "Great grace" was on the church at Jerusalem: (Acts iv. 33,) the faith of the Roman believers was "spoken of throughout the world;" (Rom. i. 8.) Paul thanked God on every remembrance of those at Phillippi; (Phil. i. 3;) and remembered without ceasing the Thessalonians in their " work of faith, and labor of love, and patience of hope, in our Lord Jesus Christ in the sight of God and our Father;" (1 Thess. i. 3.) The scattered strangers whom Peter addressed, (1 Peter i. 8,) though they had not seen the Lord, loved him; and believing, rejoiced with joy unspeakable and full of glory. The church at Smyrna in its tribulation yet was "rich" (Rev. ii. 9;) and the church of Philadelphia had "kept the word of patience" amidst much surrounding evil. There were degrees of grace and holiness, and probably then, as now, very few eminent believers. We know that there were corrupt practices; evil men crept in unawares; some turned aside from the faith; and there were old remains of former superstitious habits; but the spirit of the Lord made the preaching of the word effectual; qualified native evangelists, pastors, and bishops, as Philip, Apollos, Timothy, and Titus; animated each church to strive to send the gospel to regions beyond. (2 Cor. x. 15, 16.)

We have seen in these sketches, a history not dissimilar: and shall we say that we are straitened in the Lord; that He cannot extend the experience of this mission, and cause others to share its fervor and its reward?

Well may we "think on these things!" We greatly need a quickened zeal, a stronger faith, a firmer confidence. If the love of Christ were shed abroad in our hearts by the Holy Spirit, animating us to prayer, causing us to count ourselves, and all that we have, as His alone, we should not labor languidly any longer; but sowing in hope, should look for that promised time when not only all the tribes of Burmah, but all mankind shall bow before the Saviour's feet; when every hand shall bring its willing tribute; and every lip utter its song of praise; and when holiness, purity, and love, shall mantle, like a robe, the universe of God, and the whole earth be filled with his glory.

THE END.

# Sheldon and Co.'s List.

## Hermann Olshausen, D.D.

| | |
|---|---|
| Commentaries on the New Testament. 6 vols., 8vo. Ed. A. C. Kendrick, D.D., | 12 00 |
| The same. 8vo., sheep, | 13 50 |
| " "  Half calf, gilt or antique, | 18 00 |

## Augustus Neander, D.D.

| | |
|---|---|
| Planting and Training of the Christian Church. Edited by E. G. Robinson, D.D. (*in press*). | |
| Commentaries, John, Philippians & James. 8vo., | 1 75 |
| History of Christian Dogmas (*in press*). | |

## Adolphe Monod, D.D.

| | |
|---|---|
| The Life and Mission of Woman. 12mo., | 50 |
| Sermons—Monod, Krummacher, Tholuck, &c., | 1 00 |

## W. W. Everts, D.D.

| | |
|---|---|
| The Bible Manual. 12mo., | 1 50 |
| Childhood, its Promise, &c. 12mo., | 75 |
| Manhood, its Duties, &c. 12mo., | 1 00 |
| The Pastor's Hand-book. 18mo., | 50 |
| The Sanctuary. 18mo., | 42 |
| Scripture Text Book and Treasury. 12mo., | 75 |

## Rev. Chas. Buck.

| | |
|---|---|
| Anecdotes—Religious and Entertaining. 8vo., | 1 50 |

## Mrs. H. C. Conant.

| | |
|---|---|
| History of the English Bible. 12mo., | 1 25 |

## Rev. C. H. Spurgeon.

Sermons, 1st Series. 12mo., . . . . 1 00
" 2d " 12mo., . . . . 1 00
" 3d " 12mo., . . . . 1 00
" 4th " 12mo., . . . . 1 00
" 5th " 12mo., . . . . 1 00
" 6th " 12mo. (*in press*).
The Saint and Saviour. 12mo., . . . 1 00
Gems Selected from his Sermons. 12mo., . . 1 00
Life and Ministry. 12mo., . . . . 60
Smooth Stones from Ancient Brooks. 16mo., . 60
Communion of the Saints (*in press*).

## Francis Wayland, D.D.

Sermons to the Churches. 12mo., . . . 85
Principles and Practices of Baptists. 12mo., . 1 00
Domestic Slavery (Fuller & W.). 18mo., . . 50

## Richard Fuller, D.D.

Sermons. 1st Series. 12mo. (*in press*).

## Mrs. Emily C. Judson.

Memoir of Sarah B. Judson. 18mo., . . . 60
An Olio, Poems. 12mo., . . . . . 75

## Geo. C. Baldwin, D.D.

Representative Women. 12mo., . . . 1 00

## Mrs. S. R. Ford.

Grace Truman. 12mo., . . . . . 1 00

# Sheldon and Co.'s List.

### J. P. Thompson, D.D
The Christian Graces. 16mo., . . . . 75
Memoir of the Rev. D. T. Stoddard. 12mo., . 1 00

### S. Irenæus Prime, D.D.
The Bible in the Levant. 16mo., . . . 75

### William J. Hoge, D.D.
Blind Bartimeus. 16mo., . . . . 75

### Rev. W. P. Balfern.
Glimpses of Jesus. 16mo., . . . . 60
Lessons from Jesus. 16mo., . . . . 75

### Rev. Henry M. Field.
From Copenhagen to Venice. 12mo., . . 1 00

### Rev. Alfred S. Patton.
Losing and Taking of Mansoul. 12mo., . . 1 00

### Mrs. Maria T. Richards.
Life in Israel. 12mo., . . . . . 1 00

### Manton Eastburn, D.D.
Thornton's Family Prayers. 12mo., . . . 75
" " " Fine ed., red edges, . 1 00

### John Dowling, D.D.
The Power of Illustration. 18mo., . . 30
The Judson Memorial. 16mo., . . 60

# Sheldon and Co.'s List.

## David Benedict, D.D.
History of the Baptists.  8vo., sheep, . . . 3 50
Fifty Years among the Baptists (*in press*).

## E. T. Hiscox, D.D.
The Baptist Church Directory.  16mo., . . 50

## Rev. D. C. Haynes.
The Baptist Denomination.  12mo., . . 1 00

## J. B. Jeter, D.D.
The Life and Writings of Rev. A. Broaddus, . 1 00
Campbellism examined.  12mo., . . . 1 00
The Mirror.  16mo., . . . . . 60

## Rev. J. D. Fulton.
The Roman Catholic Element.  12mo., . . 1 00

## John Clarke Marshman.
Life and Times of Carey Marshman & Ward, . 5 00

## Edward B. Underhill.
Struggles and Triumphs of Religious Liberty, . 75

## Rev. Francis Mason.
Memoir of Mrs. Helen M. Mason.  12mo., . 60

## William Dean, D.D.
The China Mission.  12mo., . . . . 1 00

# Sheldon and Co.'s List.

## Mrs. Thomas Geldart.

| | |
|---|---:|
| Daily Thoughts for a Child. 16mo., | 50 |
| Truth is Everything. 16mo., | 50 |
| Emilie the Peacemaker. 16mo., | 50 |
| Sunday Morning Thoughts. 16mo., | 50 |
| Sunday Evening Thoughts. 16mo., | 50 |

## S. G. Goodrich (Peter Parley).

| | |
|---|---:|
| The Cottage Library. 10 vols., 18mo., | 3 75 |
| Picture Play Books. 4to., | 75 |

## Francis L. Hawks, D.D., LL.D.

| | |
|---|---:|
| Richard the Lion Hearted. 16mo., | 75 |
| Oliver Cromwell. 16mo., | 75 |

---

| | |
|---|---:|
| Aunt Mary's Stories. 12 vols., | 3 00 |
| The Little Commodore. 16mo., | 75 |
| A Treasury of Pleasure Books. Gilt, | 1 50 |
| Indestructible Pleasure Books, each, | 20 |
| The Illuminated Linen Primer, | 20 |
| The Farmer Boy's Alphabet, | 20 |
| The Scripture Alphabet, | 20 |
| Little Annie's Ladder to Learning., | 40 |

# Sheldon and Co.'s List.

## John F. Stoddard, A.M.

| | |
|---|---|
| Juvenile Mental Arithmetic, | 12 |
| American Intellectual Arithmetic, | 20 |
| Practical Arithmetic, | 40 |
| Philosophical Arithmetic, | 60 |
| Key to Intel. and Prac. Arithmetic, | 50 |

## Stoddard & Henkle (Prof. W. D.)

| | |
|---|---|
| Elementary Algebra, | 75 |
| University Algebra, | 1 50 |

## J. Russell Webb, A.M.

| | |
|---|---|
| Normal Primer, | 5 |
| Primary Lessons, a Series of three Cards, | 1 00 |
| The Word Method Primer, | 15 |
| Normal Reader, No. 1, | 12 |
| Normal Reader, No. 2, | 25 |
| Normal Reader, No. 3, | 38 |
| Normal Reader, No. 4, | 50 |
| Normal Reader, No. 5, | 75 |

## Edward Hazen, A.M.

| | |
|---|---|
| The Speller and Definer, | 20 |
| Symbolical Spelling Book. Complete, | 20 |
|     "    "    "   Part 1st, 288 Cuts, | 10 |
|     "    "    "   Part 2d, 265 Cuts, | 12 |

# Sheldon and Co.'s List.

**Rev. Louis L. Noble.**
    Life and Works of Thomas Cole. 12mo., . . 1 25
    The Lady Angeline and other Poems. 12mo., . 75

**Rev. Sidney Dyer.**
    Songs and Ballads for the Household. 12mo., . 75

**Mrs. Mary A. Denison.**
    Gracie Amber, a Novel. 12mo., . . . 1 25

**Harriet E. Bishop.**
    Floral Home; or, First Years of Minnesota, . 1 00

**Rev. Joseph Barnard.**
    Wisdom, &c., of the Ancient Philosophers, . . 75

**Mrs. A. Lincoln Phelps.**
    Ida Norman. Illustrated. 12mo., . . . 1 25

**David Millard.**
    Travels in Egypt, Arabia Petræa, &c. 12mo., . 1 00

**John McIntosh.**
    The North American Indians. 8vo., . . . 1 50

**Rev. William Arthur.**
    Origin and Derivation of Family Names, . . 1 25

# Sheldon and Co.'s List.

### Eliphalet Nott, D.D.
Lectures on Temperance. 12mo., . . . 1 00

### Robert Turnbull, D.D.
Life Pictures from a Pastor's note book, . . 1 00

### Rev. Matthew Mead.
The Almost Christian. 18mo., . . . . 45

### John Frost, LL.D.
Wonders of History. 8vo., . . . . 2 00

### T. J. Farnham.
California and Oregon. 8vo., . . . . 1 50

---

Life of Spencer H. Cone, D.D., . . . . 1 25
The Life and Works of Lorenzo Dow, . . 1 50
Father Clark, the Pioneer Preacher, . . . 63
Homœopathic Practice, by M. Freleigh, M.D., . 1 50
The Napoleon Dynasty. Illustrated, 8vo., . . 2 50
Marble Worker's Manual, . . . . . 1 00
Memoir of Thomas Spencer, . . . . 60
The N. Y. Pulpit, Revival of 1858, . . . 1 00
The Baptist Library. 8vo., sheep, . . . 3 50
The Living Epistle. Tyree, . . . . 60
Rollin's Ancient History. 8vo., . . . . 1 50
The Words of Jesus and Faithful Promiser, . 37

# Sheldon and Co.'s List.

## Prof. Jean Gustave Keetels.
A New Method of Learning the French Language, 1 00
A Collegiate Course in the French Language, . 1 00
Key to the New Method, . . . . .
Key to the Collegiate Course (*in press*).

## J. R. Loomis, D.D.
Elements of Anatomy, Physiology, and Hygiene, . 75
Elements of Geology, . . . . . 75

## Oliver B. Goldsmith.
Copy Books in Five Numbers, each, . . . 12
Gems of Penmanship, boards, . . . . 2 00
Double-Entry Book-keeping. 8vo., . . . 75

---

Exhibition Speaker, Fitzgerald, . . . . 75
Normal School Song Book, . . . . 38
History of the United States, Peabody, . . 75
Nelson's Copy Books, 5 numbers, each, . . 10
United States Speller, Miles, . . . . 12
Fitch's Mapping Plates, . . . . . 30
Parley's Geography, . . . . . . 30
The University Drawing Book, . . . 3 50

---

\* Sample copies of Sheldon & Co.'s School Books are sent to Teachers by mail for one half the prices annexed.

## HOUSEHOLD LIBRARY.

| | |
|---|---|
| Life and Martyrdom of Joan of Arc. By Michelet, | 50 |
| Life of Robert Burns. By Thomas Carlyle, | 50 |
| Life and Teachings of Socrates. By George Grote, | 50 |
| Life of Columbus. By Alphonse de Lamartine, | 50 |
| Life of Frederick the Great. By Lord Macaulay, | 50 |
| Life of William Pitt. By Lord Macaulay, | 50 |
| Life of Mahomet. By Gibbon, | 50 |
| Life of Luther. By Chev. Bunsen, | 50 |
| Life of Oliver Cromwell. By A. de Lamartine, | 50 |
| Life of Torquato Tasso. By G. H. Wiffen, | 50 |
| Life of Peter the Great. Compiled by the Editor, 2 vols., | 1 00 |
| Life of Milton. By Prof. Masson, | 50 |
| Life of Thomas A'Becket. By H. H. Milman, D.D., | 50 |
| Life of Hannibal. By Dr. Arnold, | 50 |
| Life of Vittoria Colonna. By | 50 |
| Life of Julius Cæsar. By Henry G. Liddell, D.D., | 50 |
| Life of Mary Stuart. By A. de Lamartine (*in press*). | |

www.ingramcontent.com/pod-product-compliance
Lightning Source LLC
Chambersburg PA
CBHW030001240426
43672CB00007B/785